A RAMBLE
THROUGH
MY WAR

The author in 1942
Photo by Ralph Zaionz

A RAMBLE
THROUGH
MY WAR

Anzio and Other Joys

CHARLES F. MARSHALL

LOUISIANA STATE UNIVERSITY PRESS

Baton Rouge

Copyright © 1998 by Louisiana State University Press
All rights reserved
Manufactured in the United States of America
First printing
07 06 05 04 03 02 01 00 99 98 5 4 3 2 1

Designer: Michele Myatt Quinn
Typeface: Trump Mediaeval
Printer and binder: Edwards Brothers, Inc.

Library of Congress Cataloging-in-Publication Data:

Marshall, Charles F., 1915–
    A ramble through my war : Anzio and other joys / Charles F. Marshall.
      p. cm.
    ISBN 0-8071-2282-3 (cloth : alk. paper)
    1. Marshall, Charles F., 1915– . 2. World War, 1939–1945—
Secret service—United States. 3. United States. Army Biography.
4. World War, 1939–1945—Personal narratives, American.
5. Intelligence officers—United States—Biography. I. Title
D810.S7M274 1998
940.54'8673—dc21   98-24711
                                                CIP

To my cousin, Staff Sergeant Henry Kromer,
who lost his life in World War II;
and for all the fallen I knew
and those I didn't know

CONTENTS

PREFACE

This is not a book about the broad scope of World War II, the Church-illian view. Rather it is a firsthand account of the actions of one serviceman, myself, a battlefield intelligence officer attached to the G-2 (intelligence) section of the U.S. Army's Sixth Corps headquarters, and is primarily concerned with the campaigns in Italy, France, Germany, and Austria in which I had a hand. It is intended only as a microcosmic view of that compelling blood bath, the ripples of which extended to every corner of the globe, and in which 60 million people lost their lives and untold other millions were left wounded, homeless, starving, and without families. It conveys only my modest role in the total effort to beat into submission the German people, who had been swept off balance by Adolf Hitler's hypnotizing oratory and had surrendered their moral and intellectual equilibrium to a regime of unparalleled evil.

Inasmuch as a half century has passed since the end of that tragic drama, a distorted recollection of those turbulent days might be suspected from a participant's book drawn from memory alone. This chronicle, however, is based on the voluminous diaries I kept throughout the war. They are a reliable bank of observations, memories, and comments of those days. Time and again they have jogged my memory while simultaneously preventing any unbridled departure from the facts. Although the diaries were intended at the time only as a record of what was happening in my personal life, an incidental primer on corps-level battlefield intelligence gathering emerges from these pages.

Recorded is the day-in, day-out life of one member of a breed whose behind-the-scenes achievements were rarely acknowledged, never glorified, and habitually obscured. Yet theirs was often the hidden hand that influenced the course of battle, sometimes dramatically. It was to his intelligence chief, Major Edgar Williams, that Field Marshal Montgomery in his memoirs gave the credit for the idea that played a large part in winning the Battle of El Alamein in North Africa, one of the pivotal battles of the war. While good intelligence, even when properly evaluated, does not necessarily win battles, poor intelligence is almost guaranteed to lose them. Like Montgomery, Lieutenant General Edward V. Brooks, last commander of the Sixth Corps troops, also paid profuse tribute to his intelligence chief, Colonel Joseph Langevin, at the end of the European hostilities.

Langevin had been the G-2 and my boss. The accuracy of his "crystal ball"—as Brooks referred to Langevin's daily estimate of the enemy's situation, capabilities, and intentions—was the result of his acute evaluation of the intelligence overtly and covertly extracted from the enemy side. As this story moves through war-torn Europe, I am sure the veteran who took part in these campaigns will often be moved to say, "Yes, that's how it was," or "Yes, that's how I remember it." He will also develop, I think, a retrospective appreciation for the battlefield intelligence people who tried to reduce his peril and speed his victory. Before that victory could be acclaimed, 16 million Americans were called to the colors. Of that number 1 million became casualties, 400,000 didn't come back, and the remains of 80,000 have never been recovered. Since most of the surviving veterans of the Great Conflict are now in their late seventies and eighties, not too many more documented firsthand accounts are apt to be written. So perhaps those of us still alive may be forgiven if we have the temerity to offer our individual experiences to the historians of the future.

ACKNOWLEDGMENTS

I wish to thank Stackpole Books for permission to reprint Chapter 22, "An Emissary and More Field Marshals," from my book *Discovering the Rommel Murder*.

To the editors of Louisiana State University Press I am indebted for their enthusiastic reception of the manuscript: to Sylvia Frank for getting the ball rolling, to Gerry Anders for his eagle eyes and wise guidance in overseeing the editorial process, and to Jack Rummel's masterful copy editing.

The military authority Charles P. Roland, to whom the manuscript was sent for expert evaluation, I thank for his wholehearted recommendation that LSU Press publish this work.

To my wife Mary I owe a debt of gratitude for her diligence in keeping our two-year-old granddaughter from underfoot while I worked, and for her forbearance in holding or delaying dinner when I felt I was "on a roll."

And lastly, to my son John and son-in-law Mark Larson, who together dragged an old Underwood into the computer age at the start of my writing endeavors a few years ago, I would like to express my appreciation.

Introduction

On a cloudy afternoon in June 1946, I sat on the deck below the bridge of the SS *Sea Flier* as it plowed its way across the Atlantic with a load of returning World War II troops. With little to do and much time to think, I reflected on my army career that was now coming to a close after four and a half years of service, by far the most interesting years of my life.

I had been strenuously opposed to America's entry into the war, but about to be drafted, I volunteered. After basic training with the Fifth Armored Division in California, and another month suffering through the rigors of maneuvers in the Mojave Desert, I was sent on to officer candidate school and then, as a second lieutenant, posted to the Fourteenth Armored Division in Arkansas.

Up to this point mine had been a normal army career. Then, because of a fortuitous knowledge of the German language, I was transferred to the Military Intelligence School in Maryland for four months of intensive study before being deployed to Italy. There Allied and German forces were bitterly engaged in the Apennine Mountains.

As the ship bulled its way through the choppy sea, I stared out over the water and memories tumbled forth. There were the trips to the stalemated front where both sides were bloodily contesting every foot. Then my sudden transfer to the Anzio beachhead, the operation that was intended by Churchill to be an end run that would bypass the resisting German troops and result in the quick capture of Rome.

To mind came the memory of all that savage fighting at Anzio and how we intelligence people used the information filtered from captured maps, codes, field orders, letters, and assorted other documents, plus the information gained from prisoner interrogation, in an effort to whittle down the Nazi forces trying to drive us back into the sea.

Never would I forget the breakout from the beachhead and the capture of Rome, the search of the German embassy and the blowing of its safes. With satisfaction I recalled my help to the FBI in its hunt for the treasonous propaganda broadcaster, the renowned poet Ezra Pound.

Interspersed with the somber memories were pleasant ones: friends made in Rome, golf at a Roman country club, swimming at Tivoli, visits to Vesuvius and Pompeii, to Paris, and to innumerable places of interest in Germany, including Hitler's chalet at Berchtesgaden.

There were recollections of the relaxed days in Naples as we planned the invasion of southern France. And then the not-so-relaxed day of the actual invasion as, hanging on to a rope with the naval guns firing over us, we waded ashore through shoulder-deep water.

There were flashes of the eclectic mix of places I had slept: among others, caves and cellars, palaces and grand chateaus, barns and orchards, tents, and even for a while in a house with a feather bed.

Disappointments there were many, sorrows many, and far too many friends were killed. And worrisome days when the Battle of the Bulge was going in the Germans' favor and forcing us, although distant from the action, into a strategic retreat.

Surprises there were too. One occurred when I escorted General Vlasov's emissary to General Patch's headquarters so that he could arrange the surrender of 100,000 Ukrainian troops, allies of the Germans, only to have the surrender rejected.

Another was my interrogation of the widow of Field Marshal Rommel and her revelation that her husband, the most famous general of the war, the chivalrous unconventional wizard of desert warfare, had been murdered on Hitler's order.

As the ship fought its way through intimidating swells, I hung on to the rail and with lurching steps worked my way back to the stern. I watched the swirling wake trail into the distance, but soon again I was lost in flashbacks. There were the lengthy conversations I had had with

Field Marshal List, commander of a million German troops on the Russian front, and the oddity of the night I spent at his home as his guest while the war was still in progress.

To mind came my questioning of other senior generals, among them Field Marshal von Leeb, commander of German forces in France and Russia, and Field Marshal von Weichs, commander of the German forces in the Balkans.

One person I knew I would never forget was Doctor Theodor Morell, Hitler's personal physician, who, in the War Crimes Camp at Stuttgart, told me of the medications he had routinely administered to the Führer and described the injuries Hitler had suffered in the abortive July 20 bomb plot.

Unpleasant memories, much as I would have liked to repress them, often surfaced. At the end of hostilities, when I was supervising the screening of prisoners of war before releasing them back into civilian life, the days were marked by the tremendous numbers of pitiful young men, ill and half-starved, with missing limbs, sometimes one arm or leg, sometimes one arm and one leg, sometimes both legs. Not infrequently a soldier with a poorly matched glass eye came by. At other times there was not even a glass eye, just a bare eye socket. There were boys of fifteen and sixteen, and broken-down men in their fifties and sixties.

Weaning my thoughts from the disagreeable, I recalled pleasant memories of lengthy visits with Mrs. Rommel after the war as she assisted me in my research for a book on the field marshal's life and death.

Particularly pleasant was the recollection of the warm friendship developed with General Hans Speidel, Rommel's chief of staff during the fighting in Normandy and one of the plotters against Hitler. (This was the man who was later to become one of the chief architects of the new German army, its first four-star general, and NATO's first commander of the Allied Forces, Central Europe, and with whom I would maintain a correspondence for years after the war.) Never would I forget the many weekend visits with him and his family as he helped me unearth the true story of Rommel, giving me unstintingly of his time and gratefully accepting my offer to act as mail conduit between him and his American friend, Colonel Truman Smith. Smith had been the prewar U.S. military attaché in Berlin, friend of Colonel Charles A. Lindbergh, and valued adviser to General George C. Marshall, chief of staff of the U.S. Army.

As the ship's meal call sounded, I was struck by a thought: As a die-hard opponent of America's entry into the war, at what point had I changed my mind and decided our entry was right and necessary? I couldn't put my finger on it.

Perhaps the reader can.

1

To War via North Africa

I came to World War II by way of French North Africa during the Mediterranean rainy season. I was part of a contingent of eight officers and sixteen enlisted men, all but two fluent in the German language. Of the officers, three were first lieutenants and the other five of us second lieutenants. The enlisted men were all sergeants except for two or three corporals.

After eight days of zigzagging designed to frustrate German submarine attack, our ship, a fast one, and sailing without escort, ended its Atlantic crossing at Casablanca, Morocco, on December 2, 1943. Two years before, propelled by the wizardry of German field marshal Erwin Rommel, German and Italian forces had swept across the deserts of Tripolitania, Cyrenaica, and Egypt to within spitting distance of their goals, Alexandria and the Suez Canal. Then, short of manpower, ammunition, artillery, tanks, and particularly gasoline, and subject to overwhelming British and American air superiority, Rommel had to forsake the objectives so tantalizingly close to his grasp. Further disadvantaged by the Allied decryption operation, code-named Ultra, which revealed messages to and from the German High Command, he was forced into a long retreat.

The Afrika Korps's retreat ended in the surrender of the Axis forces in Tunisia in May 1943, leaving control of all North Africa in Allied hands. Rommel's early successes, however, forced the scrapping of General George C. Marshall's plan for the invasion of Europe in 1943.

As Rommel had predicted to Hitler in beseeching reinforcements, the Axis loss of North Africa would be followed by an Allied invasion of Italy. And that had occurred.

Our little group had graduated from the army's intelligence school at Camp Ritchie, Maryland, and after a briefing at the Pentagon, was now en route to the battle in Italy.

At Ritchie we had been put through a two-month course in prisoner of war interrogation, followed by an intensive four-week postgraduate course in "order of battle." This is the study of the enemy's organization and equipment, but in actual battle it becomes the pursuit and evaluation of the collective intelligence gained from all possible sources. Some of this information, often much, comes from the interrogation of prisoners and military and civilian deserters. This is enhanced by the study of captured enemy documents such as field orders, codes, maps, field manuals, memorandums, newspapers, letters, and photographs. Other data comes by way of espionage, counterintelligence, radio intercept, fighter pilot reports, aerial reconnaissance reports, and aerial photo interpretation.

Although all these means are not always operating simultaneously, some combinations of data gathering are always in play. From this cumulative data, much is known about the enemy, his capabilities, and often his plans. Sometimes order-of-battle (usually abbreviated OB) practitioners can even construct psychological profiles of enemy commanders.

While the enlisted men might be more or less restricted to specific chores, the OB officers quickly become enmeshed in the whole intelligence picture. Once involved in a campaign, any OB man worth his salt soon knows infinitely more about the enemy than he knows about his own forces.

None of our group had ever been in North Africa before. Much of the construction in Casablanca surprised us. Many of its buildings were elegant and modern. On the other hand, the Arab component of the population came up (or down) to our expectations. Every child seemed able to say, "Gimme smoke! Gimme candy!" Teenage youngsters would offer surprisingly high prices for blankets, shoes, mattress covers, and other army matériel. Although eighty cents for a pack of cigarettes would seem a poor offer today, at that time a pack of cigarettes in the States sold for fifteen cents or even two packs for a quarter.

After five days encamped in tents in a field ankle-deep in mud, we boarded the famous French "40 and 8s" (forty men or eight horses per car) for Algiers in Algeria, the second French colony. The train chugged along at a snail's pace and often spent an hour or two idling at small stations for no good reason that we could discover. Nor could the American engineers running the train shed any light. They had their orders. It was the French way of doing things.

Our group was lucky. Unlike the hundreds of other men who suffered the discomforts and indignities of the boxcars, we were assigned a coach.

For meals during our four-day, 700-mile journey, we were given C rations. The C ration was the ration for one day in the field and consisted of three cans of meat and vegetables, three cans of crackers, sugar, powdered coffee, and a confection. Eaten cold, C rations would win no epicurean prizes, but quickly a bit of American ingenuity came to the rescue. A candle was put into an empty can, and a can of the rations placed on top to be heated. As time went by the "stoves" improved, two or three candles side by side simultaneously firing the heating unit and warming the processed contents closer to gastronomic acceptance.

When we arrived in Algiers, site of AFHQ (Allied Force Headquarters), the enlisted men went off to a camp and the officers were quartered in Pullman cars at a railroad siding. An obliging native orderly would get a girl to spend the night in the compartment of any officer with romantic yearnings.

The next day Major Holsten, the commanding officer of our unit (2680 Headquarters Military Intelligence Service), which was attached to AFHQ, came to welcome us. When he had finished with the formalities, he told us he needed a couple of officers to accompany the drivers taking a batch of two-and-a-half-ton trucks to Oran, a seaport some 220 miles to the west. There the drivers were to drop off the trucks and pick up the jeeps that had been allotted to the order-of-battle contingent. Tired of life in trains, I, along with a Lieutenant Alfred Pundt, volunteered for the assignment.

In civilian life Pundt had been a professor of history at Penn State. Known as Doc among the officers in deference to his Ph.D., Pundt had come by his commission via the ROTC. About thirty-eight, with a fair complexion and bald except for a fringe of wheat-blond hair, he was six feet tall, well built, and had an energetic stride. Rarely hesitating to break regulations if they inconvenienced him, he often affected haziness about what an officer's duties and privileges were, usually determining them in his own interest. He was divorced from the German woman he had married while a graduate student studying in Germany, and the marriage had soured him on women, although it had not diminished an insatiable appetite for priapic adventure.

Doc Pundt was a man with whom I would be closely linked in the campaigns in Italy, France, Germany, and Austria. Although on the surface we did not have much in common, we would become good friends. We were ten years apart in age, and whereas I was a practicing Catholic with a conservative background from the world of business, he was an atheist and, like so many in academia, an apostle of socialism, whose cause he sought tirelessly to advance.

Once, early in our association, when he was pontificating on the virtues of socialism and castigating the iniquities of capitalism, he sought to clinch his diatribe with, "Now all right-thinking people know . . ."

At this point I interrupted: "Cut the crap, Doc! If anybody disagrees with you, they are not right-thinking. Is that it?"

Startled, he quickly backpedaled. But thereafter, for whatever reason, he sought out my company at every opportunity and gave up proselytizing in my presence.

The trip proved enjoyable and the scenery delightful, the green rolling hills reminding me of southern California where I had received my basic training with the Fifth Armored Division. Stops for meals and to answer nature's call were often enlivened by Arab youngsters peddling oranges that we were afraid to buy, having been warned of the danger of contracting dysentery from their unwashed fruit.

Mid-journey, we stopped the first night in a town named Orleanville, and Pundt and I went in search of entertainment. The first public building we wandered into turned out to be a steam bath. Neither of us interested in a steam bath, although it was a cold drizzly night, we resumed our wanderings, using flashlights to find our way through the pitch-black streets. Against my better judgment, which was eroded by Pundt's persistent cajoling, and somewhat emboldened by the security of the pistols at our hips under our trench coats, we left the French quarter and ambled into the dirty native quarter. Here our attention was drawn to a building from which a racket was coming. As we drew closer, we recognized the sound of tambourines and boisterous singing.

Doc rapped on the door. It opened a crack and a voice asked in French what we wanted. Pundt, whose French was better than my two years of college French, responded. Inside the door, in a vestibule, a panel was slid open and Pundt paid some kind of cover charge. Another door was unlocked and we found ourselves in a large smoke-filled room. It was a combination bar, social club, and house of prostitution, we quickly gathered.

The patrons, mostly men, many of whom were seamen of various nationalities and in various stages of inebriation, were seated at tables bearing bottles of wine. Some had girls on their laps, presumably negotiating sex, while others gazed through the haze of smoke at two scantily clad dancers gyrating suggestively to the beat of their tambourines.

A bosomy barmaid brought us a bottle of red native wine, for which I am sure I was charged as a "rich American." Concerned by the suspicious, even antagonistic, eyes focused on us by some of the patrons, who obviously were wondering what the hell two American officers were doing here, I moved my chair to sit with my back against the wall. While our search for entertainment had no specific goal, this sailors' dive was certainly not it, and halfway through the second bottle we left.

It was now late. I had a cold that I had been nursing for days and that wasn't helped by the bone-chilling dampness of the country's rainy season. I proposed we rejoin our group, but Doc was intent on a further exploration of the town. So we parted.

The next morning he told me he had an Arab boy, a young pimp, take him to the home of a French-Arabian girl, the hour costing him 500 francs. Back in Algiers later he was to go into the "off limits" *Medina* (native quarter) and lie with a twelve-year-old Arab girl. His mania for collecting sexual experiences, I reflected, could not have been an asset in his wife's eyes and was probably one of the causes for his failed marriage.

Arriving in Oran, we delivered the trucks and started back to Algiers with the jeeps. It was another drizzly day, and en route one of the jeeps skidded on the slippery road, pushing an Arab and his donkey into a ditch. Neither was hurt, but the Arab immediately began a series of wails interspersed with calls on Allah. We lifted the jeep off the donkey as the Arab pulled the fear-stricken animal out of the ditch by its ears.

Army regulations required an accident report, but since the donkey and its owner were unhurt, and since the Arab spoke no English and we no Arabic, we moved on only to be involved in a second incident shortly after. One of our drivers, in going around a blind curve in the mountains, pushed a French army vehicle into a ditch. A captain and two lieutenants emerged, the captain bleeding from a cut suffered from the shattered windshield. The French vehicle's fender and spare tire had been ripped off.

This time an accident report was filled out. In the later stages of the war, when I had become somewhat disenchanted with the French, whenever I thought of the incident I wondered if some day the French government, with typical Gallic reasoning, wouldn't bill the American government for the damages to the vehicle, although it was the American government that donated the vehicle to the Free French forces in the first place.

We arrived in Algiers without further mishap.

While Doc Pundt and I were destined to work closely together during the war, the man who was to become my closest friend in the OB group was Alex Shayne, a twenty-six-year-old burly Polish-born Jew with a lumbering gait who spoke no German but was fluent in Polish, Russian, and Italian. His face had five o'clock shadow at seven in the morning. Although his complexion called for dark eyes, he had disconcertingly blue ones. He had grown up near the Polish-Russian border and then for several years lived in Italy before coming to America. He was gifted musically and with a sense of humor that often had me in stitches.

One night during our stay in Algiers, to kill some time, Shayne, a British officer, and I went into the entertainment district to see a show. As we left the theater, two ladies of the evening crossed the street and fell in with us.

The girls ignored the Englishman, experience probably having taught them that American officers had deeper pockets. One grabbed Alex's arm and the other mine, importuning us to partake of their charms, assuring us that their sexual favors were like no others ever experienced by man, while we tried to shake them off by pleading that we were due back at quarters, a story they refused to buy.

The ignored Britisher, determined to get some fun out of the situation, insisted that the "ladies," emphasizing "ladies," were entitled to introductions, whereupon he introduced us by our first names as Lieutenant Alex and Lieutenant Charlie. As a consequence of this nicety, and despite our rejections, for the next ten minutes the more curvaceous of the two girls hung on my arm and kept up a refrain of, "Pleez come, Sharlie. Collette luffs you! Collette luffs you, Sharlie!"

Thereafter, for the duration of the war, whenever Alex and I met, and we were to meet many times in Italy, France, Germany, and Austria, his greeting to me would be a mile-wide smile followed by a hearty bellow, "Pleez come, Sharlie! Collette luffs you, Sharlie!"

Delighted to see him, I always joined in his laughter, despite his roaring this greeting through the whole G-2 section. Earlier requests of "Come on, Alex, knock it off!" had no effect and in time I gave up. For Alex, this greeting had become a Pavlovian reaction. Years later, when I was newly married, he came with his wife and daughter to visit me, and his greeting was no different, causing my bride, I noticed, some curiosity. He, too, noticed the questioning look and mercifully explained, something he never did during the war.

Alex was a great friend. More about him later.

In Algiers, the port, dotted with sunken ships, only their tops visible above the water, was something of a mess. While the impression was one of clutter, the city as a whole was clean and bustling with the activity of Allied Force Headquarters. Traffic was fast and furious. One formed the impression that a bounty was awarded for every pedestrian a driver could hit. Forty miles an hour down side streets was just standard operating procedure.

After a few days we left the city. It was raining again and seemed a good time to leave. Major Holsten shook hands heartily, wished us well, and promised us lieutenants that we would probably never be promoted. On that cheerful note, we mounted our jeeps and headed for the next stop on our way to the war in Italy.

After driving four hundred miles through the coastal mountains of Algeria, we entered Bizerte, a port city at the northern tip of Tunisia. The outskirts were marked by piles of captured enemy equipment, much of it battle-damaged, the detritus of the two-year Allied battles with Rommel's forces.

We stayed in Bizerte four days, during which time Christmas came and went. While there, Doc suggested we find a restaurant and experience a taste of the local cuisine. The cuisine, it developed, was unembellished black market, standard U.S. Army rations, for which we paid a fancy price.

Some of us took the opportunity to drive the forty miles to Tunis to the site where the remnants of the Axis forces in North Africa, 230,000 men, had surrendered. Something more than half were Italians. The rest were stragglers from Rommel's Afrika Korps, who, we were told, had marched into captivity singing, their spirit unbroken.

Our time in Bizerte up, we boarded a navy LST (Landing Ship, Tank) for the voyage to Italy where the Allied armies were locked in tenacious battle with Hitler's forces. The ship had surprisingly good accommodations for men and officers, but what astounded us more was its practicality. Powered by two diesel engines, it was able to carry 2,100 tons through rough waters and could be beached in water so shallow that its cargo could be unloaded or driven off. On this trip it was filled with vehicles.

With the new year, 1944, just ahead of us, we were now headed for "sunny Italy," glad to forsake the bone-chilling rains of North Africa. The Mediterranean crossing proved uneventful, and on New Year's Eve we drove our jeeps off the LST in the port of Naples.

We were met, of course, by another bone-chilling rain.

2

The Palace: This Is War?

Our order-of-battle group had orders to report to General Mark Clark's Fifth Army headquarters in Caserta, a town fifteen miles north of Naples. In our ignorance of the battle situation, we had half expected to be strafed en route to headquarters and to spend the night in foxholes. Our amazement, therefore, knew no bounds when the drive passed without incident and the headquarters itself turned out to be the Royal Palace, an enormous structure with a reputed 2,500 rooms, built between 1752 and 1774 by the Bourbon kings of the old Kingdom of the Two Sicilies.

It was resplendently set in enormous formal gardens adorned with cavorting nymphs and gods sculpted in stone amongst cascading streams. In the foreground were broad lily-strewn pools at different levels. In one floated Clark's pontoon-equipped cub plane, a somewhat incongruous sight midst the ornate statuary.

Taking advantage of the immense marble edifice, the army had transformed it into a self-contained city. In addition to harboring the vast network of offices that make up an army headquarters, it housed mess halls, bakeries, officer bars, laundries, recreation rooms, a chapel, a dispensary, and innumerable other facilities, plus sleeping quarters for men and officers, not to mention an opera house whose beauty must have taken one's breath away in its candlelit heyday. In the

month I was to spend here, I saw the San Carlo Opera Company per-
form *Barber of Seville, Madam Butterfly,* and *Rigoletto,* missing *Tosca*
because I had to work that night.

My billet was a room off a corridor that was so lengthy the drafts
sweeping through could actually blow a cap off a head. And yet this
was indoors! All the palace lacked in creature comforts was central
heating.

Instead of spending that evening—New Year's Eve—in foxholes, the
officers spent it at a ball in the royal drawing rooms, toasting the advent of 1944 with champagne. Such is war. For some.

"If this is war," said Alex, "it ain't bad."

"I could get used to this," I agreed.

It was not to be. After a few days our contingent was divided into
teams of one officer and two enlisted men, the normal complement for
OB units. During wartime these OB teams are attached to the G-2 sections at division, corps, army, and army group levels. Meant to supplement the G-2's capabilities, since G-2 sections are often manned by
personnel who do not speak the enemy language, they quickly become
so valuable to the G-2 chief that he will fight to the death to keep his
OB people from being reassigned.

At this time there were only six assignments for the eight teams, and
they were parceled out by our senior officer. Flabby, gawky, and tem-
peramental, he was a physically unimpressive fellow with a sarcastic
tongue and watery eyes, about thirty years old, with a personality that
repelled many of us. It was said he had spent much of his life in Europe,
had come from a wealthy family, and was a stage designer by profession. He assigned himself, of course, to headquarters here at the palace,
the place farthest from the killing.

In fairness, I could not blame him. All the men, in their hearts, I felt,
wanted to get through the war without sweating through any more
danger than necessary. No man in his right mind could look forward to
participating in the bitter combat that was going on in the mountains
a few miles to the north.

The second assignment went to another first lieutenant, Henry
Pleasants, about thirty-two, a witty, winsome chap, a joy to be around.
A singer of rollicking sea chanteys, he could have shivered the timber
of the orneriest seafarer with his colorful cussing, which was his hobby.
Intellectual and practical, he was a good friend and a first-rate man in

The Royal Palace in Caserta and one of its many fountain pools. The palace was my first foxhole. Life could be tough.

every way. By profession he had been the music critic with the *Philadelphia Evening Bulletin*, and when the war ended he returned to music criticism. Married, he did not believe in condoms as a method of birth control. "Using a rubber," he would proclaim, "is like washing your feet with your socks on." Attached to the G-2 section of the Second Corps, then fighting in the Apennine Mountains, Henry's path would take him away from me, and regrettably we never again met during the course of the war.

The third assignment went to our third first lieutenant, William Peebles, about thirty, who, though sober as a judge, always looked as though he were recovering from a hangover. Peebles was attached to one of the divisions, and we were to meet once in Paris after the war.

The youngest of the officer group was Rocco Ciffereli, twenty-five, a generous fellow, free with money—his and others'. He was a splendid audience, listening attentively to every word spoken. He had a gift for gambling and was in fact a compulsive gambler, continually seeking partners for his gambling forays. Effervescently optimistic, he would shoot craps and in five minutes lose two hundred dollars, about four thousand in today's dollars. We kept in touch by phone and letter during much of the war.

Another of the group was a professional photographer who aspired to be a writer. From my perspective I saw no gifts in that direction, but he glibly spouted the approved views of the intelligentsia of the day and in my view lacked common sense. He had been married and divorced twice and, like Doc Pundt, had eclectic sexual tastes. At the intelligence school he was often late for classes and meetings. In France he was to lose an arm tinkering with a German shell.

Doc Pundt's team was sent to Sixth Corps headquarters, which, although we did not know it at the time, was planning an invasion of Anzio, a seaport thirty-three miles south of Rome.

As things worked out, there were no assignments for Alex Shayne and me. So while the others went off to battle, we two were left temporarily unassigned and condemned for the time being to the rigors of further palace life.

I was disappointed at not receiving an assignment. Now that I was in the war zone, I was itching to get involved and get the war over with. "What's wrong with us?" I griped. "Are we misfits or something?"

Alex, on the other hand, had a laid-back philosophy. "Listen," he would say soothingly, "right now you and I are in this jeep headed for Naples and a good dinner with a family I know, and maybe the opera after. What the hell is the hurry to get your ass shot off?"

A few evenings later at one of the palace's bars, I bent elbows with Captain Ian McLeod, a British officer with whom I had become acquainted on the LST while crossing the Mediterranean. He, too, was an intelligence officer, and we had discussed order-of-battle work. He was now involved in organizing something to be known as "S Force." This S Force was to be an organization of British and American intelligence personnel of every kind and was to join the forward combat troops entering Rome. It was to immediately search all strategic buildings and gather up the thousands of documents the army hoped had been left behind before they were burned, lost, or destroyed by our inexpert fighting men. The documents would then be sent to examiners at Fifth Army headquarters, who would evaluate them and order any necessary action based on information found in them. McLeod asked me to head the force's documents-evaluation section.

S Force was quickly put together, and my documents section was organized and ready to go. It included Alex, whose knowledge of Italian could be most helpful, and our four sergeants. In working with the British on this project, I soon found they used their pipe smoking to advantage. Whenever my opposite number wanted to avoid an immediate response, he would first puff on his pipe, stuff it with fresh tobacco, light it or remove it from his mouth and look at it critically, or fiddle with it some other way. And since I was going to be dealing with the British in the future, I took up pipe smoking to put myself on an equal footing in these mental duels that so often occur when one is negotiating with an ally. I was learning, and I was enjoying my association with the British officers, many of whom were engaging company.

One evening as I was coming from the mess, Captain Irving-Bell, a fine Brit, called me into the bar. As we drank, he told me with a straight face that he had just seen an AFHQ order resulting from the pregnancy of two WACs. The order read, he said, "Hereafter officers will not dip their wicks in WACs."

The captain had a bottomless fund of jokes and anecdotes. When told something he didn't know, his favorite expression, which never ceased to amuse me, was, "Well, bless my belly and tits!"

While on a march with S Force during its organizational phase, a British major told me of his days in the earlier fighting in North Africa. He was in charge of hiring mercenary tribes to fight the Italians. There was, though, one African tribe whose men he always tried hardest to hire, because the Italians had a deathly fear of these people. When a tribesman killed or wounded an Italian, he would cut off the Italian's penis. In this tribe the desirability of a young warrior to the young lady of his choice was measured by the number of male organs he could present to her.

While S Force was champing at the bit, ready to rush to the papal city, whose fall was thought to be imminent, the Germans were not cooperating. The overall enemy command in Italy was under the redoubtable and resourceful Field Marshal Albert Kesselring, an air force general, a gifted, versatile officer who had led Luftwaffe units in the battles of Britain and North Africa. With an impressive build and an optimistic nature, he was known in the higher military circles as "Smiling Albert" and was a favorite of Hitler. He was now conducting a brilliant and ferocious defense of Italy, extracting a high price for every foot of ground he yielded.

It was in the Apennines, with Monte Cassino as its hub, that he used the natural barriers of the Rapido, Garigliano, and Sangro Rivers to build the formidable Gustav Line, a virtually impregnable string of defenses running across the Italian Peninsula from the Tyrrhenian Sea to the Adriatic. Consequently, the battles in these mountains, with their cold drenching rains, were incredibly bloody, with as much as 65 percent of some American units becoming casualties.

The effort to shake loose the Nazis' grip on the crags and outcrops of these mountains was to involve the Allies in some of the bitterest battles of the Second World War. Only the fighting on Anzio beachhead would be worse. These engagements took place in deep, sticky mud, often accompanied by icy rains and snowstorms. Since neither side could significantly budge the other, they were locked in a dismal deadlock that would last through the wintry months.

Although technically a member of S Force, I quickly tired of killing time at the palace while waiting for the Holy City to fall. It was mid-January now and Rome was not to fall until June 5. Seeking out Captain Shewbridge, chief of the Fifth Army's advance document section, I offered to accompany him on his next trip to the front.

The following morning we jeeped to the combat zone in the mountains and searched for documents in a small, newly captured village, Mignano, and I was shocked to find that it had been thoroughly destroyed by the Germans and not by our shelling. The enemy was pursuing the scorched-earth policy of the Russians.

At the intelligence school we had been taught by training films to be aware that the enemy often booby-trapped houses and headquarters sites when leaving them. We were taught to probe behind a picture on a wall, to open a desk drawer by tying a string to the handle, moving a safe distance away behind a wall, and only then pulling open the drawer; and there were cautionary measures for other situations.

Observing that Shewbridge moved about quickly, disregarding all safeguards, I asked why. He and his men, he said, had so far not run into any booby traps in their searches. I decided that when my men and I began our independent document hunts, we too would ignore the time-consuming safeguards unless there were grounds for suspicion. (This was admittedly a gamble, but not once in all the searches in all the campaigns we were to fight in did we encounter a booby trap.)

Another trip to the front with Shewbridge took us to a town called Cevaro. The wine casks in the cellars were full, indicating the Germans had left in haste. The first house we entered was that of one of Mussolini's Fascist Party captains. The place was quite destroyed, but we were able to unearth some documents, mostly of long-range value.

The next house, which had suffered less damage, had been a platoon headquarters in which we found some German material, mainly small-town newspapers. These, of course, had no intelligence significance for the current tactical situation. In the big picture, however, they had value. The army's statisticians in the Pentagon studied the obituary columns of great numbers of such newspapers with keen interest. The number of military dead, their ages, their previous civilian occupations, and where they had fallen yielded insights and pointed up trends in the Wehrmacht's manpower situation. Therefore we packed them up for high-echelon study.

The third building was a church that had been the headquarters of a German general but was now occupied by an American field hospital. The documents had already been sent to headquarters, we were told by the curate.

Outside the church-hospital was a heap of bloody American combat uniforms. When a casualty was brought in, the medics often cut the uniform off to quickly get to the man's wound. Although I badly wanted a warm combat suit, the weather in the mountains frequently being vile, with snow and pelting rains, and the jeep trips back shivery ones, I could not bring myself to pick up one of these damaged but salvageable suits. I felt it would be cheating. I did not yet consider myself a combat man, and these suits were issued only to combat men.

It was pitiful to observe the inhabitants of these obliterated villages in which hardly a house escaped the scars of battle. At some houses women cooked on little open fires while babies wailed or sprawled among the remains of furniture. At others they huddled in the one remaining room or in the corner of a couple of walls that remained standing. Despite the poignant scenes wherever one looked, I saw no women weeping, but despair was etched in their faces. They had long since accepted the destruction of their homes as inevitable, and they had wept themselves out.

I could not help but reflect on the powerful force of motherhood as I watched these women suckling their babies, often wrapped in newspapers for lack of diapers, seated on a pile of charred rubble, shells still bursting uncomfortably close, shrapnel flashing through the air. These women and their men were reduced to a most straitened existence. A long period of acute misery would have to be endured before life took an upturn.

Deeply carved in memory is one of these early forays to the battlefield. As I drove up to a little village that had just been captured, a company of infantrymen was being relieved by another. As the boys came out of the line, they gathered on a small road, hardly more than a goat path, and began the march back to temporary shelter, rest, resupply, and possibly some medical attention. Slowly and wearily they slogged through the ankle-deep mud, lifting each foot from the suctioning slop only with great effort. They reminded me of struggling flies on a glue strip. Some were so tired they were walking in their sleep. The glazed eyes of others told how much fighting they had seen. With helmets askew and uniforms tattered, they dragged their bodies rearward with the last vestiges of their strength. Each leg weighed a ton. No man spoke to another. There was no energy left for talk.

Not for days had soap and water touched these faces, not to mention razor blades. Every so often a bandaged man would come along being supported by another, sometimes also bandaged. A few had cigarettes dangling from their lips. Intermittently mules would come down from the mountain with dead men lashed to their backs.

When Shakespeare cried, "O war thou son of hell!" I thought he knew whereof he spoke. What he didn't know was the degree to which the horrors would be magnified in the centuries to come. These dough-

G. I's is the term

boys, or "grunts" or "doggies" as they were more often called, had to contend around the clock with every infernal device invented by man to kill or maim. If their lives were not in jeopardy from the action of planes or tanks, they were subject to being snuffed out by rifle, mortar, or artillery fire, not to mention mines, grenades, and flamethrowers. And if the grunt or the *Landser* (the German foot slogger) was lucky enough to come through unscathed, he might well find himself called on for a nighttime reconnaissance patrol and a slithering crawl through barbed wire entanglements.

Even the simple acts of toileting could be dangerous to the frontline infantryman. One of my cousins crawled out of his foxhole to defecate, only to be cut down by mortar fire. To this day a shard of shrapnel remains in his forehead, over an eye, and is considered by surgeons too risky to remove lest the sight in that eye be lost.

Those among them who survived all this, and if they didn't come down with pneumonia and could surmount their trenchfoot, might be lucky enough once in a great while to get a three-day pass to a city swarming with rear-echelon troops who didn't have the faintest idea of the rigors of infantry battle. Oblivious to the fact that their battle-battered frontline brethren existed day to day on cold canned rations, the support troops' biggest gripe was that the mess sergeant too often served "shit on a shingle," chipped beef in a creamed sauce over a slice of toast.

One evening as we were driving back down a mountain on a narrow, muddy, deeply rutted road, the dim bluish glow of a string of blackout lights came toward us in the rainy darkness, trucks headed for the front, enemy shells falling hither and yon. One of the vehicles, a three-quarter-ton truck, had been hit, forcing the column behind to halt.

As we came up to it, the tense, swearing GIs were trying to shove the crippled vehicle off the mountain so the column could continue. We hopped out of our jeep to help, and I can still remember an overwhelming surge of pride, such as I have never felt before or since, in being an American and working with other Americans for the common good, as we slipped and slid and fell in the mud, struggling in the dark, not daring to use headlights lest we target ourselves for the German artillerymen.

Shewbridge and I, too, shivered from the penetrating cold of sleety rains, although he less than I, for he had wangled a combat suit. But, as night fell, we were able to return to dry rooms and hot meals, unlike the chilled, mud-encrusted doggies squirreled in some hole.

From those days in the inhospitable mountains of Italy and forever after, the combat infantryman, more than any other serviceman, was my hero. After the war General Omar Bradley would write, "The rifleman fights without promise of either reward or relief. Behind every river there is another hill and behind that hill is another river. After weeks or months in the line, only a wound can offer him the comfort of safety, shelter and a bed. Sooner or later, unless victory comes, this chase must end on a litter or in the grave."

I appreciated the engineer, the tanker, the flyboy, the artilleryman, the mariner, and all the other members of the various branches and services that made up the country's fighting forces. But my experience throughout the war only reinforced my opinion that nobody, but nobody, gives as much of himself as the combat infantryman. It is he who bears the burden of the battle. It is he who does the face-to-face killing. In the rueful phrase of the day, he had good cause to be "nervous in the service." Of the ground forces killed in Europe, 85 percent would be from the infantry. Their sacrifices would be way out of proportion to their numbers.

As S Force impatiently waited for a penetration of the Gustav Line and a race into Rome, it occurred to me that because Japan was an ally of Germany and Italy we might find some valuable Japanese documents once we got there. And inasmuch as we had no one in the section who could read Japanese, we wired to Allied Force Headquarters in Algiers that we would need a Japanese reader. AFHQ wired back that the only man who could meet the requirement was a certain major. Further inquiry revealed that this major was on the island of Corsica and that he would be hard to get.

Then, accidentally, I learned there was a whole battalion of Japanese-speaking boys at the front, the 100th Infantry Battalion from Hawaii. After considerable red tape, I got permission to go up and bring back one of them. He turned out to be a smart PFC and every inch a soldier. The 100th Infantry won more awards than any other unit of its size. These boys and the 442nd Regimental Combat Group, all volunteers, were the two Nisei groups fighting in Italy. They suffered more than nine thousand casualties, were awarded more than a thousand Purple Hearts, and did not have a single case of desertion, a record no other unit could match. Some of these men actually escaped from hospitals to rejoin their units.

The troops of the 442nd were second-generation Japanese Americans. Yet many of their parents were among the 112,000 citizens and residents of Japanese ancestry forcibly interned after being removed from a 150-mile strip along the Pacific Coast, and despite the fact that not even one act of sabotage was known to have occurred. Not until September 1945 were they released, testimony to the fragility of civil rights in wartime.

With the belligerents stalemated at the front, the departure of S Force was delayed. I took the opportunity to take two of my sergeants and the Hawaiian boy to visit the ruins of the old city of Pompeii, fifteen miles southeast of Naples, smothered centuries ago by the flow of lava from the nearby volcano of Vesuvius. The streets were paved with flagstones, and the city had been laid out as a grid, making it easy to find one's way about. The ruins and statuary conveyed a vivid sense of the opulence of civilization at the height of the Roman Empire. Sometimes scratched into the soft stones of the villas were raunchy Latin inscriptions. Particularly entrancing were the houses of prostitution with their frescoes on the walls depicting the various coital positions. Above the door of each room within was a picture of the position the man was to assume with his partner. Obviously it was not Henry Ford who had first hit upon the efficiency of specialization.

Having learned a bit about negotiating with the British, I now also had to learn how to negotiate with Americans, especially the mechanics in the motor pool. The jeep of those days had a windshield wiper that had to be moved by hand, not the safest operation when returning from the front on a rainy night. I had noticed an occasional jeep with electric wipers and was determined to have such wipers as soon as I could remove a pair from a wrecked civilian car.

The secret of getting motor pool cooperation was to dispense German military items picked up at the front. The soldiers in the rear wanted something to show when the war was over "from the Nazi I killed." When I discovered this, I got wonderful cooperation from the mechanics when my jeep needed servicing.

In discussing with Alex Shayne this GI hunger for souvenirs, he suggested that we buy cloth and pay an Italian woman a few lire to make up some "genuine" Nazi battle flags. We laughed but never followed through.

One morning Alex and I went to the motor pool to get his jeep for a trip to Naples. I climbed in behind the wheel and as I started the vehicle, it stalled. A beginning driver, Alex was afraid something was mechanically wrong. "No," I said, "it's just cold."

"It shouldn't be," said Alex in all seriousness. "It's got antifreeze."

In 1944, it must be remembered, cars were much less common than today. Most young men did not know how to drive, unlike today when a newborn comes out of the mother's uterus waving a driver's license.

Every one of my sergeants had to be taught to drive. Because I had been driving a car for six years before entering the army, and because I did not trust my life to these beginning drivers, I always drove my own jeep. This in turn resulted in periodic reprimands from my superior officers. The enlisted man was supposed to drive when in a car with an officer.

The original jeep weighed 2,200 pounds and, because of its four-wheel drive and short wheelbase, had tremendous versatility in rough terrain. On good roads it had a maximum speed of over seventy miles per hour. It had a canvas top that gave the illusion of protection from rain, but that was it, an illusion. The top was commonly kept down. Toward war's end, some ingenious GIs in the rear areas added plywood bodies that did offer some protection from the elements.

The Germans also had a jeeplike vehicle called a *Kubelwagen* (roadster). Eventually I was able to test drive one. Ours was superior.

Returning from the front one evening toward the end of January, I was told that Captain Reining of the G-2 Section wanted me to lend my noncoms for interrogation work at the Fifth Army prisoner of war enclosure. In the last two days, three thousand prisoners from the Forty-fourth Infantry Division had been bagged, 65 percent of whom were Austrian conscripts, sick of the war and glad to be in captivity, as I noticed in reading interrogation reports at the prisoner of war cage. At times the enemy was captured in such large numbers that interrogators at division level and the next level, corps, were overwhelmed by the size of the catch and could only sample it. This was one of those times when even the interrogators at army level were swamped.

I decided that the next morning I would study the interrogation methods at the cage and volunteer my services. About to leave Captain Reining's office, I was informed that the army G-2, Colonel Howard, had directed that a second order-of-battle team be sent to Sixth Corps

Headquarters, which would now have two OB teams, Doc Pundt's and mine. I was ordered to take my two best sergeants and report there pronto. Two weeks earlier, on January 22, the corps had made a successful landing at Anzio, thirty-three miles south of Rome. After the hoped-for capture of Rome, I was to revert to S Force again.

The Allies had landed in Italy in September 1943 and in October captured Naples, the first European city to be liberated. By the end of the year they were facing the German lines in the mountains seventy-five miles south of Rome. The fighting there developed into a deadlock. In an effort to break it, Churchill conceived the plan of trying an end run by landing at Anzio, a rocky promontory and seaport. Neither the Fifth Army commander, General Mark Clark, nor the general designated to lead the Sixth Corps, John Lucas, was enraptured with the scheme.

Nevertheless the Sixth Corps, comprising at that time the U.S Third Infantry Division, the British First Division, and ranger and parachute units, landed at Anzio. So big a strategic surprise were the landings that only 150 of the 36,000 troops became casualties. The entire force was put ashore on the first day in addition to three thousand vehicles and vast quantities of ammunition, supplies, and equipment. To assist, the Allied air forces flew 1,200 sorties to seal off the landing area against German intervention, whereas the Luftwaffe was able to fly only 140 sorties against the invaders.

That was the good news. The bad news was that after only seven days herculean efforts by the German High Command enabled the Wehrmacht to seize the initiative.

Wisely, or unwisely, a matter that will be debated whenever this campaign is studied in military academies, General Lucas did not immediately push out into the Albano Hills, a volcanic mass twenty miles inland from the sea. These hills dominate the area, and—of great importance—they bisected two railroad lines and Highways 6 and 7, the lifelines used by the Wehrmacht to transport supplies from Rome and the north to their southern front.

The delay enabled Hitler to meet the threat by rushing infantry and armor from his reserves in northern Italy, swiftly sending more from the Balkans and France, and pulling some units from the stalemated area in the Apennine Mountains—all for deployment in the Albano Hills. Within ten days Lucas was hemmed in by ninety thousand Germans in a semicircle across the corps's front with the mission of driving the Allies into the sea. "The beachhead," railed the Führer at his generals, "is an abscess that has to be lanced!"

From their dominating positions in the hills, the field-gray-clad soldiers of the Reich sought to make life insufferable for the penned-in doughboys and British Tommies. The naval vessels supporting the assault, and the merchantmen supplying the beachhead, were kept under withering attack. The dream of some, that Rome could be taken in ten days, swiftly evaporated. By February 3, the reality had set in that the Sixth Corps would be fighting for its life. Together with sergeants Joe Lowensberg and Ernest Rothschild, I drove to Naples and boarded LST 408. And when one of the crew told us that LST did not stand for Landing Ship, Tank, but really for Large Slow Target, it of course raised our spirits no end.

3

An Anzio Cave:
Time for Reflection

February 6, 1944 *The ship left shortly after midnight and about noon
we arrived at Anzio, where the Sixth Corps has its headquarters. As
we came into the harbor, German planes were flying overhead, and
some were engaged in dogfights with ours. One was shot down into
the sea by our antiaircraft units. The town was being heavily shelled
and the coastal road interdicted by shell fire as we drove along it.
Some shots fell not far from us as we followed the signs to Sixth Corps
Headquarters, where we reported to the G-2.*

That diary entry was a precursor of what lay ahead.

We had missed the good part—the successful, surprise, unopposed
landing. We arrived in the midst of the enemy counterattack, and a
dilly it would be. Losses were heavy. Typical was the fate of a picked
force of 767 British Rangers sent on a mission. Only 6 came back.

The G-2, as the chief of the intelligence section is often referred to,
was crusty Colonel Joseph Langevin. In his forties, with average build
and a cavalryman's walk, he had dark slicked-down hair carefully
parted in the middle. He spoke French, but no German. Since our enemies were principally Germans, fortified with Austrians, Czechs, Poles,
Italians, and a sprinkling of other nationalities, his linguistic ability

was of little use, but came in handy later when dealing with our French ally. A West Pointer and a stickler for military formalities, he insisted that an officer not go to a sergeant's desk, but instead, that the sergeant be summoned to the officer's. He rarely laughed, but when he did, the high-pitched laugh approached a cackle. Although he was a gruff and demanding curmudgeon, not one for easy intimacy with his staff (his taciturnity certainly no help), his competence and professionalism were highly respected. Destined to be my boss till the war's end, he was a man I came to genuinely admire.

I reported to him in the midst of an air raid alarm, but this did not prevent him from dumping two foot-high piles of printed matter on my desk area, opposite Pundt's, on a boardroom-size table, with a cryptic, "See what you can do with this stuff."

Anzio speedily assumed a different form from other campaigns. With the entire corps bottled by the Germans into a minuscule parcel of real estate, it became a soldier's nightmare. Cooks, chaplains, doctors and nurses, artillerymen and infantrymen, engineers and truckers, headquarters clerks and staff officers, privates and generals—all were within range of the enemy guns. No man on this strip of land could be sure he would still be alive the next day. There was no such thing as safety in the rear areas. In the later stages of the battle, the German determination to pulverize Anzio caused the frontline troops, who had come to the rear for relief and refitting, to hasten back to the front, where they felt safer.

Out on the water it was no different. Day and night a steady rain of missiles from long-range German guns peppered the harbor, splashing among the ships and sending up fountains of spray. When a vessel was fatally hit, boats from nearby ships would race to rescue the survivors. The British and American naval vessels supplying gunnery support sought to protect themselves with wired balloons to discourage the enemy's electronically directed glider bombs, low-flying dive bombers, and mine-laying aircraft. Despite antiaircraft barrages, the swastika-marked planes at times successfully broke through the barriers. At the front much of the fighting was a mixture of trench warfare reminiscent of World War I and the house-to-house fighting, even room-to-room, redolent of the eighty days and nights of hand-to-hand fighting that marked the battle of Stalingrad. Compounding the misery of the men were long periods of drenching, lashing rains that occasionally subsided into drizzle. They seemed never to stop, and they filled the trenches of the doughboys and their Tommy comrades to a point where men were knee-deep in water. The dead, who had been hastily buried in shallow graves, had the mounds of dirt covering them, and the crude crosses marking the temporary interment sites, washed away by torrents.

This misery and carnage were to continue until the end of May as both sides struggled valiantly to capture some of the most purgatorial terrain in all of Europe. A sizable part of the battleground consisted of wadis, gullies that in the dry season were dry but in the long rainy season filled with water and in spring sprouted overgrown foliage. Not far from the wadis were caves, and woods occupied another section of the disputed battlefield. Still another sizable part was a large segment of the Pontine marshes. A ten-year program by Mussolini's government had drained some of the ground, but much still remained to be reclaimed.

The terrain could not have been better designed for defensive operations. The Germans fortified every farmhouse, barn, and outbuilding. Machine guns, antitank guns, and even tanks were hidden in these structures, and their capture (and frequent recapture by the other side) came at high cost. Some companies suffered casualty rates of 50 percent and more.

In palmier days, Anzio had been a pleasant resort town with orange trees and sea breezes, a favorite summering place for affluent Romans looking to escape the city's heat. It was here that Mussolini often brought his mistress on summer afternoons.

A mile-long, crescent-shaped beach, with brightly painted bathhouses, joined it to the neighboring town of Nettuno. From its excellent port a fleet of fishing boats plied the cobalt blue Tyrrhenian Sea seeking catches in the pristine waters. Some of these fish were served in the many waterfront restaurants until German bombing and artillery fire demolished them.

Anzio also had historical interest: not that the average GI cared a damn, but it was the birthplace of Caligula, the emperor of Rome from A.D. 37–41. It was also the birthplace of Nero, and it was in the theater of Anzio that Nero supposedly fiddled while Rome burned. To the GI, however, Anzio was no vacation resort. By early February when I was ordered there, the Allied troops faced a perimeter of tough German forces bent on annihilating them.

Since Field Marshal Kesselring now had a second front to contend with, he switched some of his Rapido troops to the Anzio struggle. The Allies, in turn, countered by sending in the Forty-fifth Infantry Division and half the First Armored to bolster the breakout effort. As each side sought to frustrate the other's aim, the sultry-voiced radio propagandist Axis Sally would gleefully describe us hemmed-in beachheaders as "the largest self-supporting prisoner of war camp in the world." Sadly, this wasn't far from the truth.

At the end of my first day at headquarters, Doc Pundt invited me to share his sleeping place, a nearby wine cellar. *It is damp, but it will feel good tonight considering that the shells from a German railroad gun are crashing all around,* says my diary.

After a few days we moved out of this cellar, which we considered vulnerable to heavy shells, for a new home in a hill of limestone through which the railroad had cut a passageway. From the track level one climbed a ladder to a height of twenty feet and entered a large excavation. The one drawback to our new sleeping quarters was its distance from headquarters. This required a trot of half a mile, often through rain and falling shells. One night a truck ahead of us suffered a direct hit, the parts blown over an area a hundred yards wide.

Doc and I felt secure in our new cavernous sanctuary, as did some of the thirty or so enlisted men who had also discovered this haven. The older among them nightly celebrated their security and dulled their fears by getting noisily drunk. Others, the younger ones, less raucous, did not feel secure, especially during the first nights when we could hear the drone of the German bombers overhead and then the drumroll of heavy explosions, some so close that the reverberations shook the limestone refuge. Caught in the maelstrom of war, many of the youngsters, eighteen and nineteen years old, cried unashamedly and called for their mothers. Others prayed aloud. I prayed too, but silently, and thought of my parents and brothers and wondered what, in the Great Scheme of things, I had done to be here.

Unable to sleep because of boozing GIs on one hand and the young GIs wailing for their mothers on the other, I turned to ruminating, as was my habit when I went to bed, in the hope that it would lead to sleep. But each wave of Luftwaffe bombers elicited cries from the fear-stricken youngsters of "Mother!" "Mom!" and "Mommy!"—some mournful and some panicky.

These cries brought to mind my own mother. Born to poor peasant parents, she was the youngest of eight children and only sixteen when, with an older sister, she left home and family in a German-speaking village in Hungary (ceded to Rumania after World War I) to come to America. I can picture her then, with light brown hair, gray eyes, and vivid in her youthfulness, full of anxiety and hope for a better life. Like so many immigrants, especially Italian and German, she found a home with friends from the Old Country in Hoboken, New Jersey, across the Hudson from New York City. Two years later she met and married another immigrant, who was to become my father.

My call to the army had left her most unhappy. She had lost a brother and cousins in the First World War and had a foreboding I would not survive this one. Our leave-taking was tearful, and for her heartbreaking. I knew that I would miss her love and care, and her cooking and baking. Her *Apfelstrudel* was unsurpassed. It was made from scratch. Her rolling pin flattened out the dough until it was tissue thin—no store-bought phyllo for her. The basement shelves sagged with the products of my mother's energy and economy. They were laden with canned tomatoes, peaches, plums, pears, cherries, crabapples, quinces, string beans, and a myriad of other fruits and vegetables, not to mention the produce she pickled.

Her talents were equally on display in the garden. Year after year it was fully in bloom from April through November. When one group of flowers wilted, another group took its place, and this went on all spring, summer, and fall. No queen, princess, or society dowager ever derived as much pleasure from her jewels as my mother got from her flowers. To her, every leaf, petal, pistil, and bud was a gem to be admired and wondered about. "How," she would say, "can anyone not believe in God?"

Mom had a green thumb and intuitively knew if a plant needed more or less water, more or less sun, or just a little perking up and talking to. Or maybe it was in need of a little fertilizer. The peasant in my mother was a believer in the use of natural fertilizers, and her flowers and shrubs responded joyfully to her doses of cow, sheep, and horse manure.

As a boy growing up in the 1920s, I regretted that not all transport was automotive. There were still horses pulling wagons. If a horse dropped a load of steaming, stinking manure on our block, I could be certain that Mom would spot it and, over my protests, shoo me out with a broom and shovel to retrieve it for her garden. It was too precious to waste. It was easily understandable to me that her flowers and bushes flourished. She would have taken umbrage had they not.

Mom was a law-abiding citizen and scrupulously honest. As a young boy, if I returned from the grocer with a dime too much change, I would be sent back to return it. But in the famous Brooklyn Botanical Gardens she was not above looking around to see if a guard was in sight and, if not, snipping a bit from a plant, wrapping the slip in a wet handkerchief, hiding it in her handbag to be planted and nurtured when we returned home. In spite of the park's warning signs, and in spite of my father's frowns, head shakings, embarrassment, and remonstrances, he never succeeded in breaking her of this habit. "Oh," she would say, waving him away, "nobody will miss it." Subject closed.

As Mom gave all to her garden, so she gave all to her children. When my brother Frank was five years old, he contracted pneumonia, usually fatal in those days. Penicillin was then unknown. Despite the ministrations of the doctor, he developed a lung abscess. A specialist was called in. Frank was rushed to the hospital, where a rib was removed and a tube inserted to drain the pus. For two weeks it was nip and tuck whether the little boy would survive. He would take no food from a nurse, so Mom installed herself in a chair in the hospital room and for three weeks, day and night, nursed him until he was well out of danger. When she left with Frank, the nurses gave her a certificate awarding her the title "The Hospital's Best Nurse."

In the midst of my recollections, another flight of German planes delivered its message of death and debilitating fear, and again there were ejaculatory pleas for God's mercy and terror-laden cries for mothers. Why always for mothers, I wondered. Why not for fathers? Much as I loved my mother, I loved my father equally, and my thoughts turned to him. I had never known a man I admired more.

While my mother came from a poor peasant background, my father's family was somewhat different. His father, my grandfather, had inherited a sizable estate. He was a prominent landowner and judge. This, to him, justified his proclivity for wine, women, and song, plus gambling and fast horses. The horses had to be the spankingest in the region. To pay for his extravagances, he was periodically forced to sell off pieces of his lands. When most of the lands were gone, he conveniently

died, leaving much debt and, by the law of primogeniture, the oldest
son as head of the household. That was my father, age fourteen. After
struggling for three years with the impoverished estate, my father decided that fortune could better be pursued in America. He arrived at
Ellis Island with five dollars and a fourteen-year-old sister in tow.

Pop had only six or eight years of traditional schooling, but he had
an acquisitive mind and his education never ended. In the evenings
after work he read the *Staats Zeitung*, a German-language newspaper,
and then an English paper. He read several magazines, his favorite being
the *National Geographic*. Traveling was his great pleasure, equaled
only by his love of classical music. He had a large record collection and
was especially fond of the Italian tenor Enrico Caruso and the violinist
Fritz Kreisler, particularly his recordings of *Liebeslied* and *Liebesfreud*.
On Sunday afternoons he listened to them for hours. He could play the
accordion, if one could get him to play it.

Dark haired and brown-eyed, he was a handsome, well-built man.
He had no bad habits, causing my mother's friends to envy her openly.
He did not smoke and only occasionally drank a beer or a cocktail,
being partial to liqueurs, especially *Kümmel*, a liqueur made from car-
away seed. Even tempered and slow to anger, he had a voice that was
firm but never imperious. I could remember as a youngster being
spanked by him only twice, and both times I had it coming.

Pop's word was his bond. His family knew it, and when he started
his own knitwear manufacturing firm, so did his employees. A promise
to him was the giving of his sacred word, and the promise was kept no
matter how difficult it might be. This attitude he also sought to incul-
cate in his children. In my teens I often visited my cousins in the
Bronx. They were caddies and had introduced me to the game of golf.
On winter Sunday afternoons, though, we played penny poker. But one
Sunday the sky was dropping rain in buckets. The sewers couldn't handle the flow fast enough. Streets were flooded, and the subway station
was three blocks away. As my father listened to his records, he noticed
my impatient glances out the window. "Are your cousins expecting
you?" he asked.

"Yes," I said, "but look how it's raining. I'm not going."

"Yes, you are," said Pop. "You've got a raincoat and rubbers. You
won't melt. Go!"

Pop was a keen observer of social movements and had an uncanny sense for predicting the consequences of political acts. He would have been a good adviser to a president. The older I got, the more I came to admire his wisdom and philosophy, and at Anzio I often reflected on them.

While the German gunners and bombers punctuated the long nights with their deadly missiles, there was one perhaps dubious benefit to being holed up: The hours were conducive to introspection. How did I get here, and why? The Fourteenth Armored Division, in which I had served for six months after being commissioned, and from which I was called to the intelligence school, was still in the States and far from battle-ready. But apparently graduation from the intelligence school had been my ticket to the war, and I pondered the obvious. Would my life be snuffed out at Anzio at the age of twenty-eight? If so, who, other than my family and a few friends, would miss me? Certainly I would be no great loss to the world. It would not be losing a Galileo, a Michelangelo, a Mozart, a Rembrandt, or a Shakespeare. Surely God didn't owe me any favors. There was nothing special about me. Why should He watch over me any more than all these other guys sweating it out here on the beachhead? What was I but just an ordinary Joe who had been born in Hoboken, New Jersey, and raised in Ridgewood, New York.

Yes, it happened that I spoke German, an accident of birth. My parents had emigrated from two German-speaking villages in Hungary before the First World War. These villages had been settled many generations earlier by farmers from the Swabian region of Germany, the area consisting of Württemberg, Hesse, and Bavaria, the lands on both sides of the Black Forest in the valleys of the Rhine and the Neckar.

To prepare themselves for citizenship, and to learn the language of their new country, they had gone to night school. At home, though, they still spoke German in the Swabian dialect, and I, as the first born, naturally learned this as my first language. Then, after my graduation from grammar school, my mother had taken her three sons to visit her family in Europe. We spent two months in her village, except for a few days when we visited my father's relatives in the village he came from, and a couple days when we went on a religious pilgrimage. All that time, unless talking with my brothers, I spoke only the German Swabian dialect, the language that had come down through generations from the town's Swabian forebears.

On returning to America to start high school, I had to choose a foreign language for study in the course in which I was enrolled. Taking the path of least resistance, I chose German. After studying the formal language, usually called high German, for two years, I transferred to a newly built school nearer my home. Here there were only two students in the third-year German class, a German girl who was placed there to learn English and myself. For the next two years I had what amounted to a private tutor, a six-foot-tall, forbidding spinster with an acidic tongue, a martinet. I dared not go to class without knowing my assignment cold. Not only was there no place to hide, but I did not want to look bad in comparison with the girl. Little did I dream how that tutelage would shape my destiny.

With only two students in the class, study was intense and progress rapid. Ten years later when tested for competency in German at the Military Intelligence School, I outscored many of the native Germans in the written exams.

When I graduated from high school in 1933, the depression was in full force. Hard times had hit the knitting business, but I had saved enough money for my first year's university tuition from my after-school and Saturday work in the mill. When I asked my father for my savings, though, he told me he had had to use the money to meet the payroll. "But when your tuition is due," he said, "I'll have it for you." And he did. (What I did not know then, and did not find out until forty-one years later in cleaning out his desk and files after his death, was that he had borrowed the money at a usurious rate of interest with our furniture as collateral.)

Having heard that Columbia University had an outstanding school of journalism, and a career in journalism now being my goal, I applied there. At the interview with the dean of admissions, I nervously watched as he opened the folder with my application, essay, and photograph. The photograph turned out to be a sepia-colored blank. To save the cost of a picture, I had submitted the proof of my high school year book picture, and it had almost completely faded away.

"Your photograph doesn't do you justice," said the dean charitably.

I wasn't so sure. Embarrassed by the failure of my misguided economy, I was blushing so deeply that I felt my face must also be a sepia-colored blank.

After looking over my application and reading the essay, affording me time to regain my composure, the dean asked me a few questions, and then, finally, "To what other colleges have you applied?"

"None," I said.

"None?" he asked, startled.

"I guess I should have," I said lamely, taking the cue from his tone and raised eyebrows.

"Yes," he said. "You should have. We admit only a small percentage of those who apply."

"I didn't know that," I said dejectedly.

"Well," he said, putting the contents back into the folder, "We'll see. You will hear from us."

Leaving the office, I was sure my ship was sunk.

It wasn't. A few weeks later I received a letter of acceptance.

My four years at Columbia proved to be tough ones. I commuted daily by subway from Ridgewood to the school in Manhattan. There was no time for extracurricular activities. After classes I would rush home, grab a bite, and go off to the knitting mill to earn money for current expenses and the following year's tuition and books.

My studies centered around economics, literature, history, government, and politics. To be the renaissance man was the goal. But on finishing college, I was unable to go on to the graduate school of journalism. The knitting business, like so many during the depression, suffered serious losses. My father was nearing a nervous breakdown, and my mother suggested that I forget graduate school, that it might be wiser for me to help out my father. In good conscience I had to agree.

For the next five years, with Adolf Hitler's star in the ascendancy as national socialism captured the German imagination, my energies were directed to helping my father get the mill back on its feet. Gradually I became resigned to leading a businessman's life and not a journalist's.

Hoping that the last flight of German bombers, with its staccato rain of death, would be the final one for the night, I lay on my bedding roll and confessed to myself that I had a problem. This war was not in my life plan. I hadn't yet lived. There wasn't a soul in this world that I hated, there was really nobody that I wanted to kill, but here I was on Anzio with the mission of using my knowledge of German to kill Germans.

4

"Like Shooting Fish in a Barrel"

Sorting through the stacks of reports, mostly from AFHQ, that the colonel had dumped on my desk, I saw the latest information about German weapons, tanks, vehicles, planes, ammunition, and personalities, as well as assorted other data. I set about familiarizing myself with the material and categorizing the information for quick retrieval. Air raids occurred with disconcerting frequency. Headquarters are high-priority targets if they can be located and are vulnerable to attack, and evidently we met the criteria. Usually we ignored the sirens and went on with our work.

February 7, 1944 *Sixth Corps Headquarters was housed in a big stone structure, probably once a town administrative building. Apparently it was located by the Germans, because this morning we were strafed and bombed.*

The attack came unexpectedly. There had been so many air raid alerts that we paid no attention to another. Suddenly bombs fell around the building and bullets came into the window next to me. One of them would have hit Pundt, who worked opposite me at a long table, had he stayed in his chair one second longer. We all hit the floor and a few got down into the cellar, including the corps commander, General Lucas, who could usually be seen unperturbedly smoking his corncob pipe. Some of the boys in the courtyard were wounded. None of the officers were hit.

In the afternoon headquarters was moved to a big, deep wine cellar nearby, obviously the storage facility for a large vintner.

This facility consisted of an enormous maze of passageways with alcoves chiseled out of the soft rock. In these recesses were stored huge vats of maturing wines. Removal of the vats opened the space for office cubbyholes.

The evening of the day that our command post (the shorthand reference for it was CP) was targeted, the town hospital, taken over by the military and clearly marked, was bombed, killing twenty-one doctors, nurses, and patients. This event was deeply resented at headquarters, particularly inasmuch as the Germans had earlier one night sunk a British hospital ship lying out to sea, a ship that had been fully lit up in conformity with the terms of the Geneva Convention. In fairness to the enemy, it had to be admitted that bombs don't always land where they are intended. Our own men were at times bombed by our own planes.

How fairly both sides fought the war is debatable. As the German transportation situation worsened in Italy and later in France, the enemy was not above using his ambulances to transport ammunition in violation of the rules of the Geneva Convention, designed to keep war within moral boundaries. On the other hand, in the later stages of the war, to break civilian morale, the British and American fire bombing of Dresden, a Wehrmacht hospital city, in which 135,000 were killed, could hardly be considered a saintly act.

The entire beachhead was subject to bombing attacks. To the day and night shelling I quickly adjusted. Just as at home one could learn to sleep through the noise of street traffic in the early morning hours, so here, too, one learned to sleep through the nightly rumble of artillery barrages. The adjustment, in my case, was sped by a hefty slug of rye from the bottle in the pocket of my bedding roll.

February 8 *Shelling and bombing of the town continues day and night.*
   My job is
   1) Charge of captured documents.

The order-of-battle section in the Sixth Corps's underground headquarters at Anzio as sketched by an army artist.

2) *Check translations.*
3) *Examine all captured maps.*
4) *To be the expert on all German tanks, guns, and equipment.*

February 9 *This morning a shell from an unlocated 210-mm railroad gun landed a few feet from the entrance to our cave command post, wounding the MP and three others and wrecking a jeep.*

We located the First Parachute Corps headquarters from a captured map, and they'll probably get a working over like the one they gave us the other day in our first command post.

Two days later, from another captured map, I located another head-quarters, that of the Third Panzer Grenadier Division. A pilot was briefed and sent to bomb it.

It was a cardinal principle of both sides that the brains of an army are its staff—army, corps, and division headquarters. Wipe out these nerve centers and the units they control will quickly collapse of paralysis. In bygone eras, headquarters were not easily assailable even if the location was known. In modern warfare, however, they are vulnerable to air attack. Hence my gloating over discovering a German corps head-quarters and a division headquarters, all within three days.

February 10   *The MP stationed up the street from the headquarters entrance, who was hit yesterday, died today.*

In walking through the streets of Anzio, a town much prettier than anything I had seen in southern Italy, I noticed there had been much looting of the houses. Troops felt that in a combat zone anything of value or comfort in a house rightfully belonged to them. For someone with a sense of property rights, this seemed regretful, yet I couldn't blame them. The houses with cellars offered some safety from the shelling and bombing, and the men naturally availed themselves of the wine and other comforts.

Three weeks after the initial landings, prisoners told interrogators that a very high ranking officer had said that Hitler had given orders that we had to be driven into the sea by the twelfth, the next day. This confirmed what we had earlier learned, that a Nazi attack was in preparation and was due to begin that night. And sure enough, that evening their big guns boomed away. Anzio rattled to the thunderous explosions of shell fire, a prelude to the main attack that would start four days later.

The German Fourteenth Army, under the command of General von Mackensen, now numbered 125,000. On the Allied side reinforcements brought the number of troops crammed onto the beachhead to 100,000. So crowded had it become that German bombers able to penetrate the air defenses and make their runs across the beachhead were almost certain to hit rewarding targets. As for the German gunners, a reconnaissance pilot who flew over the Albano Hills was to tell me, "The way those Krauts can shoot down at you guys is like shooting fish in a barrel." As a fledgling, I was fascinated by the daily morning General Staff meetings at which Colonel Langevin briefed the division generals and their G-2s. We junior intelligence officers attended when our duties permitted, and in due course Doc Pundt and I would take over some of the briefing. These sessions took place in front of a large detailed map covered with acetate in the war room, the nerve center of operations, where information is received and from which it is disseminated. In blue grease pencil our units and operations were indicated, while the enemy dispositions and vital information were shown in red.

There are many factors a commanding general must take into account before issuing his orders. First, of course, is his role in the grand plan. To carry out his mission he must factor in the strength and condition of the forces available to him, including air and possibly naval support. His supply situation, the weather, the road network, and terrain must enter his thinking.

War has been described by the great German military theoretician von Clausewitz as basically a mistake-ridden exercise conducted in fog-like conditions. While this is particularly true once the battle has been joined, there is also a heavy preliminary fog as the opponents gird for battle. The commander wants to know how many of the enemy he is facing, where they are positioned, what type of troops they are, and how they are equipped. Are they seasoned fighters or new conscripts? What percentage are native to the enemy country and what percentage are men from countries the enemy has conquered and pressed into service under duress? What kind and number of tanks and self-propelled artillery oppose him? What type of antitank weapons must he take into his calculations? Does the opponent have air support? Does he have a tactical reserve? What is his supply situation? How is his morale?

In short, the commander wants to know what he is up against. Consequently, his demands on G-2 are insatiable. What are his opponent's options? His intentions? If an enemy attack is planned, when and where will it be? If the enemy decides to defend, is it merely to delay the advance or to make a last ditch stand? Or is it to retreat? If so, is there a prepared line at which he will make a new stand? And if he retreats, will the newly conquered area be safe for the advancing soldiers or will they encounter guerrilla resistance?

To befuddle his opponent and to checkmate his possible moves, the enemy commander tries to prevent his opponent from finding the answers to these questions. It is G-2's function to penetrate the resulting murkiness, so that the general is not left in the situation of a blind boxer unable to deflect or counter his opponent's blows.

Supplementing these meetings was the distribution of the daily G-2 journal, which contained summaries of the reports from the various intelligence sources, such as the OSS operatives (forerunners of the CIA) working behind the enemy lines, the counterintelligence agents, and the nightly reconnoitering patrols. Included would be the fruits of prisoner interrogation and information derived from captured documents, sometimes of devastating import to the enemy. His passwords, regularly uncovered from captured documents and prisoner of war (PW) interrogation, were included for the benefit of our patrols before they went on their missions. The segment dealing with information gathered from the air included the results of the photo interpretation of pictures taken over enemy territory, plus the reports of the pilots describing what they had seen, what actions they had taken, and where they had encountered flak.

These were the main sources of intelligence funneling in to the G-2 section, but there were others, particularly important being radio intercept, the findings from which were distributed only on a "need to know" basis.

Initially I was a bit puzzled when the colonel had us relocate a German unit on the enemy situation map when we had no evidence of such a move from PW reports or captured documents. His action, however, invariably proved correct, and was corroborated by subsequent prisoner interrogation. With the passage of time I discovered his actions were not based on intuition, but on the contents of an envelope that was left on his desk by an officer who routinely came and left at dawn. The contents were the product of our radio intercept unit, a van with powerful radio intercept equipment. It was well camouflaged, strategically located in a wooded area, and manned by highly trained German-speaking technicians.

While in general the enlisted men and officers in the section worked smoothly together, there were occasions when I was appalled by the irreverence and cavalier attitude of some of the clerks. One day a stenographer, a bit frazzled, said to another, "Gimme a hand, will you? I got a whole mess of shit to type up."

"What have you got?" said the other.

"The colonel's G-2 Estimate of the Situation," was the answer.

The estimate was a summary and evaluation of the work of the whole panoply of intelligence gatherers. Its purpose was to depict what was happening on the other side. Men often lost their lives to get the information going into it.

February 12   *Today the major from Grave Registration came down to our section in G-2 and showed us an arm insignia—a streak of lightning going through an eagle—and asked us to identify the unit. We didn't recognize it as American, British, German, Italian, or French.*

The major's problem was where to bury the man, in the Allied section of the cemetery or the enemy section. The body had been washed up on the beach. So, reluctantly, I accompanied him to the cemetery outside of town and found about 1,000 graves (800 American, 200 enemy) and 20 or so unburied bodies. Except for the crushed bodies in a tank accident during training at Camp Chaffee, this was my first close-up encounter with death in the war.

From a distance these unburied bodies appeared to be statuary thrown on a heap.

My first impression as we approached the burial area in the jeep was shock at the grotesque positions in which the bodies lay, rigor mortis having long set in. The second impression was the waxlike artificial look about the figures. But some of the bodies were just a mass of meat. It was a truly grisly scene.

The man whom I came to try to identify, it developed, had just been identified by one of the Italian grave diggers, who had lived for a time in Hungary. He recognized the shoes of the dead man as the kind worn by Hungarian sailors. They have a round attachment to the heel and this revolves. Its purpose is to aid the wearer in doing facing movements in marching drills.

During World War II, Hungary, landlocked, had no navy. The government, however, was led by Admiral Horthy, a World War I–era naval officer from the days when the Austro-Hungarian Empire sprawled over much of Europe and boasted a navy. Apparently some units of the Hungarian defense forces were still designated "sailors," since Hungry had a few small river gunboats.

The cemetery was located at the seaside, and as the major and I talked, troops coming off the boats were being driven past it, a chilling introduction to the fate Anzio might have in store for some of them.

On February 13, after a night in which thirty enemy planes dumped their bombs on us, a navy officer who was attached to S Force with me, and was now also temporarily attached to Sixth Corps headquarters, told me he had heard that the force had been dissolved, leading me to wonder what my next assignment would be once Rome was taken.

The railroad gun that had been firing at us several times a day and then gone into hiding—and for which we had sent out fighter-bombers time and again—was supposed to have been found and put out of action. No sooner had the air officer gleefully reported it neutralized than it again shelled the town. The German employment of their monstrous railroad guns, thorns in our side, was devilishly adept. We thought there were two. Only after the breakout did we learn there had been four. These elusive behemoths would fire their 562-pound shells and then withdraw into a tunnel before they could be detected from the air. During clear daylight hours the technique was to fire a few rounds and

A German railroad gun used at Anzio. Captured photo.

scoot back into their tunnels for cover and concealment before our spotter planes could take off in search of them. Darkness and bad weather were the favorite times to bedevil us. To some of the men these guns were known as Anzio Annie. To others, because the projectiles hurtling through the air made a sound similar to that of a speeding train roaring by, they were dubbed the Anzio Express. At headquarters we referred to the guns as "Whistling Pete."

The greater the butchery, the larger was the capture of documents. I was always a bit repulsed when handed a batch of bloody papers with a buck slip reading, "From good Germans—dead ones." This was our Third Infantry Division's trademark.

The study of documents was engrossing work, because one never knew what one would find. There was also a tantalizing element: In which batch would we hit the jackpot? Meticulous examination leavened by serendipity and voilà! There it could be!

Most of the document perusal was done by the sergeants, three of whom were native-born Germans and one an American of German ancestry. They sorted the wheat from the chaff. Any papers or maps they thought might have value were culled out for my evaluation. When the fighting was particularly heavy and there were many dead and wounded and large batches of prisoners, the document haul was so large it was brought in mailbags. Even at such times, when we felt like miners panning a ton of silt to find an ounce of gold, our searches were never haphazard, but as thorough as time would permit. Consequently, a significant amount of shelling and bombing was not willy-nilly, as it may have appeared to the frontline soldier, but directed at targets ferreted out by behind-the-line intelligence.

For us laborers in the vineyards of intelligence, some aspects of our work were unpleasant. Bloody documents were no joy to inspect. And when they were both bloody and wet, which was often, because so much of the weather during the fighting was rainy, they were particularly revolting. Sometimes they were not removed from the fallen soldier's pockets until he had lain dead for days in a rain-drenched field or ditch. Yet, onerous though our task was, we intelligence personnel could not get rid of these papers without examining them, lest there be a clue in them as to how to kill more of the enemy and, conversely, cut American and British losses.

As recompense for our slightly sheltered lives at field headquarters,

"Gosh, I didn't know we'd have fo walk . . . Where the hell's that Anzio Express?"

This cartoon appeared in the *Beachhead News* on July 1, 1944, at the time of the breakout from the beachhead and the capture of Rome.

we felt a moral obligation to the frontline soldier to do a conscientious job so as to shorten his travail and possibly save his life. That was our motivation. No matter how bloody and wet the document, no matter how repulsive, it was scrutinized. It just might be that nugget of gold.

Before eating, and at times at considerable inconvenience, I scrubbed my hands thoroughly, not only for sanitary reasons, but to get rid of that odor of death that, no matter how much I scrubbed, seemed to linger with an irritating pervasiveness.

We thought then, and I still think now, that we were making a significant contribution to the battle to undo Hitler. Our work revealed that Germany was running so short of manpower that sixteen- and seventeen-year-old kids were being drafted and given only two months of basic training before being thrown into the front lines. This policy was criminal. Sometimes I felt like weeping as I went through their papers and pictures. To my parents I wrote: "They're not soldiers. They're just children in uniform. They are now pulling their kids directly from the Hitler Jugend. I can't help wondering how long before they take them from the kindergarten. I don't see how Germany can go on much longer. We have overwhelming air power, manpower, and production."

The Hitler Jugend was more or less similar to our Boy Scouts, although rigidly organized, superficially trained militarily, and politically oriented.

Most German boys carried enough documentation to write their biographies. Among the items they surrendered were their wallets, birth certificates, baptismal certificates, family pictures, pictures of their girlfriends or wives, diaries, driving licenses, and any of a hundred more or less standard items—including as a rule a batch of personal letters.

Some carried nude pictures of their wives or sweethearts, stimulating reminders of the joys awaiting their return. One PW had half a dozen seductively posed shots that, according to the letter found with them, had been taken by the woman's father. Such photos, triggering salivating appraisals, lightened the day's chores and were gleefully passed around, getting as much critical inspection as a captured map.

Other pictures had a morbid interest. A couple pasted into my diary were typical of those taken from soldiers who had earlier served on the Russian front. One depicts two civilians hanging from a lamp post, a uniformed German standing by, and a crowd of civilians that had seemingly been summoned to witness the hangings. The other shows a man being hanged and another lying on the ground, already hanged. Such photos we forwarded to the War Crimes Commission.

Some of the items found among the documents were considered souvenirs. As I had discovered at army headquarters, and quickly found at corps, a sergeant's whistle or compass, or the lapel patch from the uniform of an Italian parachutist of the Nembo Regiment, produced instant service on my jeep.

However, in the ordinary course of events, in the absence of maps or

We often found photos like these on German PWs who had previously served in Russia. In one, an SS officer stands at a gallows where one victim still swings from a noose and another, cut down, lies on the ground. In the other, two men hang from a lamppost while a German officer observes the civilians assembled to witness the execution.

field orders, the item most important to the order-of-battle specialists in the daily study of the enemy was the German soldier's *Soldbuch*, a passport-sized booklet that ingeniously encapsulated his entire military history. It had to be carried by the man at all times, whether he was a private or a field marshal. It was of tremendous help to American intelligence people in understanding how the Teutonic army operated.

The *Soldbuch* was an incredibly informative document. Starting with the soldier's photograph, blood type, and complete physical description, including distinctive marks, it gave his date and place of birth, the date and place from which he entered the service, his signature, army serial number, the name and address of his wife and parents, his religion, and his civilian occupation.

Other data included the names and dates of the successive units to which he had been posted and his current rank. Space was provided for his shoe size and every item of clothing he had been issued, plus any specialized clothing and special equipment, such as field glasses, compass, gas mask, etc. The weapon he was issued and its serial number were recorded.

There was a page for his dental record, which showed any missing teeth and tooth replacements. There were pages for his medical record, detailing the dates and places of hospitalization, even including a record of receipts for valuables turned in at the hospital for safekeeping.

One page listed the prescription of his eyeglasses, including the measurement of the bridge of his nose.

There was space for the medals he was awarded and even for acknowledgment that he had received his laundry money.

All leaves of over five days and the reason for the leaves were noted.

On the inside of the back cover were printed the soldier's responsibilities in connection with the document and a warning that unauthorized changes would be punished as falsifications.

The back cover was double-sized and folded in to create a pocket for holding other papers. Printed inside this cover was the admonition to read the rules carefully. These rules stated:

1. The *Soldbuch* serves the soldier in wartime as a personal identification, and authorizes him to receive his pay from his regular paymaster or another. Further, it is to be used as his identification to receive mail, for railroad trips, and for leaves.

2. The soldier is always to carry his *Soldbuch* in his coat pocket. To keep it in his baggage or in his quarters or elsewhere is forbidden. It is in the owner's interest to carefully guard it.

3. The *Soldbuch* must be neatly kept. It is the owner's responsibility to see that all changes in allowances due to promotion or transfer are immediately recorded by his authorized service post.

4. The *Soldbuch* is a legal document. Entries are to be made only by army duty stations. Self-made entries will be punished as document falsifications.

5. The loss or damage to the *Soldbuch* is to be immediately reported to the troop section or service post where he is currently assigned. The issue of a new *Soldbuch* is to be requested.

Through the study of the constant flow of these *Soldbuchs*, information pumped from prisoners, plus the study of captured documents of all sorts, we OB specialists developed a wide and deep knowledge of the German army, its weapons, equipment, and policies. We were immersed from early morning until late night in these studies, often uncovering trends.

The too-rapid expansion of that army under Hitler led to many inadequacies and severe strains as its leadership tried to compensate for deficiencies. A shortage of vehicles to transport its officers, for example, was offset by commandeering civilian cars.

In the U.S. Army, there was a closer kinship between officers and men, and in combat units outstanding sergeants were sometimes given battlefield commissions. This rarely occurred on the other side. There were some interesting organizational differences and policies in the two armies. If an American division, for instance, usually about 15,000 men, suffered heavy losses, the casualties would be replaced by new soldiers from replacement depots in the rear areas, referred to by the GIs as "repple depples." So American divisions were kept pretty much at full strength.

The Germans operated similarly in the early stages of the war, but differently in the later stages. Now, when Wehrmacht divisions, which at full strength numbered 10,000 men, were decimated, the remnants of two or three divisions would be united into one new one with a new name. By examining the *Soldbuchs* taken from prisoners we were able to trace which divisions had been eliminated and which new ones had been formed.

As the war went on, the firepower of Allied divisions was increased. On the other hand, as the Wehrmacht's need for divisions increased and as new divisions were formed, they were smaller and had fewer tanks and less artillery. In 1940 a panzer division's table of organization called for it to have 328 tanks. Four years later such a division, if at full strength, which it rarely was, had only 159 tanks. Infantry divisions were reorganized on a basis of seven battalions instead of the previous nine, and companies that originally had 180 men were reduced to 80.

When masses of *Soldbuchs* began turning up showing their owners were forty-eight, forty-nine, and fifty years old and at the other end were fifteen-, sixteen-, and seventeen-year-olds, it was not difficult to extrapolate that Hitler was digging desperately deep into the manpower barrel.

On the night of February 15, a few hours before the main German attack was to start, a package of documents came in with two maps. It was late, close to midnight. Pundt and I were tired, but I wanted to at least have a fast look at the maps. Doc, however, insisted I leave them for Sergeant Greiner, who was on night duty. There was still that risky half-mile lope through the shelling and darkened streets to our sleeping cave. As we rushed toward it, we flicked the flashlight on every few seconds to see the way ahead and hoped that none of the 88-mm shells whooshing overhead had our names on it. Instinctively we ducked our heads at each whoosh, but soon we adopted the grunt's credo, "If you can hear it, it ain't for you."

February 16 *One of the maps that came in last night had the locations of all the German command posts. Fortunately Greiner examined them promptly, realized what we had, and called Colonel Langevin. All day long we've been preparing overlays for the bombing missions tomorrow. It was the kind of map you dream about capturing. In our week here we've already found two like that.*

Today Major Webster came into the office and swore that as he was shaving, a shell came through the window in front of his face and through the open door without exploding.

Shells and bombs poured into town all day long as von Mackensen's men, outnumbering us by 25,000, began their all-out attack to dislodge us from our toehold, and it so happened that this was the day for my scheduled bath.

One of the privileges of being a staff officer was that of being able to get a hot bath once a week. Each officer was allotted ten minutes for his ablutions. Two GIs had the sole duty of heating water and scrubbing out the tub for the next officer. No matter how much bombing, shelling, and strafing might be going on, few officers ever skipped the luxury of that bath. As a morale maintainer it was second to none.

This day, in the middle of things, with me all soaped up, a plane strafed the street outside. By well-developed instinct now, I would have dived for cover, but I was literally caught with my pants down.

To solve the problem of a change of underwear, socks, and shirts, a troublesome matter for the frontline soldier, we gave our laundry to a townswoman. Some 20,000 civilians had been removed from the battle zone. She was one of the few who had not fled. She was given a bar of soap with the agreement that she could retain what was left of the bar after the washing. Soap for civilians was unattainable and therefore highly prized. The lira remuneration was of secondary importance to her.

One noon as I was washing up before chow, a shell screamed over my head and hit a house a hundred feet away, nothing unusual. Yet, in spite of the constant danger, Pundt and I daily went for a short walk after lunch and dinner. Spending the entire day in an office cave and then switching to a sleeping cave at night was too depressing. It was a life for troglodytes, not humans. To stay alive it was prudent to stay underground, but to see natural daylight felt so good that we took our brief walks in the full realization that any one of them might be the last.

February 17   *The Germans are attacking with increasing vigor. The shells keep plopping in. Interrogators who went through the Salerno campaign tell me this one is much worse. We attack tomorrow at dawn. Most people are beginning to get worried. The Germans have been pushing us back. They are still bombarding the town like mad and they are now trying something new, shelling us with aerial bursts. The old timers say this is the worst shelling the American army has undergone since the war began.*

Today a report came in that one of our tanks ran into a battalion of marching Germans, opened fire at 25 yards and killed 300–400 of them.

Another report was less favorable. For the fourth time certain of our fighter planes strafed a body of our own troops.

This killing of Americans by friendly fire was to happen on numerous occasions. Combat is disorienting, so much of it fought in the "fog of war."

To help the frontline units repel von Mackensen's forces, the Allies, desperate, had all available aircraft in Italy rushed to the fray.

February 18 *This noon, after lunch, there being only desultory shelling, Pundt and I walked the two blocks to the beach and sat on the porch of an abandoned house overlooking, and almost overhanging, the sea. We watched the results of German guns trying to hit some of our ships two miles out in the harbor. The shells would whistle over our heads and fall between the ships and us. We watched 10 or 12 land, all in the same area. The gunners never seemed to correct their aim, because, I believe, they were firing without adequate observation. It was a sheer waste of ammunition.*

During these same few minutes we watched German and Allied planes engaged in dogfights overhead, saw one pilot bail out as his plane went down, and then another. A Spitfire got the two ME 109s. Later the English pilot came into headquarters, peeved because he could have gotten a third, but his guns were empty.

The Germans poured everything they had into this operation and for a time it seemed they might succeed. Casualties on both sides ran high. Over in the British sector, General Penney, commander of the First Division, was wounded. We had no alternative to a spirited defense. Our backs were to the sea. There was no place to retreat to. It was more than nail-biting time. It was, literally, stand or die. Two days later, behind a shield of artillery fire, we launched a counterattack. Four hundred prisoners were taken, and it was reported exultantly, but again mistakenly, that the two railroad guns had been knocked out. The attack hardly budged the enemy. Kesselring and von Mackensen were serving notice that the Allied march into Rome was not going to be a cakewalk.

Shortly after, during the night, enemy artillerymen hit one of our ammunition dumps, blowing up four hundred to five hundred tons, sending the decibel volume into the stratosphere and shaking the town to its foundations. To a fireworks aficionado the successive bursts of exploding shells would have made a Chinese New Year seem down-right funereal.

5

A New General Takes Over

A month into the campaign, General Lucas was replaced as corps commander by Major General Lucian K. Truscott. The operation had not measured up to Churchill's expectations. He was unhappy that it had bogged down, felt that Lucas was not aggressive enough, and urged the theater commander, Britain's General Alexander, to persuade General Clark to replace him.

The new commander was a different type of leader, a man in the mold of Rommel and Patton, driven, inspiring, and visible. Whereas Lucas rarely left his CP to visit the lower units, Truscott could be counted on to consult constantly with his subordinate commanders and to turn up at the trouble spots at the front. A Texan, he was one of the few combat generals who was not a product of West Point. I never saw him without his battered leather jacket, cavalry boots, and white silk scarf, and a helmet that shone as though it had a dozen coats of lacquer. His salute was like a wave to a friend, and I tried to model my own on it.

As a colonel, he had been one of the planners and the ranking American officer on the cross-channel raid on Dieppe, a port of northwestern France. Later he commanded the Third Infantry Division during the campaign in Sicily and again in the Anzio operation. It was to become the most decorated U.S. division in World War II.

A man of steely resolution with a supremely confident commanding manner, he did not accept the word *impossible* as an answer. He'd
say, "Don't tell me it can't be done. Go out there and do it!" And he'd
bellow this in a deep, gravelly voice. The story I heard was that as a
young child he had swallowed carbolic acid. Like Rommel and Patton,
he was both admired and feared, and his raspy voice only served to en-
hance his authority. To his troops he was known as "Old Gravel
Mouth." That he had been in the mid-1930s a fiercely competitive
member of the army polo team was easy to believe and strictly in character, so much so that his weakness for fresh flowers, which always
graced his tent or trailer, seemed an anomaly to some.

At work, among other duties, I continued whipping the German
matériel literature into shape, editing it and indexing it for fast retrieval. In the process I began to catalog the German division insignias
casually mentioned in the literature and in interrogation reports, using
my imagination freely to draw "rampant lion," "eagle on a cross on a
shield," and other vague descriptions. I believed it would be possible
to immediately identify enemy divisions if we knew their symbols.
This was important because, for example, a light infantry division was
equipped differently from an armored division or a parachute division.
Consequently, if we OB people could identify the division, we could
give our G-2 a good estimate of its strength, organization, and equipment. He in turn could pass this on to the commanding general and to
the G-3, the operations chief, with a well-based prediction of what that
division's capabilities were.

Sometimes the first knowledge we had that a new German unit was
entering the fray came from OSS men behind the lines in Rome. By
means of their hidden transmitters they would describe the symbol
painted on the vehicles in which the men were being transported.

Soon I realized that the best way to identify enemy units seen but
not yet contacted in battle was by these vehicle markings. American
commanders, to prevent enemy agents from identifying their units
while on the move, often covered their vehicle markings with grease.
Apparently no serious effort had been made to catalog the German
markings until I brought the matter to the attention of Major French,
Colonel Langevin's executive officer.

The major agreed that an improved system of identifying the German units was badly needed, that the OSS reports and those of the re-

connaissance patrols and the observation posts would be immeasurably more informative if we could identify the units. He urged me to pump the PWs at the cage whenever I could find time from my other duties. Not only did I want the division markings, but also the regiment, battalion, and company symbols. The same symbol, but in a different color, I had noticed, sometimes differentiated one regiment from another. Patterns would develop, I was sure, and all interrogators were instructed to cooperate in the endeavor.

My first trip to the cage proved frustrating. I had barely begun work when the Germans were packed into trucks for shipment to the boats, starting them on their way to the PW camps in America. A fleet of LSTs shuttled between Naples and Anzio, bringing supplies to the beachhead and taking prisoners and our wounded to Naples. On other days I had better luck and, as time went on, when the OSS radioed a description of the marking, we were able to check our compilation and identify the unit. Knowing that, we would also know the type and often the history and quality of the troops being committed. We might also have data on the personality of its commanding officer. Just as Lucas and Truscott were two very different generals, the enemy, too, had very different generals.

I was grateful for Major French's encouragement. He was a meticulous man with a facile and imaginative mind, a quick stride, and a no-nonsense businesslike attitude. Before the war he had been a successful lawyer in Florida. In the many months we were to work together, I never had a quibble with him, which wasn't the case with everyone in the section. The legal eagle's perfectionism irked many, particularly the chief draftsman. The major had a vexatious knack for driving the poor fellow up the wall. While the overlay of the situation map was being run off on the duplicating machine and readied for attachment to the G-2 Report prior to distribution, French would come with a new piece of information to be added to the overlay; or, at other times, insist on some minute change, a matter of insignificant importance in the mind of the draftsman. This, however, would force him, swearing a blue streak under his breath as he passed my desk, to redo part of the overlay and start the reproduction process over again. There were times when he had to make three consecutive overlays before the major's passion for accurate, up-to-the-moment data was satisfied and the report could go out. When the sergeant later became involved in transatlantic divorce proceedings through the mails, French guided him through the tangle of red tape. The staff felt the civilian-life lawyer owed him big and that the draftsman had the free legal expertise coming to him.

One of the units under Sixth Corps command was the British First Division. It was a crackerjack outfit and was on our left flank. There was naturally considerable communication between their G-2 section and ours.

February 21, 1944 *Englishmen on the phone make me laugh. They yell into it as though the other party was miles away and there was no phone line between.*

The Germans hit one of our ammunition dumps tonight and it blew up all over the place. The racket was terrific. The whole town shook.

February 23 *Last night when I got back to my cave I found somebody had stolen my pistol—probably one of the quartermaster drivers who have been seen ransacking the place. This is a hell of a time to lose your weapon. I overslept yesterday morning, and in my haste to get to work forgot to put my gun on.*

My bosses from Fifth Army and Allied Force Headquarters, Captain Reining and Major Holsten, came today. Holsten strikes me as a loud-mouthed opportunist.

February 25 *This morning the Germans plumped a shell into a house near our CP and killed two MPs sleeping inside. The entire house collapsed, and it took till noon before they even recovered parts of the boys. The Germans shell especially heavily during our meal hours. They are now hitting close to the officers' mess. One day they'll land one in and kill a bunch of us. The damned building is too exposed. Why don't they move the mess or at least change the mess hours?*

Meals in the officers' mess, which was above ground, were adequate but monotonously unvaried: C rations usually three times a day, washed down by the local vino at lunch and supper. To supplement the insufficient vitamins in canned foods, vitamin tablets were placed on the table. Never was there a delicacy served, although steak did one day appear on the table. Apparently a cow got in the way of a shell.

Habits developed at the mess would sometimes be carried back to the States. The tables were set with checkered tablecloths. As we sat down, many of us first picked up the knife, fork, and spoon and, to wipe them clean of the soapy film left on them after washing, briskly rubbed them with the overhanging tablecloth. This became a habit, and so instilled with time that it became second nature. How much so was evidenced when a lieutenant colonel in the G-3 section, a banker in civilian life, was ordered back to the States for a course at the Command and General Staff School. Landing in New York, he went to his home on Long Island where his wife had gathered their closest friends and relatives for a welcoming dinner party. As he sat down to the formally set table, complete with candelabra, crystal wine decanters, and silver champagne bucket, what did he do, he laughingly told me on his return, but pick up the shimmering silverware and briskly rub it on the tablecloth to the astonishment of his wife and guests.

It was Doc Pundt's job to keep the order-of-battle charts. These showed the current number, quality, and nationality of the men in the enemy unit, the number and kind of weapons it had, and the type of vehicles. Most of this information was derived from the PW interrogation reports.

Sometimes I was distressed by Pundt's methods. If he had conflicting information about a company whose normal complement of motorcycles might be twenty-five, and was now reported by PWs to be both five and fifteen, he was apt to dismiss the discrepancy with, "Oh, the hell with them! Cross them off!"

The same cavalier attitude applied to weapon characteristics. When the colonel asked him the range of a certain German artillery gun, Pundt would check with me. I would give him the information, which was often not one answer, but several, depending on the type of shell being fired. Pundt would give the colonel one range.

Poring over a document a week after one of our ammo dumps had been blown sky high, I thought I found a clue to the location of a camouflaged regimental ammo and supply dump. I went over to the van in which the aerial photograph interpreters worked. The three officers, two Americans and one Brit, pulled out their latest pictures of the area and quickly confirmed my finding. They had missed it earlier. The artillery people were given the target and shortly the Germans had some fireworks of their own. "A little tit for tat," I said gleefully to Doc. But my joy was short-lived. Forty-eight hours later the enemy upped us one, hitting another of our dumps.

Mail is a big thing in a soldier's life and on the battlefield is irregularly received, so when on February 28 I was handed a batch of twenty-three letters, six of which were from a girl I loved (and would eventually marry), it should have made my day. But happiness in war is fragile and fleeting. Before I could read them, our intelligence indicated another big attack was in the offing.

February 28   *The Germans are supposed to be putting 300 more tanks into action. If it's true and they break our lines, we may be prisoners by this time tomorrow—or worse, dead or wounded.*

With the battle in the balance, there were some nerve-racking hours. Colonel Langevin directed me to a mass of papers, several boxes full, stamped SECRET and TOP SECRET. Afraid they would be captured if matters went against us, he told me to burn them. With a sergeant's help I carried them out of our subterranean office to the street above, which the gunners of the Third Reich were inconsiderately working over. There, in the yard of a gutted building, we made a pile of the papers. Seeing no point in both of us being exposed, I sent the sergeant back and tossed a phosphorous grenade into the pile, thinking the fierce blinding fire would instantaneously transform it into ash and I could quickly duck back into the safety of the cave. The incoming shells were a powerful incentive to get this job over with fast. Getting blown to bits was not high on my wish list.

I was quickly disillusioned. Loose paper burns rapidly, but sheaves, I learned, no matter how hot the fire, take their good sweet time.

To hasten the burning, I stirred the sheaves into smaller increments with a long board. The hot, fierce incendiary action, which took perhaps twenty minutes or half an hour, seemed to take forever before all was ash and I could scoot to safety. (When I related this incident to a German general after the war, he remarked, "In our army we used to say, 'That side will win the war which first runs out of paper.'")

Hitler's guns continued to pummel Anzio unmercifully. The town was beginning to look as devastated as any I had seen on the southern front in my document foraging. The ravages of battle were evident wherever the eye fell.

February 29   *The Germans launched another big attack today, and this afternoon an important map and notes were captured that gave*

away their artillery plan. We did a rush job of translation and expla-
nation for the colonel and hope it saved the lives of many American
boys.

The German planes again hit a big ammunition dump tonight.

I notice that some of the translations of German documents that
I've supervised and corrected are appearing in the Allied Force Head-
quarters Intelligence Notes publication.

The way we park our jeeps to hide them from enemy aerial obser-
vation is to run them into a store, knocking down the doors if neces-
sary.

A good batch of mail today again, mostly from [my brother] Frank.

About this time Colonel Carleton, General Truscott's chief of staff, called a meeting of the G-2 and G-3 officers. A robust man with a commanding presence, Carleton had a British handlebar type mustache and behind his back was affectionately known as "Tally-Ho." He criticized some of our work, wanting us to put forth more suggestions and options "so that the General can better fight his war."

The phraseology, I thought, was probably Command and General Staff School jargon, but the term "his war" stuck in my craw. "If it's *his* war," I muttered to Doc, "what the hell are we doing here?"

By March 1, after only six weeks of fighting, casualties on both sides were in the 20,000 range and Kesselring knew his mission to drive us into the sea was not going to succeed. Periods of good flying weather allowed the superior Allied air forces to bomb the bridges to the north and interdict the roads and rail lines leading to the front, sharply limiting the ammunition available to the Germans. There were days when every shell fired at us was answered by twenty of ours.

At this time I debriefed a young GI who had been captured and removed to Rome, where the Germans liked to parade their PWs. The boy had escaped with the connivance of an anti-Nazi noncom and worked his way back to his own lines.

March 2 *I hear today that the dead on the German side are so many*
"they are piling 'em up like cordwood." If the politicians had to do the
piling and burying, and dying, we wouldn't have much more of this.

Found what looks like a good thing for our Radio Intercept people—
namely the German artillery code.

March 3   *One of the PW interrogators, an enlisted man, was killed by a piece of shrapnel today. Died on the operating table.*

Although I was friendly with all seven or eight officers in the G-2 section, it was with Doc Pundt that I worked most closely, and since we had known each other the longest, and slept in the same cave, we tended to spend what little free time we had together. As respite from the dreariness of our molelike existence, we continued our brief walks after the noontime and evening meals, their duration determined by the Teuton artillerymen's shell supply. On these walks Doc would insist on prowling in every damned newly destroyed house we came upon in hope of salvaging some article that might be of use to us. Now and then I let him stumble about by himself while I remained outside puffing on my pipe, which provided at least a modicum of pleasure.

The forays had a secondary purpose. We were not happy with the nightly half-mile trot to our sleeping quarters and were keeping our eyes peeled for a closer sanctuary. One day we discovered to our delight that the deep wine cellar of the house across the street from headquarters had for some reason been abandoned by its previous occupants. We promptly transferred our gear to the new quarters.

While the war with the Fatherland still had over fifteen months to go, the letters from Germany to the soldiers at the front were painting a depressing picture. In captured outgoing letters, a valued source for judging enemy morale, the Germans repeatedly wrote that the beachhead fighting was worse than anything they had gone through in Russia. Well over half were veteran Russian campaigners. Certainly for the Nazi-indoctrinated youth, once giddy with the first easy victories of the Führer's incursions into foreign lands—pushovers, really—the realities of the present were painful. There was still, though, a small cadre that hid behind a facade of confidence in their Führer, but mostly this was just whistling in the dark.

Captain Ed Cap was in charge of interrogation at the corps PW enclosure. When I had cause to work at the cage, Cap and I enjoyed each other's company. We had developed an instant rapport on discovery that our fathers were both in the knitting business and that both he and I had run knitting machines in earlier days. A tall, sturdy six-footer with a cheery disposition and a broad smile, Ed had big brown eyes in a round face with dimpled cheeks. A high school teacher in peacetime, he had a talent for seeing the absurdities in army life, engendering many a laugh. He was a man impossible not to like.

When I told Ed of the GI I had recently debriefed, the man who had been a prisoner in Rome, escaped, and had seen heaps of German dead waiting to be buried, Ed said, "Many of the Krauts don't have their hearts in this any more." He had just finished with a batch of sixteen PWs who had surrendered as a group. It happened the Germans had a lot of wounded on the field and had sent out a sergeant who knew where they were, together with fifteen more to help retrieve them. The sergeant, however, had made up his mind to desert and led the whole contingent over to the American lines, where they were taken prisoner. The Americans then sent the sixteen back, under guard, to get the wounded and carry them back to the American lines, yielding further prisoners.

One day in my quest to catalog enemy division insignias and vehicle markings, I was pumping PWs at the cage. Ed Cap and I were working in the same room. Finishing with a prisoner, Ed called for the next one, and in came a corporal accompanied by an overpowering odor, hardly reminiscent of attar-of-rose. Ed and I looked at each other. "Corporal," said Ed, "have you shit in your pants?"

The German, at stiff attention, stiffened even further and snapped, "Herr Hauptmann, if you had been in my foxhole and the bombs had dropped all around you, you, too, if I may say so, would have shit in your pants!"

Ed and I erupted in laughter, and he quickly disposed of the prisoner. What little new information he might have had was not worth the stench.

Soon the units that received our G-2 report began to realize the value of the vehicle markings. To further spread the use of this tool, AFHQ republished them and circulated them among all higher intelligence units. Then on April 10 we captured a document from which we learned that the German High Command had discovered our interest, and of course deduced its purpose, and all vehicles, including those in France, were to have their markings painted out. Said Major French, "If you've done nothing else for the war effort, Marshall, you've at least cost Hitler a few gallons of paint."

For some reason, though, whether the order was countermanded, or whether the elimination of the markings caused operational problems, the German vehicles continued to carry their markings.

In many ways corps headquarters was the ideal place to be for an inquisitive officer in his first war. Close enough to the front—often too close—to be fed the minutiae of the small picture, it was strategically important enough to be kept informed of the big picture by higher headquarters.

March 5   *There is nothing to do here except work. If only you could look forward to a few spare hours once a week. But seven days a week it's nothing but work and eat. I haven't changed my underwear now in two or three weeks. At the moment my laundry is being done by an Italian woman, one of the few courageous (or stupid) enough to come back into town.*

My pipe is now nicely broken in and I do enjoy that once or twice a day.

March 7   *Heard today that a German medical lieutenant who was taken PW is being released because he was captured bearing a Red Cross aid flag and not a white flag of surrender.*

March 8   *One of the clerks told me he liked living in Maine better than Italy. "Too much iron in the atmosphere here."*

(I could agree. One morning the officers' mess was a target. I almost had Krupp iron in my cereal.)

I'm ready to start home right now—across the street to my deep cellar—but the damned 210s are hitting all around the building again. I can feel the cave shake. I'd better stay a while. Better less sleep than permanent sleep. . . . I'm more and more convinced our mess is in a bad place. Today a shell from a 210-mm railroad gun hit the house next to it—in which the officers' latrine is located—and completely demolished it. Another MP was killed and three men wounded.

Rarely could you go into the latrine without finding two or three other officers there, but luckily it was empty at the moment of the strike.

The cartoonist Bill Mauldin, who was a member of our Forty-fifth Infantry Division and went with us through the Anzio campaign and later the French campaign, described our new command post in his book *Up Front:*

> The Corps Headquarters in Anzio was set up in a twisting maze of catacombs far below the earth's surface. The tunnels had been used for wine storage for centuries, and once you got down there it was hard to leave. It wasn't only a good place to stay away from shells. Many of the little niches had big vino barrels. Only once was the peace of the catacombs and the soft sound of gurgling vino disturbed. That was when a shell hit the officers' latrine on the surface and shattered the wooden stairs which led down into the caves.

Mauldin's description is accurate enough, but in fact, one night when I was on duty, we were hit a second time, a large-caliber shell penetrating the thick roof of the cave.

As for Mauldin's potshot at our vino barrels, let it be said that liquor plays a substantial part in the life of combat soldiers of all ranks. In battle, recreational facilities are limited or nonexistent. Drinking to celebrate, contend with fear, counteract boredom, and as a social and macho custom has long been a part of the military culture. That accounts for the many references to liquor in my journals.

It also accounts for the recurrent theme in Mauldin's cartoons, such as the one showing a large barrel of vermouth with three new bullet holes out of which the liquor is pouring into three canteens: Willie says to Joe, "Go tell the boys to line up. We got fruit juice for breakfast."

Aware that the repetitive liquor theme might give a false impression of army drinking, he sought to clarify the situation in *Up Front:*

> I'm not trying to say the American army is a drunken army. Most men have the same attitude I have about liquor. I drink very little and I don't like strong liquor at all. Yet there have been times over here when I have tied one on because I was homesick, or bored, or because I was sitting around with a bunch of guys who had a bottle, and when it came around to me I just naturally took a belt at it. And there were many times that I guzzled wine because the water was questionable.

Like Mauldin, I did not worship Bacchus, but neither did I repudiate him. As we moved through Europe, I drank much champagne, cognac, vermouth, and wines from the Rhine, Moselle, and Neckar Valleys. Many a time I would have swapped the joys of the grape for a Coke, milk shake, or strawberry sundae.

Despite the easy availability of alcohol, for the army as a whole, generally speaking, sobriety was pretty much the norm.

6

The Germans Switch to Defense

March 9, 1944 *Found a remarkable document today. Von Mackensen's order changing the German stance to defense. Taken from a PW engineer officer. General Truscott demanded to see it immediately. Since the Germans are starting to dig in, I'm sure we will immediately launch an attack, because we won't let them dig in and get set.*

I also found on a captured map today that the Germans are putting their ammunition dumps next to aid stations to keep us from bombing and shelling the dumps. We've also found proof that they are now carrying ammunition in ambulances, which we've known for a while.

The document established that the Germans were no longer capable of assuming the initiative by attack. The offense had passed into our hands, a pivotal point.

March 10 *The translations I correct and edit appear with greater frequency in AFHQ publications.*

A German shell hit one of the entrances to the headquarters cave, blocking it with rubble. Happily, the place is really a labyrinth with half a dozen entrances.

Our new sleeping cellar on the other hand has only one exit, so I've taken the precaution to take down the jeep's pick and shovel—just in case.

March 11   *This noon while standing on a railroad bridge, I saw a 6 x 6, two-and-a-half-ton truck, coming from the front, pass with a load of bodies covered by a large white tarp. The bodies were piled up like a butcher's truckload of beef.*

Officers were required to censor their men's mail with a view to eliminating security breaches. My sergeant, Joe Lowensberg, was a chubby, avuncular German Jewish refugee who always looked rumpled even when he wasn't. He had a Santa Claus ho-ho-ho laugh and was a man I became truly fond of the more I came to know him. He had been a supervisor in a Manhattan textile firm, was married, and had a child. Evenings, after his workday was done, he pecked at his typewriter with the two-finger system, but produced voluminous mail. He maintained a correspondence with friends and relatives all over the world, or so it seemed. The last thing I did each night was my censoring job, and faced with Joe's mail pile, I often wished he would break those two fast-flying fingers. Something that constantly amused me, however, was Lowensberg's bawling out his wife—in about every second letter for the past two months—for not using some free movie tickets he had left her.

The other permanent man on my team was Sergeant Ernest Rothschild, also a German Jewish refugee, a bright gifted youngster. Both were workhorses, always loyal to me, and never showed signs of resentment because of the heavy load of work I constantly threw at them. Both men remained with me through the war and several months after, until they were returned to the States. To this day I think of them fondly and remain proud to have had them serve under me. They earned the citizenship that was automatically granted all honorably discharged foreign-born servicemen.

Two days after enemy shellfire scored a hit on one of the CP entrances, I got lucky and found the German 362nd Division's entire code names for its sectors. Doping the document out in a jiffy, I sent it to the signal intelligence people, who were tickled silly. Their work was invaluable to G-2, and we were happy to reciprocate. It was synergism at its best.

Knowing that not all enemy killed had their pockets searched, it occurred to me that the pockets of the unsearched dead might yield documents useful to us. To that end I went to see the graves registration officer, and learned a few things. The cemetery now held 2,466 Americans and 364 Germans. When a body was old and smelled, it was "gay." How long a man had been dead could be told quite accurately by the color of the body. If it was black, he had been dead two weeks.

To my discomfort I also learned that the Italian gravediggers knew when the Germans were going to attack. They would not show up for work on that day, afraid of getting hit since the cemetery was within range of shell fire. It showed me that information was crossing the lines via civilians.

On March 15 I queried some forty PWs on vehicle markings. Most were seventeen-, eighteen-, and nineteen-year-olds who spoke freely and even volunteered information. One of the captured was a second lieutenant and, a bit to my surprise, also talked freely. Most officers were reticent. This was a nice, clean-cut kid of twenty-two at the front only a week. He was engaged to be married, and we chatted a bit about how long it would be before we got home. I said soon, but he said no, if we beat Germany we would have to fight Russia. In the months ahead I was to find this to be a common refrain from the *Gefreiter* (private) to the *Generalfeldmarschall*.

To facilitate their work, order-of-battle teams were issued various items such as cameras, binoculars, telephones, typewriters, magnifying glasses, map-measuring instruments, and so on. Cursorily examining an enemy training film that came into our possession, I held it to the light. As I studied the frames, I noticed excitedly, yet regretfully, that we had a gem. The film showed a new tank of which we had no knowledge, leaving me no alternative but to forward it to higher headquarters for study. An item not issued to us was a movie projector.

March 16   *Had a bath today. Suspect I may be getting lice. Lice are very very common in Italy.*

Dull day. Spent a good part of it going through a technical book on railways to get some dope for the colonel on bridges across the Tiber.

I'm told an item we dug out of a captured letter was broadcast from London by BBC. A sabotaged train resulted in the killing of 800 Germans.

March 17   *Interrogated a batch of twenty prisoners this morning. They then left for Naples, and as they were leaving five Polish deserters were brought in. Captain Cap decided they should be held over for* *interrogation tomorrow. Tonight Cap got a phone call that a German shell hit the enclosure and killed one of the Poles. Fate is funny. Had they been interrogated yesterday, that Pole, who surely thought the war was over for him, would be alive.*

The amount of military secrets that are casually passed around in the office is immense. Yet everybody, including the lowest noncom clerks, gets so numbed to them that it takes something really tremendous to arouse interest.

Tonight I'm duty officer. So in a certain definite sense I'm liable for the safety of 60,000–80,000 Allied troops on the beachhead. Everything that happens will be phoned in to me and I'll have to evaluate each report and decide who is to be informed. It's a helluva big responsibility, especially if the Nazis drop a few plane loads of parachutists on us as they did four days ago, or if we have a bad night with air raids, ammunition dumps blowing up, ships being hit, etc.

March 18   *Had a fairly quiet night as duty officer. At 2300 (11:00 P.M.) the army headquarters assistant G-2, Colonel Welles, called. He wanted a copy of the Signal Intercept Station report of the day before. Unfortunately, we had already burned it.*

Fifteen minutes later an excited British officer called and asked me to verify the identification of a messenger named Matthews. I contacted six parties before I could verify him as okay. But since the British officer had already given the fellow the documents, it was much like locking the barn door after the horse has been stolen.

At 2345, just before midnight, an excited British boy with the damnedest Limey accent called from a signal station to say that during an air raid then going on he saw a blinking light.

At 0400 the Fighter Control headquarters called to tell me one of their night fighters had shot down a JU 88 [Junkers 88 bomber] which went into the sea in flames. He didn't know the fate of the crew. They had tried to send a launch to the spot, but the launch hit some rocks and was stranded. The navy was trying to free the launch. So in case the crew had safely bailed out, I notified both divisions defending the coast to be on the watch for the crew, who would be trying to get back to the German lines.

About this time a German shell, delayed action, scored a hit over the cave, blew a deep hole above it and smashed in the part over the

Ordnance section. Luckily, no one was sleeping there this night.

Another call reported the shooting down of another JU 88 over the front lines.

After that the divisions began sending in their morning reports of the night's activities over the phone and teletype, and everything else was just routine until I was relieved.

After three hours sleep, I went on duty interrogating PWs.

7

A Night to Remember

After that night of little sleep, I was looking forward to a better rest the following night. Instead, at 5:40 in the morning a German shell hit the shed containing the entrance to our sleeping cellar, and two large wine vats, along with tons of debris from the adjoining buildings, came roaring down the steps to the foot of our cots. Pundt and I would have been on the casualty list were it not for our foresight in having moved many of the barrels away from the entrance to the steps and having put our cots not in the middle of the cellar, but rather into two bins carved out of the soft rock.

When the last of the debris had fallen, I called out to Pundt through the thick dust, "Doc, are you okay?"

"I'm okay," he yelled back. "How about you?"

"I'm okay too," I shouted. "I can see light. I think we can dig out."

Happily, the debris had fallen on the stairway in such a manner as to make escape possible. With the aid of the pick and shovel and tricky maneuvering among fallen beams, bricks, plaster, and wires, we were able to crawl out.

The last hours had not been pleasant ones. Just before we went to bed, a shell had hit next door to us and set the American Military Government warehouse afire, burning an Italian civilian to death.

Shelled out of our sleeping sanctuary, Doc Pundt and I were forced to find another. Forgoing lunch, we made a hasty search of the houses still standing in the headquarters area and came on a cellar not occupied by other men or officers. It was roomier than the previous lodging, but not as deep. Carved out of the porous stone were the usual niches for storing vats and barrels of maturing wines. It was also devoid of wine, which we reasoned may have been why it was empty.

Hastily we transferred our belongings to the new Ritz and returned to our destroyed quarters to retrieve the last item, a large demijohn of wine. Unfortunately the demijohn broke as I pushed it up the litter-strewn steps, and the wine cascaded over me. Doc, waiting at the landing, went alternately into fits of laughter and bursts of irritation at the loss of the vino, for the stuff was becoming scarce.

To me the episode was not that funny. In a few minutes I was due for duty in the war room and had no time to change clothes. By the time I was relieved, the war room smelled like a winery.

When the troops first landed in the fertile Anzio-Nettuno vineyard region, the wine-laden cellars quickly came to serve as combination shelters and bistros. Hemmed in by the Germans after a few days, many a boozy GI thought the ideal tactic was to stay put until the place was drunk dry. But eventually the surfeit of wine, which gave our soldiers what we called "catacomb courage," was diminished to a point where it became a precious commodity. This drought inspired a famous Mauldin cartoon. It depicted a "vino" shop demolished by the retreating Germans. From smashed and bullet-ridden barrels wine is flowing onto the floor, and Joe cries, "Them rats! Them dirty, cold-blooded sore-headed stinkin' Huns! Them atrocity-committin' skunks!"

None of Mauldin's cartoons was more heartily laughed at and empathetically received on the beachhead.

March 21, 1944 *Corrected the order of battle charts of two of the German divisions. It is vital that these charts be as accurate as possible, since so many of our tactics are based on them. Since there is often much information that we lack, we must often rely on our knowledge of German Army organization and on trends within it. If we evaluate badly, it can cost lives.*

A commanding general's orders and the conduct of operations by G-3 are significantly influenced by the information supplied by G-2. In fighting the Germans in Italy, our side needed to know what percentage of a division was made up of Germans and what percentage were men drafted from lands Hitler had occupied. The Poles and Russians conscripted by the Wehrmacht were, not surprisingly, proving unreliable soldiers, as were the Austrians, Czechs, and other drafted nationalities. By studying our copies of the interrogation reports, we tried to ascertain how well an enemy unit would fight. Would it fight fiercely or just perfunctorily while looking for an opportunity to surrender or desert?

In the service, "assigned" means a man is permanently allocated to a particular unit, whereas "attached" means the man is temporarily placed with a unit that requires his specialty. When there is no longer a need for him there, he may be transferred to another unit. Doc Pundt and I, therefore, as intelligence specialists, were attached to Sixth Corps, a designation that had its drawbacks.

When a shipment of liquor arrived from the United States, the officer designated to distribute it allotted one bottle for every assigned officer, two for colonels, and none for the attached officers. Doc and I were miffed and I wanted to complain to Colonel Langevin, but Pundt refused to make waves. I then bitched to Major French, telling him it was not the liquor that mattered, but the offense. Not only were we doing the order-of-battle work, I pointed out, but we had been given all sorts of other duties. French agreed we had been shortchanged and promised to see that it would not happen again, and it didn't. While I was not much of a drinker, certainly not one to take refuge in alcohol, a nip of rye or scotch in the evening before turning in would have been nice.

After the war, Sixth Corps headquarters held annual reunions. Although I served with them until the war ended, I was not on their roster of assigned officers and consequently never received invitations to their reunions—something that annoyed me for years.

After the demijohn calamity and now with no hard liquor ration, we resorted to pulling a fast one. Hearing that the CIC (Counter Intelligence Corps) people had wine in their cellar quarters, we sought out the location and lifted a few bottles. "It's like picking a policeman's pocket," chortled Doc.

However, instead of rustling up vino, and considering that our last shelter had been blown to smithereens, we would have been wiser to give our new quarters a closer look. But Doc and I felt reasonably safe in our new haven until the building next door was hit and demolished. In the hasty occupation of our new quarters we had not checked all sides of the building, unaware there was no structure behind us to afford protection from fire on our right flank. "God must be generous in his protection of fools," I said to Doc.

"No," replied Doc, who didn't believe in God, "we were just a couple of lucky horses' asses."

Once again we had to prowl about in search of nighttime sanctuary.

March 25 *Major French added to my job. Wants me to keep track of all German antiaircraft guns on the front.*

I had already been doing this without instructions.

When I made my first estimate I found it was only one gun off from the estimate of the artillery office.

March 26 *Still another addition to my work. Now supposed to keep location of all artillery, amount and types on the whole front. That's sure a ticklish one.*

It was indeed a challenge. After firing for a time, a battery's location, although camouflaged, was often spotted by the other side's artillery observation planes. Or its location may have been found in a study of the pictures taken by the photo reconnaissance planes. Or it may have been ferreted out by the PW interrogators who routinely asked where the enemy guns were situated, often learning their locations from blabbing prisoners seeking to ingratiate themselves. Hence it behooved the gunners to shift their positions from time to time.

To add another factor to the problem, after a hiatus of several days, the gargantuan railroad guns were back in action. Our constant aerial search ensured that they could fire only at night and during overcast conditions. These behemoths did more psychological than material damage.

March 27 *Duty officer tonight. This leaves me in charge of collecting and disseminating all the information coming to us in a constant flow from all our intelligence sources. One source, though, Signal Intelligence, is so secret that we don't give the derivation of the information when we disseminate it.*

So far tonight it's been quiet. Some shelling, the usual flare reports.

This afternoon at about 5:30 the Germans came over in twenty-five planes. Our antiaircraft shot down four and accidentally one of our own. I saw one plane dive into the sea, his tail burning. Another pilot bailed out, but his chute didn't open.

Allied antiaircraft defenses and air superiority forced the Luftwaffe to restrict its operations over the beachhead largely to nighttime sorties. On occasion, however, the Luftwaffe raided Anzio during daylight hours, assuring the ground troops a spectacular and mesmerizing sight. As our antiaircraft guns directed their frenetic fire at the intruders, and the Allied planes engaged them in dogfights, many of us forsook our cave havens to stand in doorways and, eyes glued to the sky, watch the dueling pilots. In so doing one day, one of our noncom interrogators was killed when struck by an unexploded antiaircraft shell.

Got a typhus shot and a smallpox vaccination. In addition I took the prescribed Atabrine tablet to ward off malaria and the vitamin pill designed to ward off everything else. I've put more drugs into myself today than a pharmacist carries on his shelves.

Some of the battleground was swampland. We had heard that of five thousand Italian troops stationed in this area last year, three thousand had contracted malaria. One of the headquarters clerks now came down with the disease, no doubt prompting the dispensing of the Atabrine.

Lieutenant Colonel Weber, the assistant G-2, left today to take command of a battalion. Major French is replacing him and Major Dixon is taking French's job. A Captain Joseph Haines 4th, just arrived, is taking Dixon's.

The newcomer to the G-2 section was a handsome, virile, six-footer plus with dark hair prematurely flecked with gray, who was to become one of my closest friends. Haines had been a regimental S-2 (intelligence officer) when a loaded rifle was accidentally knocked over in the S-2 tent and he was shot in the leg. He now limped a bit. After his release from the hospital, he was assigned to Sixth Corps headquarters.

8

Hitler's Secret Weapon

With the Wehrmacht retreating in Russia, Hitler sought to bolster badly sagging German morale by repeatedly boasting of invincible secret weapons being developed and about to be committed. We were skeptical of these miracle weapons, and in a quiet period during my last stint as night duty officer, I wrote a satirical story about a mythical, new German tank. While I don't find it particularly humorous a half century later, in the mood of the time it apparently struck a chord. In the morning I casually showed it to Doc, who laughed uproariously, showed it to Major French, who showed it to Major Webster, who showed it to the colonel, who read it at the press conference and then passed it on to the *Beachhead News*, the Sixth Corps newspaper. Many army and civilian publications reprinted it.

When, owing to delivery difficulties after the Anzio landings, the official army newspaper *Stars and Stripes* failed to arrive, the troops felt cut off from the rest of the world. Sixth Corps Headquarters started its own publication and continued it until the war's end.

The clipping is pasted in my diary:

By far the biggest news of the day was the uncovering through questionable channels of a document giving the details of Hitler's secret weapon. This appears to be a 400-ton tank, the Berchtesgaden MK

XXVIX, having a max speed of 25 mph—45 mph in reverse, 60 mph
when used in Russia—and mounting a 3000-cm rocket projector with
a very much baffled muzzle brake. Designed by Dr. Kraut von der Sch-
naut, it has a coaxial machine gun of radical design, firing two boops
to every burp. However, one PW report states that extreme care must
be taken to keep this gun clean, or else it will not fire two boops to
every burp but two burps to every boop. A careful study of a similar
gun captured in Tunisia revealed that this weapon cannot be fired sin-
gle shot because the two boops could not be separated when the
weapon was clean, nor could the two burps be separated when the
weapon was dirty. How Nazi inventive genius will solve this problem
remains to be seen.

Aside from its rocket projector and double-booping single-burping
machine gun, this tank is equipped with 3 smoke dischargers and one
lawn mower—reflecting the Nazi manpower shortage—and is there-
fore a formidable weapon.

According to the table of organization there are 5 to a platoon, 17
to a company, and 6 for a nickel.

Editor's note: Suggestions for a weapon suitable to combat this tank
will be gratefully received by the Beachhead News, c/o SSO, Sixth
Corps Headquarters.

Two days later, bursting into his cackling laugh, Colonel Langevin
waved me over to his desk. In his hand he held a drawing, the Forty-
fifth Division draftsman's version of my description of Hitler's new secret weapon, including the lawn mower. I joined in his laughter. As the
drawing was passed around, it evoked further merriment from the rest
of the staff, and the colonel ordered it sent to the *Beachhead News*, the
sketch and description to be reprinted, encouraging reproduction by
other service publications.

Laughter, I reflected, was one of the opiates that enable men to en-
dure the grimness of war. There were units with natural-born jokesters
and clowns, and these men were gems. A soldier who could retain his
sense of humor in battle and lift the spirits of his mates made a contribution to the effectiveness of his unit that was not to be valued
lightly, and I treasured stories about them.

One such involved a master sergeant who was in a strafing path, but
jumped into a ditch and escaped unhurt. Rising to his feet, he shook

his fist at the departing plane and yelled, "Goddamn it! Cut that out! You crazy sonofabitch coulda hurt somebody!"

Another story concerned a sergeant whose men were lagging behind during an attack. "C'mon, you bastards," he called back, "ya wanna live forever?"

A third involved a GI who was always saying, "War ain't so bad." Then one day he was hit, but hardly scratched. His buddies asked him what he thought of war now.

"Hell," he said, "that ain't war, that's murder!"

War, terrible as it is, has occasional humorous moments. Sometimes such moments occurred in the interaction of the soldier and the civilian. One of the AMG (American Military Government) officers told me of his efforts to make some refugee civilians comfortable. Since there were six hundred refugees and only fifteen mattresses, he decided to pick out the sorriest-looking specimens—sick, old, crippled—and give them preference. He gave out six or eight mattresses and then told the sergeant to issue one to a woman who had her breast out nursing her baby. Upon getting her settled, the officer turned around to find several other women had taken out their breasts and were hastily looking for infants to "nurse."

Because we were under constant artillery fire, we often found letters from home sardonically amusing. One of our stenographers read one aloud. The writer had gone camping and "slept in a pup tent last night."

"Listen to that," cried the stenographer. "He slept in a pup tent last night. Whoop-de-doo!"

March 30, 1944   *The Germans are now shooting 280-mm guns into town again.*

French now gave me the job of figuring out how many guns would face us if we attacked in one direction, how many if we attacked in another, and how many the Germans could use as antitank guns in each case.

In connection with the last, this largely boiled down to how many 88-mm guns the enemy had. The 88-mm gun was the most effective multipurpose weapon produced by any army during the war. It was used as an antiaircraft, antitank, antipersonnel, and field artillery weapon, besides being mounted on many German tanks. Its one negative feature was its high profile. It was difficult to camouflage. Our photo interpretation team readily picked it up on the air reconnaissance pictures.

March 31 *By means of a series of prophylaxis receipts found on a dead man, I traced the route by which a unit from Germany came to Italy. After a visit to a bordello the man goes to his pro station and is given a confirmation slip.*

The route to the battle front taken by this Casanova and his comrades was given to our air force to target.

Innocent-appearing minutiae were often helpful in filling in the blanks in the intelligence picture. Like a jigsaw puzzle, the picture was made up of big and little pieces, and every piece, no matter how seemingly insignificant at the moment, properly placed, could help to complete the picture.

April 1 *Major Holsten sent a letter today in which he tells Pundt and me that we were lucky, that we had fallen into ready-made jobs, and giving us no credit for developing the section, which we did from a pathetic skeletal set-up.*

I wrote Holsten a letter, tactfully straightening him out.

The fault is Pundt's—as Pundt admits. When the major first visited corps, Pundt, in the presence of Colonel Langevin, from whom recommendations for promotion would have to come, praised the original, but actually nonexistent, corps setup.

Despite Doc's sycophantic gushing, Langevin knew better. In the two months we had been on the beachhead, the two order-of-battle teams had made themselves indispensable to him. That sharp old bird was in no way ever going to allow us to be transferred elsewhere, as we were to find out. The day the war ended we were still attached to Sixth Corps headquarters.

In our two months, we had so impressed Colonel Langevin, our actual commanding officer, with our work that he recommended our promotion. Unfortunately, because we were attached and not assigned, he did not have the power to promote us, only the power to recommend our promotion. His recommendations had to go to the 2680 Headquarters Military Intelligence Service Company, the unit to which we were assigned, and which was headed by Major Holsten, our nominal commanding officer and the one with the power of promotion.

Hardly had my letter to Holsten been sent off before we heard he had been promoted to lieutenant colonel, angering Pundt and me.

"Here we are," I said to Doc, "getting shot at day and night, working our butts off seven days a week from seven in the morning till ten at night, not counting night duty every few days, and that palooka sits in Algiers, working three or four hours a day five or six days a week, if that, and refuses to promote us."

"He's a phony, incompetent jackass," railed Doc.

And that he was, affirmed by an asinine directive he had sent us the day before concerning the disposition of documents. He had no order-of-battle experience and no authority to issue such a directive. When I showed it to the colonel, he countermanded it.

The liaison officer between the two British divisions and our headquarters was British captain Bill Guest. A sandy-haired, freckled Yorkshireman, about thirty-eight, Guest was fluent in German. A well-known soccer player in England, he kept track of the American sporting scene and could rattle off without error the big league baseball team standings that the *Beachhead News* periodically printed. He presciently saw the imminent disintegration of the British Empire, loved America and things American, and at times talked of emigrating to the States after the war if he could persuade his wife. He was generous and helpful to a fault. When my clothes needed laundering and there was no Italian washwoman available, he would insist that I make use of his batman, his soldier servant.

Bill was one of the finest men I was to meet in my service career. He was the kind of man the British call "top drawer." My contacts with British officers were mainly at army and corps headquarters and at the two British divisions. With one exception, a supercilious, snaggle-toothed major, I liked them all. In general the officers of both armies got along with a minimum of friction, although I understand this was not always true at the highest levels. But on the beachhead, the dough-boys and the Tommies both fought valiantly and by some strange alchemy got along well together.

Guest invited me to visit the two British divisions with him, where I was cordially received. Their intelligence sections thought we OB people were doing a fine job and couldn't suggest any way to improve our work. They indicated some resentment, however, at G-3's abbreviations of the names of their division units. Whereas our regiments were numbered (Seventh, Fifteenth, Thirtieth, etc.), the Brits had the King's Royal Artillery Lancastershires, the King's Own Yorkshire Light Infantry, the Royal Inniskilling Fusiliers, the First Duke of Wellington's Regiment, the Second Sherwood Foresters, the London Irish Rifles, and so on.

Despite an initial impulse to brush the matter aside, I listened to the complaint gravely, for it was clear that they took great pride in their regiments, which were mustered from particular regions and had long, rich traditions. Often generations of a family served in the same regiment. The emasculation of these proud and historic regimental names was clearly an important matter for the Brits. I promised to take up the issue with the G-3 people.

I found I was also a bit uncomfortable leisurely having tea with officers of the First British Division, who were the embodiments of spit and polish, while guns were booming and Tommies were dying in the mud two or three miles away. This feeling of incongruity was heightened when I overheard one officer tell another that he had loaned the general a book of poetry, which the general had read the previous night while the battle raged. Poetry, even amidst belching guns, was apparently his relaxation. Earlier, ironically, after returning from the midst of battle to his headquarters, First Division's commander, Major General Sir Ronald Penney, was wounded when the Germans scored a hit on his van, putting him out of action for a time.

Arriving back at corps, I found that in my absence there had been a scare. Radar had indicated forty-three ships headed to attack us. There had been much excitement in the G-2 and G-3 sections until it turned out to have been "an atmospheric disturbance." The last thing we needed was a Nazi seaborne attack on the rear of our precariously held toehold on the beachhead.

In early April Doc and I again heard that Colonel Langevin had recommended us for promotion, but the recommendations were stymied by Holsten on the grounds that the table of organization was filled.

April 4 *It's a bit unnerving to see the lack of safekeeping documents stamped SECRET and TOP SECRET get here. We have them lying on desks day and night. Yet regulations say they should be kept in a* *three-combination safe. But if anybody had a three-combination safe in the battle zone, it would be used to safeguard cigars and whisky.*

Every six or seven days my name would come up on the night duty roster, but by this time I was an old hand at the job and felt comfortable in the role, so much so that I would often make only a brief, bored note in my diary:

April 6   *Pulled duty officer. Usual stuff. Greatly increased artillery fire tonight for some reason.*

After dinner, and before returning to work, Doc and I continued to take our walk to stretch our legs, breathe fresh air, and enjoy a brief respite from cave life, the length of the walk depending, as always, on the activity, or lack of it, of the German gunners. On one walk we found a new cellar to hole up in.

In times of quiet, when fighting was light, some men dug up potatoes to add variety to their usual chow. Others went so far as to plant gardens. One day in digging for potatoes a GI dug up a brand new bicycle hidden by its owner before fleeing. Soon the whole countryside was dotted with GIs digging for bikes. In some areas bikes proliferated.

April 9   *Easter today and surprisingly little shooting. I don't think it's the spirit of Christianity as much as poor visibility. It's raining, as usual.*

Spent the day preparing estimates for the war room and G-3 of German guns and trying to get them to jibe with the artillery overlay.

We had a funny report today. The Germans sent out stretcher bearers with Red Cross bands, but armed, and they wandered very close to the British lines, so the British took them prisoner. The next day a propaganda shell burst over the British command post with a note saying, "You have taken so-and-so, so-and-so and so-and-so prisoners. This is contrary to the Geneva Convention." So the British sent a propaganda shell over the German command post with: "True, but so-and-so, so-and-so and so-and-so were armed, contrary to the Geneva Convention rules, please be reminded." And signed by the British commanding officer.

Generally speaking, despite all the bloodletting, both sides abided by the rules of the Geneva Convention. Our release of the German lieutenant who had wrongfully been taken prisoner while bearing a Red Cross aid flag was a case in point.

From time to time in the infantry fighting there were brief truces—initiated by opposing lieutenants—to allow each side to remove its wounded and dead. This might be considered normal, but as in all wars, there were anomalies. There were instances when the dug-in troops, to vary their diets, exchanged foods during pauses in the fighting. At other times, a soldier hanging laundry to dry and an excellent target would not be shot at. On both sides there was empathy for the suffering of the other. And then, minutes or hours later, someone would blow a whistle, and the ritualistic butchery would resume, quickly reaching its earlier level of intensity.

Every so often as I drifted off to sleep I would wonder what the future held in store for me and my team if we survived Anzio, succeeded in taking Rome, and our S Force service came to an end.

A letter from Alex Shayne seemed to have the answer.

April 11   *Alex says that he has information that after the Rome assignment my men and I are to be transferred to Fifth Army headquarters Documents Section, which would be a swell deal, too good to be true. Have my fingers crossed.*

There one could exploit documents and sleep without having to duck enemy fire. One could eat without fearing that a German shell might inconsiderately put an end to the dinner and the diner. The next day the prospect of such a transfer seemed even more desirable when the railroad gunners sent us one of their 550-pound lethal greetings, which traveled forty-seven feet underground before stopping not far from us, fortunately a dud. "If that thing had gone off," said Major Dixon, the G-2 section's artillery expert, "we'd all be sprouting angels' wings."

Don Dixon was a midwesterner with a brush-cut, a man of serious mien who could look at a piece of shrapnel, do some measuring, and announce the caliber of the shell. He was initially suspicious of us six German-speaking additions to the G-2 section, a unit that before our arrival could not boast of even one man familiar with the enemy's language. He may have felt there was a mole among us, since three of the six spoke English with a German accent. The three were sergeants, refugee Jewish boys from Germany. He was more at ease with the fourth sergeant; Fred W. Luck, who hailed from Minnesota, of German parentage, planned to study for the ministry if he survived the war and spoke English without a Teutonic trace. It was some time before Dixon fully trusted us.

For several days we had been receiving reports from one of our divisions that night after night they heard clanking sounds and in the morning would find gaps in their barbed wire defenses. The colonel asked me if I had an answer. Some weeks before I had seen a photograph in a captured German army publication. It described a miniature tank, called Goliath, that was equipped with chains dragging grappling hooks. The tank was to be run by remote control into the enemy's barbed wire, the hooks would engage the wire and the tank would break it while returning to its station.

I told Langevin I thought it was the so-called Goliath and explained how it worked. Several days later we captured one that had developed mechanical trouble.

The Goliath was not the only miniature remote-controlled tank used against us. There was another called the Beetle. This chirpy little fellow was loaded with explosives set to detonate at a predetermined point. The GIs and the Tommies, however, quickly learned to blow it up before it reached its target.

I wrote a report about the Goliath for the *Beachhead News,* and both the army and the civilian press picked it up, took pictures of it, and had themselves a good story.

April 14 *Duty officer tonight.*
Spent much of the day plotting the location of all enemy artillery for the general. An attack must soon be coming off.

After having worked out a good system for tracking the German artillery, I was asked by Major French, the executive officer, to turn the job over to Major Dixon, our artillery specialist, after explaining the system to him. I was now to tackle the problem of keeping track of the enemy tanks and assault guns.

On April 16 one of our companies took sixty-three prisoners with-

out sustaining any casualties. These PWs, who had lost the will to
fight, were from a division commanded by a general named Greiner,
who had told his men that they would defend the line until the last
man, even if he had to be the last man. So his men composed a jingle:

Division Greiner
Wird immer kleiner
Da bleibt nur einer
Das ist der Greiner

which translates as:

Division Greiner
Gets steadily smaller
There remains only one
And that is Greiner

April 19   *Noticed again in PW interrogation reports that the Germans
are drafting sixteen-year-old kids. That indicates a desperate state.
Surrender can't be too far off.*

How wrong I was! The end was to take another year.

Doc and I were unhappy that we had not yet been promoted, so
when some officers from Fourth Corps headquarters arrived for a visit
and were intensely interested in our work, I told one of them I'd be glad
to have them put in a request for me.

A few days later, as we sat in the latrine together, Colonel Langevin,
perhaps intending small talk, asked me how long I had been in grade
and was astonished to hear it was now sixteen months. I was now fix-
ated on moving up the ranks and knew from Major French, the executive officer, that I had twice before been recommended for promotion.
I said bitterly, "Colonel, I think I must be the most recommended un-
promoted lieutenant in the whole damn army."

"You should have been promoted long ago," said Langevin. "Let me
try again."

My spirits were not substantially raised. As an attached officer, the
colonel did not have the power to promote me, only to recommend my
promotion. Holsten, I was sure, would tell him that the T.O. (Table of
Organization) was still filled.

April 23 *Bad news. Heard two order-of-battle teams are coming to Italy, being flown over—one to go to Fourth Corps and the other to a division. Which means the following may happen: when we are through in Rome, S Force will be dissolved and Holsten will recall me and my men. So, since the Fourth Corps job will be filled, we'll probably wind up at one of the divisions.*

The following day the G-2 of the Fourth Corps came visiting and, I was told, asked to have one of the two Sixth Corps OB teams transferred to his G-2 section. But that didn't happen. It would have been a logical move, rather than to have Fourth Corps serviced by a newly arrived inexperienced team. The U.S. Army actions sometimes defied comprehension. Langevin, we knew, would resist such a transfer, even if it was necessary to get General Truscott to intervene. Measured by results, Doc Pundt and I and our men were more than earning our keep.

Going through a batch of newly captured material, some of it the most pornographic literature I had ever seen, I came across an envelope marked IMPORTANT! IMMEDIATE ATTENTION! It had come to us from SSF, the First Special Service Force.

9

Deciphering a Dress Pattern

The First Special Service Force was a brigade of 2,500 tough volunteers, many of whom had previously been discipline cases in various army units. Allowed to volunteer for the SSF, they formed an elite guerrilla brotherhood. A third were Canadians.

The organization had a distinguished lineage. A couple of years before, General Truscott, then a colonel, had trained and fought with the British commandos at Dieppe. When the U.S. Army Rangers were established by Truscott, he brought along the commando's *Handbook of Irregular Warfare.* It contained such tidbits as "the days when we could practice the rules of sportsmanship are over. For the time being every soldier must be a potential gangster. . . . The vulnerable parts of the enemy are the heart, spine, and privates. Kick him or knee him as hard as you can in the fork. . . . Remember you are out to kill."

The Rangers evolved into the SSF and at Anzio were led by Robert Frederick, the youngest general in the army. Earlier, in southern Italy, they had locked horns with the famed Hermann Goering Division, where their unorthodox methods had proven so effective the Germans dubbed them the "Devil's Brigade." Their black-faced nighttime recon patrols penetrated deeply into the enemy lines and invariably returned with valuable information. Their skill with a myriad of weapons, of which their razor-sharp knives were one, was legendary. They were widely conceded to be a rough, tough bunch of cookies, the best and cockiest in the army bar none. They were the forerunners of the Green Berets.

The German forces defending the Mussolini Canal on our right flank were opposed by the SSF. They quickly discovered in skirmishes that they were up against a resolute group of ruthless, savage infighters, and withdrew a cautious distance, leaving a half-mile no-man's land between the two sides. Within the enemy ranks the word spread that these fearless men took no prisoners, which was not true, although there were times when they didn't, as one of my diary notes validates: *An SSF patrol last night captured a German and on the way back got involved in a fire fight. "They had to run for it,"* the report continues, *"and they couldn't take the German. So they slit his throat."*

Opening the IMPORTANT! IMMEDIATE ATTENTION! envelope, I found a large sheet with lines running in all directions and many numbers and names. The names were words associated with clothing, such as *Naht* (seam) and *Muster* (pattern) and *Faden* (thread). At first glance, the diagram appeared to be a clothing pattern, but scattered on the sheet, in crayon, were some of the German units we were up against. Interspersed were various numbers.

Captain Bill Guest, the British liaison officer, happened to be in the office at the time, and rather sanguinely at first, we tackled the apparently coded sheet.

We added the numbers, multiplied and divided, combined them, inverted them. We used every trick we could think of to break the code. No luck. As Bill and I lobbed ideas back and forth, others of the staff came over, studied the markings, saw no solution, and drifted off. Frustrated and disgusted after three hours, I said to Guest, "Maybe this damned thing really is just a clothing pattern."

"Or a suit," said Bill. "Maybe a zoot suit."

We laughed and resumed work, goaded on by the tantalizing promise of priceless disclosure. Finally, after another half hour and no progress, I said, "Bill, I think this thing is really nothing more than a dress pattern."

Just then the phone rang and SSF reported that the thing was a gag. It actually was a dress pattern. One of their regiments had marked it up and sent it to them as a joke. Everybody around found the episode hilarious, and chagrined though we were, even Bill and I had to join in the mirth. The occasional humorous interplay between intelligence sections served to lighten a bit the grimness of battle.

The SSF were such great troops that it was easy for us to forgive them their time-consuming practical joke. It would not have surprised me to learn that General Frederick himself had initiated the hoax.

Frederick, a man of average height with a small dapper moustache, would habitually arrive at corps headquarters early in the morning before the General Staff conference began. Although the weather was damp, drizzly, and cold, he would appear in his open jeep and would not be wearing anything over his shirt, not the warm combat jacket, nor even the light field jacket. After checking the war room map, he would kid around a bit with us junior officers.

One morning as we lieutenants and captains were bantering with him, Doc Pundt said, "Sir, how can you drive here in this cold rainy weather without even a jacket?"

"Betcha," I said, "he's got two pair of winter underwear under that shirt."

With an expressionless face and never taking his eyes off mine, Frederick slowly unbuttoned the shirt and pulled it open, revealing no undershirt of any kind, just a bare chest.

It was legendary that Frederick could always be found where the action in his section was toughest, accounting for his eight or nine Purple Hearts and two Distinguished Service Crosses.

April 25, 1944   *I picked up a typewriter and the carriage slid and almost hit me in the eye. Couldn't help thinking how ironic it would be to have Mom and Pop get a telegram reading, "The War Department regrets to inform you that your son Charles was wounded by a typewriter in the service of his country."*

Sometimes headquarters was a point of interest to outsiders. Toward the end of April, during a period of minimal incoming shellfire, the day was enlivened when a group of nurses came through the CP on a guided tour. They seemed to be unsure whether to be proud or embarrassed by the frank stares and attention lavished on them by men and officers starved for female companionship. I was reminded of the old chestnut about the GI stationed in a faraway land who writes his girlfriend that he is marrying a native. To which she angrily replies, "What has she got that I haven't?" To which he responds, "Nothing. But what she's got is here."

Another day a group of war correspondents turned up, not unusual, for they were given frequent briefings. This day, however, to the consternation of several of the staff, one was a female. Today women war correspondents are not oddities, but in those days Marguerite Higgens of the *New York Herald Tribune* was a novelty. Growled an incensed Major Dixon, "Jesus, what the hell next! They won't take her to the front, and she'll need special toilet facilities wherever she goes. The next thing you know they'll forbid the men to swim in the nude. After all there are only 130,000 of *them* here!"

At this time the German navy sent a few midget submarines into the harbor, but they were quickly sunk. With the fighting at an ebb, the enemy shooting in only occasional lethal greetings to remind us of his presence, an almost peaceful air descended on the beachhead. It was the calm before the storm. Kesselring had found at great cost that he could not break our tenacious grip on the beachhead. The battle had turned into a war of attrition, and in such a war, he knew, the odds were stacked against him.

Although the initiative had been briefly held by the invading forces, Kesselring had quickly retaken it with his hemming-in operations. Now it reverted to the Sixth Corps forces. They were preparing for a major onslaught and a race to Rome, and he was bracing to foil it.

For many, many weeks a penetrating dampness—sometimes a thin drizzle, at other times heavy downpours—had hung over Anzio. At the end of the day I would wearily fall onto my cot, and the lulling patter of rain would quickly induce sleep if it was not challenged by the countervailing dissonance of close-hitting shells. On those nights the duel would be settled by a swig from the bottle of whisky in the pocket of my bedding roll, usually sufficient to tip the balance in favor of Morpheus.

But now the weather was changing. There was warmth and sunshine, clear nights and stars, and chirping birds. Volleyball games broke out and athletic contests took place. Men swam in the sea and dove into the soft combers rolling in as gulls wheeled overhead. British bagpipers toured the American-held area, and one of the division bands entertained the troops with a program of modern songs, much enjoyed by men whose only music for three months had been the deadly tune of

"Whistling Petes" and the whooshing of the many German 88s.

Doc Pundt and I emerged from our subterranean shelter, and after a short search found a beautiful, undamaged little house on the coastal bluff overlooking, and almost overhanging, the sea. As we toured the rooms, a colonel entered and began a similar inspection. We held our breath, for as every conscript quickly learns, rank has its privileges, and we feared he would pull rank and claim the house. For some reason he didn't, possibly considering it too exposed should the Germans resume full-scale shelling.

Not only did we now sleep above ground, we slept on the second floor. The house had three bedrooms and a living room with a balcony in addition to the bathroom and kitchen.

We invited captains Joe Haines, Ed Cap, and Bill Guest to move in with us. It made a congenial group and was marked by much good-natured banter.

One evening during these halcyon days, as we sat on the balcony and watched the setting sun paint the sky, we speculated on what it would be like to be home again. "I don't think I could handle it," said Ed with a laugh. "It would be too difficult to get out of the habit of cutting the phone wire in the house to wrap a bundle because no cord is handy."

"Or knocking a nail into the wall to hang up your jacket," said Bill.

"Or just walking into a house and taking anything you have a use for," chimed in Joe.

"Or what about just pissing in the street when you have to go?" asked Doc.

The list of cavalier practices went on and on.

Since the house was built on the edge of a bluff, it afforded us an opportunity to sharpen our shooting skills. We recorked our empty liquor bottles and threw them as targets into the water below. Using a carbine, we took turns popping away at the bottle bobbing at the mercy of the waves, quitting only when the target was hit, the waning light made further effort fruitless, or the wind caused a rough surf.

Fueled by liquor, laughter, comradeship, and the high spirits of men in their prime, evening bull sessions on the balcony ranged far and wide. At one session, as the sun dipped over the horizon, Doc Pundt, who liked to think of himself as a socialist, went into one of his cockamamie, proselytizing spiels. In the course of it, he berated American medical practice as opposed to the meritorious socialized medicine practiced in some countries. "We've got socialized medicine right here in the army," he crowed, winding up his diatribe, "and what's wrong with it?"

As the night wore on, the merits of socialism versus capitalism were debated, and Doc found himself the loan defender of socialism, the rest of us ganging up on him in defense of capitalism. Then, the following day, Doc went to the dentist with some minor complaint, and the dentist refused to do any work on him. That evening, fuming, he excoriated the army dental system and, forgetting his position of the evening

The two Sixth Corps order-of-battle teams. Clockwise from top left: Sgt. Joe Lowensberg, Lt. Charles Marshall, Lt. Alfred Pundt, Sgt. Fred Luck, Sgt. Thomas Greiner, and Sgt. Ernest Rothschild.

before, finished with a vigorous denunciatory, "And that's why, god-damn it, socialized medicine will never work!"

Unwound, he glanced about for approbation, only to find his bilious rant greeted with hysterical laughter. Overnight Doc's admiration for the army's socialized medicine had turned to contempt, and capitalism had acquired a convert.

There were some curious facets to Doc Pundt's personality. While I did not wear my Catholicism on my sleeve, he enjoyed twitting me about it while prating of his atheism. Once, to flaunt it, as we inspected the ruins of a shelled church on one of our evening walks, he made a point of urinating on the altar despite my protests and discomfiture.

After the long months of cold and clammy days, of mist, rain, and artillery-enforced cave life, the relaxed living in our seaside villa in the balmy, dry weather now prevailing was delightful. The slate-gray days had passed. The skies were no longer an infinite expanse of roiling, water-laden clouds, and the nights were no longer starless. In the evenings, in the still-light sky, a pale moon would appear accompanied by gentle sea breezes. Later, as darkness set in, the shimmering moon-beams playing on the lapping waves seemed to whisper assurance of an imminent peaceful future, however gory the present.

With the hiatus in hostilities, there was now time for frills such as inspections and the awarding of medals, and on May 6 General Clark came to corps headquarters for such a ceremony. By now I had become so immune to generals that, says my diary, *I didn't even leave my work for five minutes to watch the presentations.*

Unlike Truscott, Mark Clark, commander of all the American forces in Italy, never captured the imagination and affection of his troops, de-spite the efforts of his public relations people, said to number fifty, in-cluding a photographer who was instructed always to photograph his "facially best side."

With the fighting at an ebb, Major Dixon, who wrote the daily G-2 report for Colonel Langevin's approval and signature, went on a seven-day rest to Sorrento, and we all wondered who would inherit the im-portant job. Major Webster, a West Pointer whose comments rarely rose above the banal, seemed the likeliest candidate. But to everyone's sur-prise, especially mine, Major French, the assistant G-2, came to me, the lowest-ranking officer in the section, and said that Langevin would like me to write it.

May 3   *Bill Guest says the British have noticed a big improvement in the report. I am flattered. I like the job. I like to write and I'm willing to evaluate the intelligence pouring in.*

May 8   *Definitely not getting the Fourth Corps OB job. Heard it has been filled.*

May 9   *Alex wrote. Still thinks I will get the Fifth Army headquarters documents job—and that's one I'd really like.*

One morning I came into the office to find an envelope of documents on my desk. It had been delivered during the night and had been taken from a dead German. Inside his wallet was a telegram from his parents. It read, simply, "Your two brothers were killed in Russia."

For several minutes I stared at the telegram, engulfed in reflection. My parents would soon have three sons in the war. I wondered if I, too, or Steve or Frank might not some day get a similar chilling notification. As I went listlessly through the other papers, I asked myself why nations, supposedly civilized, send their men to kill each other, men who, as individuals, have not known each other and might even like and admire each other under other circumstances. Could God really forgive this insanity?

It did not surprise me, years later, to read that General Adolf Galland, the German aviator who had shot down 104 Allied planes, was grouse shooting with Wing Commander Robert Stanford-Tuck, the famed British Spitfire pilot.

Nor, again years later, was I overly surprised to hear from my cousin Larry Marshall, a pilot, that he had attended a convention of the National Business Aircraft Association at which the same General Galland was the principle speaker, was hospitably received, and that "all who heard him were impressed by the man."

Because both my parents came from large families, I had a goodly number of cousins in the war. One of them, Henry Kromer, was a tail gunner who had flown fifty missions over Africa and been ordered back to the States as an instructor. Missing the excitement of combat, he had volunteered for a second series of combat missions. This, I wrote him, was tempting fate. Now the letter I had written him came back with a RETURN TO SENDER stamp and marked MISSING. When I heard that Henry had volunteered for a second tour of overseas duty, I had a foreboding of his fate. In wartime, premonitions of death, one's own or another's, are natural. Unlike superstition, they are a reasoned fear based on the law of averages and the likelihood of the possibility. In papers removed from dead soldiers, it was not uncommon to find an unfinished letter that had a foreboding of imminent death. One from a paratrooper to his mother predicted "this will be my last letter" and included his own self-prepared obituary for the hometown newspaper.

Such letters caused me to sit back and reflect on the idiocy of war and the bitter price exacted from its participants. Yet I had to admit to myself that I had as big a part in this idiocy as the next man. Although vexed by feelings of ambivalence, when I came out of my reverie, I would sigh and turn back to my work, ferreting out information and looking for better ways, more productive and perhaps innovative ways, to kill Germans.

From time to time we were visited by officers from the States who had had no battle experience and whose purpose was to learn the ropes. One such was a young West Pointer, a lieutenant colonel, who was a division G-2. I found him pathetically green and dull: *How many lives, I wonder, will be lost because of his ignorance. His father and uncle, I hear, are bigwigs in the War Department, but his promotion to this rank is criminal, and the people responsible for it should be court martialed. . . . He is incredibly skittish, is afraid to sleep above ground, which most of us are now doing, and ducks for cover every time a shell lands anywhere in the neighborhood. Yet, at his rank, he is supposed to be able to lead a battalion into battle. Another sorry example of a West Pointer is a young and unimaginative major here.*

May 13 *My promotion has fallen through again. If I'm not jinxed, nobody is.*

May 14 *Our big attack from the south started and is making magnificent headway. Just when our own will start, I don't know yet, but at least I will have had a hand in the planning of it, having submitted several estimates. My job is getting bigger all the time. 1) I'm now plotting and evaluating all enemy artillery and trying to dope out what the shifts mean.*

(A month earlier I had turned this job over to Major Dixon, but after a short time the colonel had me take it on again.)

2) I'm doing the same for tanks and assault vehicles.

3) The same for flak.

4) I'm compiling enemy unit vehicle markings and have made all our units in Italy conscious of vehicle markings, plus Allied Force headquarters, which has only now put out an elaborate compilation, although not as complete as mine. That, I think, is one of my best achievements so far. We can now identify many German units in North Italy by the vehicle marking descriptions of our agents.

5) I extract and distribute the intelligence from captured maps.

6) I keep all the equipment files and anything coming up on enemy equipment comes to me. Theoretically, I'm supposed to be the boy with the answers.

7) I decide what captured documents will go into the G-2 report, and I correct the translations of the sergeants.

It all adds up to a big responsible job.

Rereading this now, I should not have been surprised when Joe Haines told me that General Frederick once asked, "How come when I have a question, I always get directed to Marshall?"

In spite of all my responsibilities, I felt in a state of limbo. Soon we would be taking Rome, I was sure, and I would then be attached to S Force until our work in Rome was finished and the force dissolved. But then what? The table of organization called for a corps to have one order-of-battle team. The Sixth Corps had two, and Pundt's team had been here first.

May 15 *In a letter Doc Pundt received from Major Holsten today, Holsten said, "In view of Colonel Langevin's recent letter, Lieutenant Marshall may soon come off the gold standard."*

And I say, "In view of how often the colonel has already recommended me for promotion, Holsten is full of crap. My gold bars should have been replaced by silver ones a long, long time ago."

May 16 *Army efficiency. The typewriter, telephone, and stapler authorized to be issued to me six and one-half months ago, arrived today.*

May 17   *Attack in south still going fine. We've taken 2,000 prisoners so far.*

May 18   *Sad letter today, although I already knew the news. Cousin Henry Kromer is missing in action. I hope and pray he was able to bail out and is still alive.*

May 19   *Heard today that the French African soldiers, called the Ghoums, are making the most progress on the southern front. They are said to have their wives and mistresses along and rape every woman with whom they come in contact. They will shoot a cow being milked right from over the farmer. They mutilate Germans, who greatly fear them, and are said to be far and away the best soldiers in the world. They are the source of innumerable amazing stories.*

The Ghoums were big, ferocious-looking Berbers who hailed from the Atlas Mountains in the French colonies of Algeria and Morocco. To these hill tribes, mountain warfare was second nature, and these slithering sharpshooters were particularly adept at night fighting. Wild, savage, and untamable, their cruelty and rapaciousness were legendary.

GIs did not shoot cows being milked. Their tack for acquiring native food was gentler, but sometimes less productive, as when a group of riflemen who sought a change of diet approached a farmer who had a dozen fat geese in his yard. When he demanded $100 per goose, they were outraged. Said one, "What the hell do these geese do? Are they the ones that lay the golden eggs?"

May 22   *Duty officer tonight.*
The big attack, for which we submitted estimates and more estimates, comes off at 0630 tomorrow morning. It will probably result in our forces joining with those from the southern front, trap many Germans between both forces, cut the remaining troops to pieces, and end in the capture of Rome. It will be the Battle for Italy, I think.

After a short nap I went back to work, soon finding myself frenetically answering two desk phones. With the attack underway, so much information had to be disseminated to so many units, I thought at times I would drive the switchboard operator out of his mind. The attack had jumped off to a good start, and by evening we had bagged over a thousand prisoners. As clouds of Allied bombers swept across the sky en route to dropping their de-Nazifying cargoes on the hapless defenders, the headquarters staff, hearing the droning planes approaching, emerged en masse from their subterranean offices, craned their necks skyward, and wildly cheered the air crews on. As the aircraft neared the front, a crescendo of Teutonic flak sent several plunging toward earth as their crews bailed out, parachutes blossoming in the sky.

As our troops forged on, the Germans continued their retreat. They were short of food, clothing, ammunition, and even oil for their guns. In the last two days our planes had destroyed or damaged two thousand of their vehicles, and the Germans were already disastrously short of transport. *It's a vicious cycle,* reads my diary entry: *They can't win. They have virtually no planes. Ours rule the skies and bomb and strafe almost uninterruptedly. I know too much about the German Army to be doubtful of the outcome. Germany is licked in Italy. It's just a matter of time.*

Another thousand PWs taken.

Probably on the theory if you want to get a thing done, give it to a busy man, for the past several days Colonel Langevin had me "temporarily" write a summary of the day's activities for the *Beachhead News.* When he called me and said he liked my "breezy, witty style, and to keep it up," I should have been forewarned that I was now locked into another job. The tally of PWs on our front had now reached 3,500, we were steadily pushing forward, and on May 25 the southern forces and the Anzio troops were joined. The official army photographer, a friend whose name I have regrettably forgotten, gave me copies of the first two pictures taken of the meeting.

Rocco, my gambling-prone, ever-ebullient buddy, came up from the south, and we gave him the latest dope on the Germans on our front.

Rocco tells me he has heard that Holsten had actually submitted my name for promotion. If he has, I think I would have got notice of it long ago. He also tells me S Force is forming up and that Alex has already been called to it. I wonder if they will request me again.

As the drive gathered steam and German units retreated in disarray, multitudinous documents fell into our hands, mailbags full of com-

First picture of the Anzio troops after the breakout meeting up with the main body of the Fifth Army forces driving northward toward Rome. Between the handshaking soldiers is General Mark Clark. This photo was given to me by the photographer.

pelling papers, dwarfing all previous hauls. Some of it was the most secret type of information, including even the plan of retreat. The large haul of captured documents led to pernicious results for the enemy: The more we learned about him, the easier he was to defeat.

How desperately the enemy needed frontline infantry reinforcements became evident when we discovered that a highly trained engineer bridging battalion was being employed as infantry. Further evidence of desperation was the committing to combat of Mark II tanks, which had been obsolete for years. In the air Allied superiority was now so overwhelming that the Germans took to digging foxholes along their supply roads for their drivers to dive into at first sight of our planes. Each safety hole was marked by a bundle of straw.

May 27 *Our forces slowed down to regroup. Will head for Rome in a day or two and probably cut the highway to the south, the main one.*

We keep getting reports that the Germans, in despair, are using their ambulances, with which they take their wounded troops north, to haul ammunition back in them. It is probably true. In fact we know it is true. We've known it for a long time, but we refrain from shooting up the ammo-laden ambulances coming south. We are in a dilemma, but I wonder if our policy is wise. On the one hand, if we legitimately shoot at theirs, they will shoot at ours, which carry only wounded. On the other hand, the ammo they haul in the ambulances is killing many of our boys.

May 28   *The PW haul is now over 5,000 on this front, 10,000 on the other. . . .*

One of Captain Cap's sergeants was up to the front today. Said the sight is unbelievable. German dead all around, thousands of vehicles burning along the road, bodies burning in and around them.

So far, thank God, our casualties have been light. The more I see of the war, the more I talk to PWs and hear their story of Nazism, the more I see why Hitlerism must go. Many things about Germany that I never believed before, this war has taught me to believe.

May 29   *At dawn this morning the second big push started.*

It was on this day, during this effort, when the leading elements of our First Armored Division were eradicating the last remnants of opposition from Campolcone Station, a railroad junction, that Lieutenant Allen T. Brown was killed. Brown was the stepson of General George C. Marshall, chief of staff of the U.S. Army. While sticking his head out of the turret of his tank to survey the situation, he was hit by a sniper's bullet.

May 30   *Heard the sad news today that Lieutenant Colonel Weber was killed this morning while leading his battalion. Death always seems more or less remote until it comes to someone you know.*

It was cheering to hear that our breakout from the beachhead was going expeditiously and that our casualties were "light." *Light* is a comforting word, unless among the "light" are some you know, and there was one that I knew. He was Lieutenant Colonel Weber, a West Pointer, who was married and had two young children. Earlier in the war he had been wounded and, while recovering, had been temporarily transferred to Sixth Corps headquarters. There he worked in both the operations and the intelligence sections.

One night we were both duty officers in the War Room, Weber manning the G-3 desk and I the G-2 desk. From time to time we consulted together on matters of joint interest. After our duty was over, he invited me to his quarters for a drink. In the course of the conversation, he said, "Marshall, if I were president, I'd have two classes of medals, one for frontline troops, and one for rear echelon. And then I'd wipe out the rear echelon medals."

I couldn't have agreed more.

The better I got to know Weber, the more I admired him. He was an officer and gentleman in the best tradition. Before his wound had completely healed, he asked to be given back the command of his battalion, and a short time before our big push started, he was back at the front.

Weber, brilliant, perspicacious, and courageous, was a great credit to his family, West Point, and his country, and I grieved for him. I was reminded of the words of Wellington: "Nothing except a battle lost can be half so melancholy as a battle won."

May 31 *Colonel Langevin called the duty officer early this morning and left a message for me to hop into my jeep and come out to the forward command post. When I got there, he handed me my notice of promotion. At long last! I am finally a first lieutenant!*

In line with our advance, we were in the process of moving our command post forward. At such times the G-2 section, as well as the other sections, were divided in two. Half went forward and set up for business in the new location, while the other half continued operating at the old location. When the communications and other vital operations were in position, word would come from the forward CP that they were ready to take over, and we could shut down. The rear section would then join the forward half.

June 1 *A sudden order. I left corps headquarters with my sergeants for temporary duty with S Force. Our troops are making rapid progress and we should soon be in Rome.*

Aside from administrative troops, the S Force we returned to was still to be the only unit permitted to enter Rome during the first days of its liberation, and it was still the same diverse group I had known back at Fifth Army headquarters. It consisted of hordes of British and American intelligence specialists. While most would be searching for technical data of all kinds—air, naval, engineering, railway, roads and bridges, propaganda, and such—the FBI man, Frank Amprin, would be looking for traitors like the American woman broadcaster for the Germans, called Axis Sally, and the renowned American poet Ezra Pound.

Amprin was passionately determined to find Pound. The poet, a leader in advance-guard art and literature movements, wrote pro-Fascist articles for the weekly newspaper *Meridino di Roma.* He was a regular speaker on the Italian propaganda radio programs, Radio Roma's "American Hour" being his main forum. As a great admirer of the fascist philosophy of Benito Mussolini, Pound was commissioned by the dictator's propaganda officials to make radio broadcasts in favor of Il Duce.

Amprin asked me to get in touch with him if in the course of my work I happened to run across any clues to Ezra Pound's whereabouts, something I deemed highly unlikely, since my job was to search the German headquarters, the German embassy, and kindred places.

It was at this time, when we were quartered in a large compound outside Rome, waiting for the word to enter the city, that an incident took place that forced me to discipline one of my men, a rare occurrence. It was the only time I was ever annoyed with Sergeant Joe Lowensberg, my lumbering assistant. Assigned to guard duty and finding the shouldering of a rifle a burdensome chore, he went to the room of Lieutenant Alex Shayne and, while Alex and I were at chow, borrowed Alex's pistol.

Alex, passing Joe on his return from the mess, and noticing that Joe was not bearing a rifle, but a pistol, asked Joe about the regulation infringement. He just hated the cumbersomeness of a rifle, explained Joe, and confessed that he had borrowed Alex's pistol.

Alex hit the roof, came to see me, and demanded that I punish Joe, since he was one of my men. To mollify him, I regretfully restricted the sergeant to quarters.

Joe was a lovable coot, but a man who thought that irksome army regulations did not contribute to comfortable soldiering. In my heart I sympathized with him because I considered the compound to be free from enemy threat, and further, I doubted that Joe, who wore Coke-bottle glasses, could have hit the side of a barn with either pistol or rifle had we been attacked.

June 4 *Our first troops entered Rome yesterday.*

The raison d'être for the Anzio operation, the capture of the Holy City, had finally been realized, but it had not been without great cost. Neither of the belligerents had had the strength to dislodge the other. In three years of island hopping in the Pacific, General McArthur suffered fewer casualties than those incurred in the gruesome three-month Anzio slugfest, considered by some military historians to have been the most savage battle of the war. Hitler was determined that the Allies be forced into the sea as a warning of what they could expect if they attempted an invasion of France. The Allies were equally adamant that this not happen. The result was a battle of attrition during which 500,000 tons of supplies were unloaded at the shallow port of Anzio, making it one of the most active ports in the world.

By the time the campaign was brought to a close, 250,000 German and Allied troops had been locked in combat, the Allies suffering 7,000 killed and 36,000 wounded, captured, or missing in action (German losses were even higher). Another 44,000 were incapable of further fighting. Some had gone mad, others suffered from shell shock. Countless men were sidelined by trench foot or frostbite. From time to time the dead had to be temporarily laid out on stretchers in the muddy streets. Morale often sank so low that desertion and AWOL rates skyrocketed, alarming the commanders. So intense was the firing of the long-range German guns that some of the masters of the Liberty ships were persuaded only with difficulty to bring their ships closer to shore so that their cargoes could be unloaded by the lighters. Indicative of the ferocity of the fighting was the rate of psychoneurosis, the highest of any battle in World War II. Between the savagery of the engagements and the inhospitable climate in which they were fought, the end of the bloodbath was prayerfully sought by all combatants. The familiar tourist advertisements of "sunny Italy" had been belied by a winter of persistent, dreary, brutal, and pitiless rain.

After the war some military theorists argued that the basic weakness of the Allied operation was that it had been carried out with two divisions when it should have been done with four, or not at all. "It was," said one, "sending a boy to do a man's job."

Whatever the merits of the argument, the battle for Anzio was one no survivor would ever forget.

10

Rome Falls: A Time of Work and Play

With each passing day, American strength increased and German muscle atrophied. As the Allied forces forged northward, Field Marshal Kesselring decided not to defend Rome, but to declare it an open city, and on June 3 the first American troops went in. The next day S Force entered to find the euphoric populace in the streets cheering and throwing flowers, the women—young and not so young—bussing the liberators. Many houses on our route displayed American flags, some on poles and others draped from windows.

We spent the night bivouacked in a park while our Long Toms fired over the city at the retreating Germans. On the outskirts, pockets of resistance remained to be eliminated. German troops in flak wagons and manning machine guns, antitank guns, and scattered tanks sought to slow the American entry while giving the Wehrmacht time to move to new defensive positions. The communists and antifascists were busy lining up fascists and machine-gunning them down. *It still won't be hard to be killed here*, laconically notes a snippet from my diary entry for the day.

I was struck by the beauty of Rome, with its colossal public buildings, monuments, and cathedrals. Intermixed with them were modern apartment houses. Yet the two architectures, the old and the new, blended harmoniously. The streets were wide and lined with trees. As an open city, it suffered no war damage, for Hitler, a master of propaganda, knew well that if Rome were destroyed he would incur the wrath of the whole civilized world.

In the morning we moved to one of the premier hotels, the Flora, and set up our offices there.

June 6, 1944   *Spent some time searching the German embassy. Took out a few pictures, one of Göring, as souvenirs. Documents of importance seem to have been removed.*

A CIC officer who arrested the courtesan of one of the German generals told me smilingly that on the way to the detention center she tried to seduce his driver.

The next day I made the acquaintance of a Czech girl. She spoke fluent French and at first we tried to converse in that language, but as my French was poor we switched to German, which she spoke well. She had studied in France, Austria, and Germany, she said. Her father had owned a factory in Czechoslovakia and been killed by the Germans. A half Jewess, she and her mother had spent ten months in a concentration camp before friends, through bribery, were able to effect their release.

Wanting to send home some souvenirs from Rome, I asked her to help me shop. I was astonished to find that a pair of sandals cost $20, a woman's tailored suit $150, a good camera $150 to $320, a pair of stockings $5, and a 60-cent New York meal $4.50. While these prices may not be out of line with today's prices in America, the comparable items in the States cost about one-tenth that. A private was paid $21 a *month*. A first lieutenant was paid considerably more, but Rome was no place for me to shop.

Soon I discovered how the Italians solved the inflation problem: Everyone dealt in the black market.

Talking with this girl, the Flora Hotel desk clerk, and other people in the course of my work, I learned German-Italian relations had never been good and increasingly soured as the war went on and Axis fortunes declined. Teutonic arrogance and domination did not sit well with the Italians, and Mussolini's acceptance of Hitler's anti-Jewish programs was deplored by most Italians. The antipathy to their partners led to widespread sabotage of everything German and to the frequent shooting of unarmed Germans. Despite the dictators' appeals and exhortations, harmony between the two peoples never exceeded a fractious working relationship.

June 7 *I get a laugh out of watching Italian policemen trying to direct traffic with their fancy ballet movements. The GIs pay no attention to them, ignore the signals, and drive right through.*

The Italians in general are fiercely anti-Nazi and have helped us in many ways. They make it a pleasure to be in Rome.

Today I was introduced to a shoemaker who was the leader of the partisans in Rome.

The partisans, underground fighters, were a considerable thorn in the Germans' side. In addition to sabotaging installations, they shot soldiers when opportunity offered. The German slaughter of 335 civilians at the Ardentine Caves outside Rome was in reprisal for the partisans' killing of thirty-three German soldiers in downtown Rome.

June 8 *Rummaged through the German embassy again in search of documents and found much good stuff. The embassy is under the protection of the Swiss, but the Swiss look the other way as we go through. There was an Artie Shaw record on the phonograph. The Germans are fond of American dance music.*

The embassy buildings are in a few acres of lovely gardens. A tennis court is included in the compound.

While slowly driving with my two sergeants down one of the main boulevards looking for a building we wanted to search, I saw a strikingly attractive girl of eighteen or twenty with a little bounce in her stride. In a flash I decided I might as well ask directions of this lovely creature as from any random Roman. Pulling over, I inquired in my best army handbook Italian, "Dove Via Nomentana, per piacere?" (Where is Nomentana Avenue, please?) and expected a flow of Italian in return. Instead, she answered in fluent English. Then soon I discovered that this girl with the large, dark, expressive eyes was equally proficient in German and Italian, and in the course of the ensuing conversation learned that she had worked for the German propaganda station in Rome in a clerical position. I decided to try to develop the relationship, offered her a lift, asked her name and address, and was invited for lunch the next day. Her name was Diana Yaselli.

Diana's residence proved to be a luxury apartment in a plush part of the city. Her mother, who also spoke English, was partially bedridden while recovering from a recent operation. She claimed, with the daughter, to have helped several American PWs to escape.

The girl had an interesting background. The mother was Italian, daughter of a prominent family. The father was an American of Italian descent, a semiretired international lawyer who was currently in Germany looking after property interests. He had been a federal attorney, in Washington, on business in Italy when he met his future wife. After the marriage he brought her back to the States, where the daughter was subsequently born. In later years they had returned to Italy to look after the mother's interests.

Diana had studied in Italy, Germany, and Switzerland. I thought her a level-headed girl, perhaps a bit spoiled by wealth. Her mother, I soon decided, certainly was. In the course of a conversation, while the maid was serving us lunch, I was shocked to have her tell me, "If I can't have servants, I don't want to live."

The remark, a bit sniffy to my mind, brought thoughts of my immigrant mother back home who had raised three boys and was always bustling about. If she wasn't cleaning, cooking, washing, or ironing, she was sure to be mending a sock, sewing a button on someone's shirt, or for relaxation, crocheting. And still she found time to help my father in his business.

After lunch Diana and I drove to the once-beautiful sulphur baths at Tivoli, the chichi watering place for the diplomatic set, only to find the Germans had wantonly wrecked them, just as they had destroyed other nonmilitary objectives.

Diana offered to give me every assistance in my work, and aside from enjoying her company, I thought she might be of help. And soon she was. She removed the pay ledgers and other books of the propaganda station from which Ezra Pound had broadcast—the turncoat poet for whom the FBI man was diligently searching.

June 11 *In the morning rummaged through the Czech embassy, used by the Germans as a headquarters, and later through the Italian Government Railroad offices, where we found mountains of valuable stuff.*

Later with Diana to the home of the Italian consul general to the U.S., a Dr. Bernadotte. He and his French-Canadian wife received us graciously. They are friends of many of the big people in Washington, including Roosevelt, and proudly showed me all kinds of letters and invitations from these people. His son, he told me, was forced by the Germans, on the threat of reprisals to his family, to broadcast propaganda for the Germans. The boy is a twenty-year-old American-educated kid, as American as Coca Cola.

In discussing the workings of the propaganda station, he and Diana agreed that of the entire staff employed there, all except three were anti-Nazi.

The Bernadotte son gave me the name of the man he thought might be able to help us find Ezra Pound, whose unpatriotic declamations have aroused fierce resentment at home.

I was invited to come again, and I would like to if I am in Rome for any length of time.

My few days here have brought me into contact with all kinds of people. Various new experiences.

June 12 *Went to Naples.*

I took Diana along so that she could see if their estate at nearby San Sebastiano had been destroyed by the March volcanic eruption of Mount Vesuvius. Since transporting civilians in army vehicles was prohibited, I circumvented the restriction by borrowing a cap from one of my sergeants and having her wear what looked like a GI raincoat. She passed for a WAC and we had no trouble. Although I carried a card issued by Allied Force headquarters requesting that I be "extended all courtesies" in carrying out my work, it seemed to me more prudent just not to be stopped and questioned by the MPs.

After completing my mission in Naples, we drove the seven or eight miles to San Sebastiano where we found the volcano, the only active one in Europe, had engulfed several towns including San Sebastiano. As we walked about inspecting the damage, still enough heat in the lava to be felt through our shoes, I observed an older man doing some repair work on his collapsed house. As he worked, apparently unperturbed by several little children underfoot, he was cheerfully singing an aria. "What an attitude of acceptance!" I thought. "I wish I could live my life like that."

San Sebastiano was almost completely destroyed, except for the church, the municipal house, and Diana's family's estate. The property consisted primarily of a handsome old house surrounded by large orchards. Inside the spacious residence were beautiful paintings and sculptures. I estimated there were at least thirty rooms.

How it was spared bordered on the miraculous, since virtually the whole town was under lava. As the molten rock came down, it split into two streams as it approached the Yaselli property, and as if knowing the borders, one stream flowed to the left of the orchards and the other to the right, doing no damage other than searing some of the trees.

Diana checked the garage to find that the Germans had taken her Fiat sports car. The radio in the house and numerous other items were also gone.

Word of our arrival quickly spread, and soon Diana's friends, relatives, the local priest, and the peasants who worked the orchards and gardens came to the house to see her. She was the young mistress of the domain, every inch of her, and they hung on her every word as she told them of her parents, Rome, the current war situation, and other news.

Supper was prepared for us by an elderly housekeeper whose dress and manner resembled that of a convent's mother superior. We had fresh eggs, my first in six or seven months, fried potatoes, bread, cherries, and peaches, a far cry from my usual army diet.

As the evening drew to a close, Diana showed me to my room, which adjoined hers and had a connecting door. As we talked, the housekeeper brought towels, went through the connecting door, and sensing perchance that this American officer might have carnal inclinations toward her unchaperoned mistress, noisily slid a heavy bolt across the door. With this blatancy she made clear her determination to spike any budding erotic yearnings I might be experiencing.

In the morning, after a breakfast that included real fresh milk, whose taste I had almost forgotten, we started back for Rome. En route the first destination was Caprocotta, a town in the mountains of central Italy, where the Yasellis had property. To get there required a long and tedious drive over narrow, curving, slippery roads, and around detours necessitated by the dozens of mostly small bridges the Germans had earlier blown up in their northward retreat.

The trip was enlivened by two episodes involving donkeys. One sprawled across the narrow road and wouldn't budge. Horn honking had no effect. We were reduced to waiting him out, a matter of ten or fifteen minutes. A short while later a second slowly ambled six feet in front of us. We had to follow behind him at a crawl for half an hour.

On the way it had begun to rain, and all I had for a roof was a torn piece of canvas that we made do and that diverted some of the water. About 4:00 P.M. we reached the town. All in all, hardly a silky journey.

At Caprocotta, which my companion said had good skiing in the winter, we found the two houses owned by the Yasellis blown up, as was most of the rest of the town. We visited Diana's relatives, those we could find. Then we stopped at the house of the town doctor (who, she told me, wanted to marry her) and dried out her clothes at the fire. This house was one of the few still standing.

We left Caprocotta at 6:00 P.M. and, after much trial-and-error driving, finally arrived at completely demolished Cassino, seventy-five miles south of Rome on Highway 6. Dominating the small town, on a hill 1,700 feet high, was the famous ancient Benedictine monastery, one of the oldest and most venerated historical monuments in Europe. It traced its roots to a structure built by St. Benedict in A.D. 529. A center of Christian monasticism, it was filled with irreplaceable treasures, many of which, to the credit of the Germans, had been removed from harm's way. Not known to the Allies at the time was that Kesselring had formally told the Vatican that he would not occupy the abbey.

In February, in a highly controversial decision, British General Freyberg ordered it bombed. Allied planes and artillery blasted it to ruins. While the Nazis were not actually occupying the monastery, it was attacked because of its strategic location. Together with other fortified hills, Cassino protected the entrance to the Liri Valley, the road to Rome. The bombardment, however, had the effect of giving the Germans an even further advantage, since rubble is easier to defend than buildings. Fortuitously, the cell where St. Benedict had lived was the only part of the Abbey undamaged, and that because a heavy-caliber shell that landed a foot away from the tomb was a dud.

It wasn't until the end of May, when the Anzio troops and the Allied forces in the south made their coordinated attacks, that Monte Cassino was finally taken. Of the 1,500 Germans captured, 377 were bagged at nearby Velletri. Interrogators found they were members of fifty different companies, a remarkable tribute to the enemy's genius for quickly melding troops from different decimated units into an effective fighting formation.

The long delay in capturing this strongpoint was largely attributable to the masterly defense of General von Senger und Etterlin, considered by military experts on both sides to have been one of the great tacticians of the war. It is perhaps the most trenchant of ironies that he was a former Rhodes scholar and both an Anglophile and a lay member of the Benedictine order that resided in the abbey.

Driving through the town in the middle of the night was both a ghostly and ghastly experience. Everything, but everything, was destroyed. Only some tree trunks were still standing.

Once on the main road to Rome, I was able to pick up speed, but we did not get back until 5:00 A.M., dog weary.

June 14 *To the Ministry of Interior where we picked up all kinds of good stuff, including stenographic reports of telephone conversations, among them the talks between Mussolini and Chamberlain, Laval, and all the other big wheels. Also picked up those between Mussolini and his mistresses, which were recorded despite, we found, specific instructions to the contrary—an indication of Italian discipline.*

When it was seen that Rome would fall, the officials of some of the offices buried important documents concerning the Italian underground anti-Nazi and anti-Fascist movements to prevent the Germans from seizing them. We also got those.

Was introduced to a marchese who, I learned from Diana, is a nobleman ranking above a count and below a prince.

Since coming to Rome I have met, besides the Yasellis, the partisan leader of the city, the consul general, big shot ministry people, a baron, a big criminal lawyer, and a crook—among others.

June 15 *Squired by Diana, Bill Guest and I toured the city's points of interest.*

Bill is leaving for Cairo.

June 16 *Again searched the German embassy. We had to blow eight safes and several hidden wall safes.*

June 17 *Returned with Diana to her home to find two CIC men wait-*

ing to question her about her father's presence in Germany. Her father is an international lawyer with both American and Italian passports and has been working in Germany.

June 18   *Frank Amprim, the FBI man whom I've helped in the partial solution of his Ezra Pound case, asked me today if it was okay with me if he asks the FBI to request the War Department to assign me to work with him. I said yes, I'd like it. He's writing a letter immediately, and I'm trying to arrange temporary duty with him till he gets an answer.*

June 19   *Found out that a man named Passamani has the books that will show what Ezra Pound was paid. He fled to Milan with the Germans upon our arrival here.*

Apparently Pound never reached Milan. En route, in Genoa, deserted by his fleeing fascist cohorts, he surrendered to a CIC unit that turned him over to Amprim. Indicted for treason, he was returned to the United States. The evidence showed that the poet had sold out his country for seventeen dollars per broadcast. Because he was considered a great artist, a national treasure, many influential literary figures, who believed that the magnificence of his poetry expiated the vileness of his politics, intervened on his behalf. His acts were termed aberrations. He was declared mentally incompetent and never put on trial. From 1945 to 1948 he was committed to St. Elizabeth's Psychiatric Hospital. When freed, he returned to Italy. There was no shift in Pound's views in his later years.

June 20   *Mr. Yaselli, Diana's father, returned from Germany today with his young son, an eight-year-old. Judging from a picture in the apartment, he has lost a lot of weight. He tells me some gruesome stories. Virtually all the Jews have been killed, many by gas. The numerous and barbaric incidents he recites have a familiar ring in view of what I've learned from PWs and other sources.*

Much of his recent work in Germany, Yaselli told me, dealt with bribing officials to allow Jewish clients to escape the country. The original National Socialist program had successfully tempered inflation (at one point in the post–World War I period, the mark had dropped to four billion to the dollar). It had built roads and railways, improved the welfare of the masses by reducing unemployment and bettering the public health system. The program that brought Hitler to power had become perverted with time and was now an abomination.

The first reports I had heard of concentration camps I found hard to believe, thinking they were probably touched up by propaganda. Yaselli disabused me.

June 21   *Drove a friend to a hospital for some medication. Upon arriving, a nurse, who was a nun, told me a long story about how the hospital was asked by the Americans to vacate 600 beds for wounded due from the north. They vacated the beds. Then came the English and said the entire hospital must be vacated. She said it wasn't possible to vacate any more beds, many of the remaining civilians were critical cases. The hospital had twenty-four hours left to obey. I advised her to see the American officer in the Rome Area Command, not the British, and that she herself, who spoke English, should go rather than the hospital director. A woman who was a nun and nurse, I felt, could do more. I wonder how she'll make out.*

Shoes in Italy today are mainly made of cork and wood. Leather is very scarce.

The fast tour of Rome's sights with Bill Guest and Diana had left me unsatisfied. There had been too much to see and too little time to see it. I returned to St. Peter's for a leisurely look and to marvel at the beauty of Michelangelo's work. Just the planning of it, no less the execution, left me agape with wonder and admiration. This was transcendent intellectual and creative power, genius, pure genius. I resolved to be careful of my use of the word in the future, and careful in my acceptance of it when used by others.

My work in Rome was nearing its end, and there was now more time for relaxation. I took Diana and her brother Georgio swimming at Tivoli and at other times at Lake Braciano. Georgio, Mr. Yaselli confided to me, was actually a half brother to Diana, the child of his German mistress. It at first struck me as odd that he would bring his mistress's son from Germany to his home in Italy, but on further thought it made sense if the boy's presence was acceptable to his wife, and particularly inasmuch as Germany was now undergoing widespread dev-astating air attacks with heavy loss of civilian life. In all the time I knew the family, I never saw the boy treated in any way but affection-ately by Diana and her mother. Since he spoke Italian fluently, it was obvious that he had previously spent time in Italy.

June 24 *Dropped in at corps headquarters to pick up my mail and shoot the bull with the boys. Colonel Langevin greeted me warmly, told me he had written Holsten to get me back, and asked me also to write Holsten requesting transfer back. I was flattered.*

The next operation, I believe, will be an amphibious landing, prob-ably France.

Two days after our entry into Rome the Allies launched the Nor-mandy invasion. Some time before the capture of Rome, Holsten had advised Pundt and me to bone up on Balkan order-of-battle informa-tion. Since we had heard no more from Holsten about a possible Balkan operation, I ruled out that we would be going in that direction. I guessed, correctly as it developed, that the Sixth Corps would now be invading southern France.

My S Force work completed, I awaited further orders. Availing my-self of the free time, I made a round of the popular tourist attractions and took intermittent trips to the beach. Then one day the gods truly smiled on me, and I had a chance to play my favorite sport.

June 26 *Golf in the morning with Diana and father.*

Learning that I was a golfer, Mr. Yaselli took us to his club. The course had not been properly cared for during the war, and there were no flags in the holes. He had a youngster go out and put the flags in, and we teed off, I with a spare set of his clubs. After nine holes we quit, the fairways and greens being in too poor a condition to enjoy the game.

In the clubhouse, as we lunched, Yaselli gave me the address of his mistress and asked me, if I should get to that area of Germany, to look her up and let him know how she was faring.

Diana did not react to the conversation. Having a mistress, I inferred, must be an accepted practice in some Italian circles.

Returning to the Yasellis for dinner that evening, I was introduced to an elderly Countess Somebody-or-other who lived in the apartment below, was hard of hearing, and spoke what she thought was English. In reality, it was a potpourri of languages liberally sprinkled with Italian and sparsely with English. It made no sense to me, so I nudged Diana, sitting next to me, who, hardly moving her lips, softly translated, enabling me to respond appropriately.

During the dinner I mentioned that while Diana and I were in Naples, en route to San Sebastiano, my camera was stolen out of the jeep and also my spare can of gas. "It seems to me," I said, "that in Naples everything that isn't locked up gets stolen."

"Yes," said the countess, "we have a saying about Neapolitans, how they make their living. Half of them steal from the other half in the morning, and in the afternoon the second half steals from the first half."

Stealing, I was to learn, was not a monopoly of the Italians. Later, in Germany, I had a package stolen out of my momentarily unattended jeep. It contained food that had been sent to me from a woman in the United States and was meant to be delivered to her relatives.

During my association with the Yasellis, I occasionally invited Diana to lunch at the officers' mess in the Hotel Flora. On one of these occasions, as we were finishing our tea, I said, "How do you say in Italian, 'May we have more tea, please?'" Instructed, I repeated it over and over until I had the words and accent down pat.

"Are you sure you can handle it?" asked Diana.

"No problem," I assured her.

Signaling the waiter, I tried out my new Italian. He, thinking he was serving a *paisan* in American uniform, burst into a joyous welcoming speech. As I frantically looked to Diana, she erupted into laughter and let the scene go on for a few more moments before coming to my rescue. Later, as we left, she said, "I was tempted to let you stew in your own juice."

June 27 *Drove Mrs. Yaselli and Diana to Naples and then San Sebastiano. While there I again examined the lava. In some places it is as deep as a three- or even four-story building. It is still hot and some of it is still smoking. Just a little of the town remains.*

Eggs in San Sebastiano cost 18 to 20 cents apiece. In Rome 50 cents.

June 28 *Spent the night in San Sebastiano. Slept well.*

The Yaselli orchards' 3,000-plus trees are yielding a fairly good crop, but apricots bring only 5 lire a kilo, which is a poor price. In Rome, even when sold in bulk, they bring 20 lire a kilo. If only one truck were to be had for a few trips, the difference would amount to thousands of dollars.

The more I see of Italy, the more I am convinced that an American businessman with the ability to organize could quickly make a fortune here. Mr. Yaselli agrees.

July 2 *Have received orders to return to Sixth Corps Headquarters.*

To Lake Braciano with Diana, Georgio, and their father for a last swim here.

Two years after the war ended I received a phone call from Mr. Yaselli. He was in New York with Diana, representing Italian wine interests, and invited me to dinner at a Manhattan restaurant. As we were being seated he asked me if I minded if he ordered a certain wine. "I want to see what they charge for it."

When the check arrived, he said, "Look at this." The wine cost four dollars. "Do you know what we got for that bottle? Twenty cents!"

The month in Rome in the luxurious environs of the Yaselli family was not only pleasant but, after the long grinding and hazardous days at Anzio, also salubrious. I was refreshed and ready, come what may, to get back into the war.

July 3 *Drove to Naples with my men to report back to Sixth Corps.*

11

Planning in Naples

In Naples, a noisy, squalid port city cradled between the hills and the sea, and seemingly thriving on its pandemonium, I was struck by the number of horse-drawn hearses not followed by mourners. The coffins in the hearses were not occupied by corpses. They were stuffed with American goods stolen from the docks and on their way into the lucrative black market. The coffins, the Neapolitans had noted, were never inspected by the squeamish military police. This was one of the many ways by which the army lost a third of the supplies landed in Naples to the black market.

July 4, 1944 *Reported to work. Warmly received. We're right in the heart of the city and planning an invasion. I've been shown the general plan, but I'm afraid to write down the area lest this notebook somehow fall into the wrong hands.*

Operation Shingle, as the plan was named, called for the invasion of southern France. It was intended to draw enemy strength away from Normandy, easing the pressure on the Allied forces to the north. Churchill was less than enthusiastic about this operation. He would have preferred that we remain in Italy and speed the advance up the

Boot so as to quickly move into Eastern Europe, thus lessening the area in Western Europe that Stalin could overrun.

The next days were a mixture of work and relaxation. Mornings were devoted to planning, and to studying the strengths and weaknesses of the German troops we would be up against, plus analyzing the coastal fortifications. The afternoons were spent swimming in the large pool in the medical center, the evenings in dancing with nurses and WACs, drinking, and chewing the fat with the other staff officers.

My first day in the pool, I swam with Colonel Langevin, Joe Haines, and a Captain John Rieger, a new addition to the G-2 section. A graduate of Fordham, Rieger was a PW interrogator, a laid-back fellow with blond hair, cornflower-blue eyes, and the kind of long eyelashes that set women's hearts aflutter. As we became better acquainted, we discovered that our backgrounds were somewhat similar. His parents had emigrated from the same region of Europe as mine, and at about the same time. We quickly formed a warm friendship.

One afternoon as the two of us were donning our trunks in the locker room of the pool, we put our clothes into two lockers at random. The long rows of lockers had no locks, but several men were always meticulously mopping the floors. "Good," I thought, "they probably also act as security."

Through swimming, we returned to discover our lockers had been rifled. The thief had taken $26 in Italian money out of John's wallet and $90 out of mine. He had removed all the 500 and 1,000 lire notes, leaving me the equivalent of $4.30 in small bills.

"I'd bet," I said, "it was one of those workers who mop up."

"Yes," agreed Rieger, "and he really mopped up!"

Recalling my previous losses by theft in Naples, the incident reinforced my impression that the population lived by stealing, lending credence to the countess's aphorism about Neapolitans.

The weather in Naples was hot, so the water had a magnetic attraction. One day I went swimming in the Bay of Naples at a beach south of the city with a Mrs. Linda Renale, a member of a family Alex Shayne had known from prewar days and with whom we dined soon after our arrival at Fifth Army headquarters. She was a comely, dark-haired, supple-bodied woman in her early twenties who moved with a sinuous grace. Her husband had been an officer in the Italian army and had been killed fighting with Rommel in North Africa.

We frolicked in the gentle waves, splashing about, diving between each other's legs, and wrestling for control of a ball, absence of a common language no great barrier.

Out of the water and sprawled in the sand, we shared a box of K rations and conversed, her smattering of English and my smattering of Italian sufficient, resorting to the army's Italian handbook only when things got too sticky. As I played with her earlobe and slowly ran my finger along her shoulder, she assured me that my heroic attempt to speak Italian was commendable, but that the only Italian an American soldier needed to know was "Voi sieta bella e mi piaceta" (You are beautiful and I love you).

My wife, a sometime reader of romantic fiction, has since told me these words are equally effective in all languages.

As planning for the invasion went on, I was convinced it would succeed if the Wehrmacht's disposition of its troops was not changed, and especially if they were not reinforced. The order of battle greatly favored us. Already, before our landing, we OB people knew that the four best divisions of the twelve defending the Côte d'Azur had earlier been rushed north to bolster Field Marshal Rommel's forces battling the Allied troops that had landed in Normandy a month earlier, on June 6, the day after our capture of Rome.

We also knew that many of the remaining troops were battle-battered men from the Russian front who had been sent to the Riviera to recuperate and, we suspected, had "had it."

A big invasion operation like ours could not be concealed. The German reconnaissance planes flew over the harbor every night and took pictures. Principally, only the time and landing area were beyond the High Command's knowledge.

July 11 *Spent the afternoon swimming at the medical center, getting a date for Thursday night's dance at the Rotunda, and drinking champagne with Joe Haines. He can drink any time of day or night.*

Sociable and fun-loving, with a winsome charm, Joseph Haines IV hailed from Philadelphia's tony Main Line and professed to having been "thrown out of more good schools than there are." He had an ulcer and was not supposed to drink, but he thought he had an answer to the problem: After every drink, he would gulp down water on the theory that it diluted the alcohol before it could do any damage. "When this war is over," he would often say, "I won't be good for anything. I'll just have to marry a rich girl."

Joe survived the war and did marry a rich girl, only to die of his ulcer-related problem a few years later.

July 12   *Colonel Langevin told me to start addressing the morning General Staff conferences on the Russian situation beginning Monday.*

Momentous events were taking place on the Russian front. The Soviets had taken Minsk. The Wehrmacht was in full flight, the field marshals often at odds with the Führer's orders that there be no retreat from areas his generals knew could no longer be held. Hitler's refusal to permit a timely retreat from Stalingrad, which cost him the loss of Field Marshal Friedrich von Paulus's Sixth Army in January 1942, had taught him nothing.

July 13   *Letter today. Kromers got War Department telegram telling them Henry was killed. Feel bad about it.*

When I had heard, while at Anzio, that my cousin's plane had been shot down, I had hoped that he had been able to bail out, but I had a premonition of his death. When subsequently one of the crew in another plane in that flight wrote his parents that he had seen Henry bail out, I was relieved, thinking he was probably a prisoner, but at least still alive.

July 16   *No swimming. Worked all day. Prepared first talk on Russia.*

July 17   *Russian talk went very well. The usual assortment of generals, admirals, colonels, and a sprinkling of lesser rank. Major French complimented me later. General Truscott was absent, gone to England, I think, probably for conferences with Eisenhower and his staff.*

For the next four weeks, until we sailed, I briefed the group about the fighting on the Russian front. My information was gained by analyzing AFHQ teletype informational reports to corps headquarters.

The map reached to the ceiling. A red ribbon indicated the front lines, red pins the major targets, and red and blue arrows the attacking and counterattacking forces. With a long pointer I explained the fighting and what I thought it all meant. I explained the German army's traditional reliance on Clausewitz's teachings, which emphasized that the capture of the enemy's territory was secondary to the destruction of his forces, and that this policy had been reversed under Hitler. I was nervous for the first few minutes and hoped it didn't show, but quickly calmed down, and then enjoyed it.

Among the audience were some Russian liaison officers, but they offered me no help. I had a sneaking suspicion that what I was telling the conference was also news to them. Weeks later, in France, when I was no longer briefing on the Russian front, the generals would occasionally stop me as I passed and ask kiddingly for an update on the Russian situation.

After these morning conferences, the planning for Operation Shingle went on. From aerial photographs and topographic information, a detailed replica of the invasion area was created out of air-foamed rubber. Every highway and street was shown; every bridge and overpass; every church, school, or municipal building; every house and gas station. In short, every feature of any kind.

Standing at this replica, in a secure room, the commanding officers and their chief subordinates were carefully briefed about their missions.

Just before we boarded the ships, this rubber replica was cut up. Pieces of it became seat cushions in my jeep, which improved the comfort of the ride considerably.

So many people had to know where we were going to land that I was afraid there would be a leak, we would be expected, and have a hell of a fight getting ashore. In fact a high-ranking German staff officer we later captured told me they had heard where we planned to land but didn't believe it because the beaches there were bad. They thought we would land between Toulon and Marseille.

Instead, we landed at St. Tropez and other points east of Toulon.

To while away the time during the three days we sat aboard the ships in the harbor, we watched movies, gambled, and indulged in other diversions aside from the obligatory safety drills. Some of these hours I spent reading and reviewing French. It had been nine years since my last college course in the language. Although I could still understand conversational French well, I could no longer speak the language with any fluency, as I had discovered in trying to converse with the Czech girl in Rome.

The ship I was aboard was a former luxury liner, the *Santa Rosa*. The food was superb and the large cabin comfortable despite holding twelve officers. The enlisted men were quartered in compartments holding 150 men each.

I drew the assignment of commander of the life rafts—for which, of course, I was ideally suited, having seen a life raft or two in the movies. I was also chosen by General Truscott's chief of staff to be one of the first ten headquarters officers "urgently needed" ashore. This was a cause for later ribbing by my friends. "Urgently needed, hell! Charlie, you were considered expendable!"

12

Invasion of Southern France

Ships, ships, ships, as far as the eye could see, among them two American and seven British aircraft carriers. The 1,500-ship armada stretched out beyond the horizon.

On August 13 the signal to set sail was given. Lifeboats were swung out as the anchors were raised and the guns manned. The water was smooth, and seasickness, the bane of seaborne soldiers, was suffered by few.

The landing zone stretched across the Riviera from Cannes to Toulon. The troops under our command were the Third, Thirty-sixth, and Forty-fifth infantry divisions, veteran components from the Anzio days, who had also fought in Africa, Sicily, and Salerno, and with whom we worked harmoniously. The Sixth Corps now fell under the command of General Patch's Seventh Army. The French supplied a naval assault group, which went into action just south of Cannes, and commandos who hit Cap Negre.

For four hours prior to the 8:00 A.M. H-hour, bombers and naval guns laid down an explosive blanket that severely reduced any German ability to hold us off. We suffered fifty dead and a few hundred wounded instead of the thousands of casualties that might have been expected.

In the vicinity of St. Raphael, the Thirty-sixth Division hit the toughest beaches, sections containing a complex series of underwater

obstacles that were heavily defended by shore batteries and lengthy entanglements of barbed wire. Other of its targeted beaches were defended
only by small guns but were suitable only for small-boat landings.

Since the Germans had placed their strongest forces at Marseille and
Toulon, where their intelligence people thought we would land, they
left only two divisions to hold the hundred miles of coast between
Toulon and Nice. The error enabled us to effect a near-perfect amphibious operation. We landed more troops on our D-day than had been
landed two months earlier at Normandy's D-day.

At this stage of the war the Germans were hard pressed to keep their
army supplied with fighting men. They were approaching the bottom
of the barrel in both manpower and matériel. With the Russian debacle, the Normandy invasion, the unrelenting and increasingly successful aerial bombings of the war plants and cities, and now with the invasion of southern France, the Fatherland had more on its plate than it
could handle.

For me, fortunately, this seaborne invasion was no great shakes, not
even especially exciting since my ship did not come under fire. At
Anzio my LST was a target. Here the shore batteries had been neutralized, and unlike at Anzio, the Luftwaffe failed to put in an appearance.

Shortly after the first troops landed, I went over the side on a rope
ladder and into a small craft that headed for shore a mile away. As it
neared the beach, it hit a sandbar, forcing me to wade a hundred yards
through chest-high water while hanging on to a hastily anchored rope
that had been cast out from the beach. My equipment got wet, I lost
my pipe, and my watch stopped—all in all, a small price to pay. Only
my wallet remained dry. I had put it into a condom issued for the purpose. (The condom was a versatile piece of military equipment. Aside
from its conventional use, GIs placed it over their rifle barrels to keep
water out and used it to protect their watches, wallets, photographs,
letters, pocket knives, and other items they felt must not get wet.)

In contrast to the indecision that had marred the Anzio assault, there
was no dithering here. We hit the ground running and pushed forward
at a blistering pace. Before midnight the advance troops of the Forty-
fifth Division had already made contact with the airborne troops that
had been dropped earlier in the enemy rear.

Our first command post was set up just outside Sainte Maxime in a beautiful chateau with orchards and lovely gardens, and that night I slept in a hotel. Within days we captured Avignon, one-time seat of the papacy, and I debriefed some paratroopers who had been taken prisoner and escaped. All had stories to tell, sometimes garnished with little anecdotes.

Two youngsters, buddies, gung-ho daredevil types, told me how they had fought with the partisans, who had a policy of no mercy shown, no prisoners taken. After killing some Germans, they had each taken a machine pistol from the dead. They waited in ambush for the next German truck to come around a curve in the road. When it came, they opened fire with their Tommy guns, but one man's gun jammed.

Said the boy with the jammed weapon, "While I'm fuckin' like crazy with my gun tryin' to get it goin', this bastard," pointing to his partner, "is poppin' away and laughin' his guts out. I yelled, 'What's so funny?' And he says, 'You dumb prick! Use the other gun!'"

These were men, and there were others, such as some of those in General Frederick's SSF, to whom war was fun. They engaged in it with a mindset like that of children playing cowboys and Indians.

During this time I also talked to a British officer who had been captured at Dunkirk and who told me of the lengths to which some men had gone to escape from Germany. One group, he said, spent three months making a compass out of nails and razor blades. Each night they assembled it and added to it, and before the morning inspections disassembled it and hid the parts in their mouths.

Not always were our command posts in comfortable places. Says my diary: *New bivouac area, an orchard. Washed by swimming in a canal of mountain water. Br-r-r.*

As staff officers we were expected to be clean-shaven every day, come hell or high water, and there were mornings when I ran my jeep a bit, and then drained the radiator for hot water to wash and shave. Ingenuity stood a soldier in good stead. If no stream was handy, men not infrequently used irrigation ditches to bathe. Later, in the Vosges Mountains, I came on one in the midst of his ablutions in an icy stream. "Must be pretty cold, soldier," I said sympathetically.

"Yes, sir," was the reply. "But man's best friend ain't a dog, sir. It's a bath."

Returning to the office from a trip to the command post of one of the divisions a week after our landings, I was handed a wad of French francs, all crisp, new bills. "What's this?" I asked.

"French money," was the answer.

"I can see that," I said, "but what's the story?"

There was general laughter. The jubilant OB section looked as happy as though it had gone to heaven without first bothering to die. It seemed an officer, new to combat, from a newly committed, unseasoned outfit had brought in a batch of documents along with the money, saying his men had captured a German officer with the company fund. Handing it to Pundt, he said, "It looks like phony French money to me."

"Yes, it does," said Doc, without batting an eye. "We'll take care of it."

And take care of it he did. My share was one-sixth of the loot.

Had Pundt forwarded the francs to army headquarters, the OB men there would have treated the swag similarly. Doc decided we deserved first dibs.

From the nature of the material received by the documents section, we could always tell when green troops were in the line. When searching prisoners, they sent back everything. As they metamorphosed into veterans, "blooded" troops, they rarely sent back anything of personal value. Wallets, for instance, were invariably empty of money.

As the fighting progressed and the enemy continued to fall back, maps and codes fell into our hands. In examining a batch of maps, I noticed that some were printed on the back of maps of England that had been stamped *Ungültig* (Invalid). The original maps had been intended for use in conjunction with Sea Lion, the German plan for the cross-channel invasion of England, but when the Royal Air Force defeated the Luftwaffe, Hitler postponed Sea Lion and was never able to put the maps of England to use. I wrote a piece for the *Beachhead News* mocking Hitler's plan to invade England, and a few days later BBC gleefully quoted it.

One of the corps's most spectacular victories at this time occurred at Montelimar on the Rhone River, seventy-five miles north of the coast, where we decimated a column of vehicles, men, and horses eleven miles long. Over two thousand vehicles, a thousand horses, and several hundred men fell victim. The retreating Germans had been caught in a defile. Our planes shot up the front and rear of the column, so the enemy could move neither forward nor backward, and being in a defile, could not move laterally. The fliers bombed and strafed back and forth at will until the slaughter was complete and the German Nineteenth Army divested of most of its equipment.

Colonel Langevin flew over the area a couple days later and told me the carnage was indescribable. The stench of the dead horses filled the air and could be smelled in the plane. "It was a real turkey shoot," he said, "a Cannae." (Cannae was the scene of Hannibal's famous annihilation of the Romans in 216 B.C. When the world's decisive battles are studied in military academies, this great Carthaginian victory is usually one of them.)

Contrary to popular American conception, the German army was largely horse-drawn, and this accounts for the large number of horses killed. A German division had five thousand to six thousand horses. In America, early impressions of German might were formed by the Wehrmacht's so-called blitzkrieg (lightning war) victories in Poland and France. Photographs and newsreels of Stuka dive bombers screeching toward their targets, panzers bobbing up and down demolishing all structures in their path, and troops racing on motorcycles toward their objectives projected a picture of invincible technical force.

Attention was rarely called to a weakness of the much-vaunted German army, namely the equine component of this juggernaut, its 2,700,000 horses. They hauled not only the bulk of its artillery and ammunition, but also kitchens, foodstuffs, and most of its supply services, as well as the forage they required for their own sustenance. In Russia alone, 180,000 horses died. (Some, during the lengthy, bitter siege of Stalingrad, were killed for food by starving soldiers.)

And never mentioned was that the enemy's mobile strategy was largely shackled by the limited speed of its horse-drawn wagons and foot-bound infantry. A supply system dependent on the horse was antiquated on the road networks of Western Europe and was no match for the gasoline-driven trucks that supplied the Allied armies, a transportation system of greater endurance, greater range, and less maintenance. Only 14 divisions out of the Wehrmacht's 103 in September 1939, at the time of the Polish invasion, were totally independent of the horse. All the rest were tethered by the umbilical cord of supply and, in consequence, their range of maneuver was sharply limited.

In contrast, gasoline was the lifeblood of the American forces. An infantry division needed six times as much gas as food, and an armored division eight times as much. Only in extremely fast, wide-ranging moves, such as some of General Patton's, did they outrun their gasoline supplies.

September 2, 1944   *American escapee pilots keep turning up with strange stories. The way the situation is evolving here, we have such superiority . . .*

This sentence in the diary is not completed. Since entries were often scribbled by flashlight, the batteries may have given out, or I may have been interrupted, the lack of privacy being a frequent obstacle to my writing. Diary keeping for one in my position was frowned on. I tried never to write anything that could be of tactical advantage to the enemy should my journal fall into his hands. Never on trips to the front, not in Italy and now in France, did I carry it, well aware that accidentally taking a wrong road might lead into the enemy lines and death or capture.

September 3   *Debriefed a French Army officer spy and got wonderful dope on the new German line being built on the Loue-Doube rivers to the north, including road conditions, artillery positions, and atrocities committed. The colonel was so pleased, he immediately dashed to General Truscott with it, just as he did earlier with the captured map I showed him, the map depicting the Nineteenth Army headquarters' plan of withdrawal.*

Tested a captured German motorcycle. Easy to handle.

September 4   *Cold night last night. Sleeping in tents on another estate.*

Our command posts have been quite good lately with their location in big estates. The last one was a place with a gilded ballroom, paintings, etchings, armor, statuary, formal gardens, etc., etc.

Debriefed two more spies, one a French Army lieutenant colonel and the other a young chemist. Information not much good and took me an hour to get them a certain map, and they needed transportation, which I couldn't get for them.

Busy studying matériel, interrogating agents, writing the daily summary of the day's action (which the chief of staff insists I do), translating captured maps, and correcting the men's translations of documents—among other things.

Had a chance to interrogate the three generals we've captured, and each damned time I was away from the command post when they were brought in.

I would like to get rid of my job of writing the daily Beachhead News story, but everybody likes the light style so much that the chief of staff insists I continue.

Sometime during the Anzio battle, Colonel Carleton, Truscott's chief of staff, told Colonel Langevin of the general's displeasure with the way the *Beachhead News* was reporting the corps's battles. Recalling my spoof of Hitler's secret tank, Tally-Ho suggested that I be assigned to write a nightly summary of the day's action. So in army officialese I was told: "In addition to your other duties, you are hereby directed . . ." My spoof had come back to haunt me.

September 5 *Got up at 5:30 A.M. in the dark, packed and drove up to a nice town, Lons-sur-Saumier, where our CP is in a park surrounding a salt bath. There are plenty of hotels in the city, but they aren't requisitioned by us—and the French would gladly give them—because we have orders to use French property as little as possible.*

Kingman took two pictures of me.

Lieutenant Kingman was one of our photo interpretation officers. He was a whiz with aerial photographs. We had a high regard for each other's work, and we often kiddingly debated the merits of his school, Yale, versus mine, Columbia.

September 6 *Debriefed some escapee American PWs. Gave me little we didn't know.*

An artillery observer pilot tells me that to hide from our air patrols the Germans are so thoroughly camouflaging their horses that from above they look like moving bushes.

Heard that Roberts, an order-of-battle officer who came overseas with me, had an arm shot off today. For an AFHQ outfit, we've had a lot of casualties. We lost several men at Anzio, and now Webb, a new man who just flew over from the States, was killed a week after getting here.

According to Captain Grimes, the editor, my column, "Today's Picture," is far and away the most popular feature in the Beachhead News, *mainly because of its humorous reporting. Yet today Colonel Langevin asked me to tone it down. I think he wants it to read like a somber G-2 estimate of the situation.*

Then along came Tally-Ho—it was in the war room—and said General Truscott would like individual companies mentioned. But I know if I do that, each of the three divisions will complain that I favor the other two.

(This is exactly what happened in time.)

Moved again—to Salin de Bains. A nice sight to see, the French lining the roads, waving, kissing, giving men wine and fruit, and everybody all smiles and laughter. The towns are decked with flags and everyone tries to shake our hands.

We are encamped in a park in tents. One would think we were in the army.

That evening Pundt and I went into town and bought several bottles of champagne. At a bull session with our friends that night, I drank a whole bottle, and then, since Joe's ulcer was bothering him, polished off the remaining half of his bottle. I slept like a log. In the middle of the night, however, I had to get up to find the latrine. That I managed. But returning was a horror. In daylight one army tent is the clone of another. At 3:00 A.M., disoriented and a bit woozy, uniformity was the last thing I needed. I stumbled about and opened the flaps of a dozen tents, flashing my light in search of my cot, before I found it. I came within a hair of swearing off the bubbly juice.

Most destruction to cities, towns, and villages occurred when there was prolonged fighting, as happened at Anzio and Cassino. Given time, everything is smashed into fragments. If, on the other hand, one side is retreating rapidly, damage is relatively negligible unless the retreating forces deliberately destroy the town. Consequently, as we moved from town to town, it was possible to measure the ferocity of fighting by the degree of destruction.

When the Germans quickly relinquished Besançon, I drove into the city and found it, according to my diary, *not badly shot up.* In the course of my inspection I noticed some girls with their heads shorn. Inquiring why, I was told this was retribution inflicted for having been friendly with the Germans. There were other strange sights. A dairy farmer whose horse had apparently been sequestered by the Germans had worked out an alternative way to deliver his milk. As I drove down the highway, I passed a huge dog harnessed to a small cart, driverless, and trotting down the road. In the cart were five large milk cans. The nearest town was three miles away. Some drivers of trucks and cars overcame the shortage of gasoline by attaching a wood burning boiler to the rear of their vehicles. No two of these Rube Goldberg contraptions seemed to be alike, and the smoke-belching appendage was often a third the size of the vehicle it was propelling. These oddities, we were to find later, were especially common in Germany.

September 7   *Today we were within earshot of the front lines and heard machine gun fire all day. Early in the morning two ME 109s suddenly flew over at tree top level, and for a few moments we expected a strafing. Don't think the pilots saw us in time though.*
    Letter from Bill Guest. Rus was killed fooling with a captured rocket.

Bill was now in the East. Rus was the youthful intelligence chief with whom we had had tea at Anzio during a visit to the British divisions, and who, Bill confided, was a titled aristocrat. At first meeting I felt that for one so young he must be over his head in the job, but as we talked at greater length I discovered he was admirably knowledgeable, cool-headed, and competent. I was sorry to hear of his death.

In its many incursions the German army lived substantially off the land it was overrunning, the spoils of conquest supporting its thrust. It did not hesitate to requisition food, livestock, and even manpower. Local needs mattered little. In contrast, the American army received almost all its supplies from home, despite the shipping lost to Hitler's submarines. Only rarely did it draw on local stocks, and when it did, it paid for them.

Despite our ample provisions, which at times even included canned orange juice, many of us sorely missed such pre-army treats as daily fresh eggs. To satisfy that hunger, the army substituted powdered eggs. But there was no way that they could be whipped into an appetizing omelet. Even when reconstituted by the most resourceful of cooks, they never resulted in anything other than an unappetizing runny mass, dubbed by one wit the Yellow Peril. Only a pugnacious mess sergeant, armed with a cleaver and backed by the firepower of the U.S. Army, would have dared to pass off the resulting concoction as scrambled eggs. This accounts for the occasional triumphant entries in my diaries, such as the one of September 9: *Getting a fresh egg every now and then and having them fry it for me at the mess.* And while this may seem a humdrum entry, to those of us starved for fresh eggs, a couple of these delicacies, fried sunnyside up and set before us by the waiter, made a lovely picture, every bit as beautiful as a Monet painting.

Because Doc Pundt and I had our own jeeps, one of the few advantages of being attached officers rather than assigned, we were independent of the corps motor pool. We did not require trip tickets authorizing the use of a vehicle and a statement of its destination. Our freedom of movement, consequently, was much greater than most of the headquarters personnel, and this enabled us, when work permitted, to dispatch a couple of our sergeants to roam the countryside bartering cigarettes, candy, soap, and other PX items for fresh eggs, cheese, bread, and wine, victuals often not available for money. In war-torn countries, barter works better than cash.

The provisions we obtained by this means we shared with our friends, and it freed us from the tyranny of day-in-day-out army chow. If no table wine was obtainable, the cheese and bread were chased down our grateful gullets by sips of champagne from bottles that cost sixty francs ($1.20 at the time).

Our living quarters varied widely in quality, from the luxurious to the incommodious. Overnight one could be transformed from a prince to a pauper and vice versa—one day a room in a palace or luxurious chateau, and the next a barn or hay loft. During a period of rapid advance, the command post might be moved every few days and at times, later in the war, every day.

As the Sixth Corps continued its vigorous pursuit up the Rhone Valley, new CP locations were needed every few days. The officer in charge of finding these sites did his best to meet the many requirements of an ideal spot, among them concealment or cover if possible, easy access to the main line of advance, and a building or group of buildings large enough for all the headquarters trappings. To find a site that met the requirements was a demanding job, and one day he was killed while reconnoitering too close to the front.

No length of time ever elapsed without learning of the death of a colleague, friend, or acquaintance, so it was always heartwarming when one heard good news, as happened one evening when I ran into a friend, Captain Kingkoff, a medical administration officer. He had been captured a week before at Valence, thirty-five miles north of Montelimar, the scene of the German debacle. Entrained for a PW camp in Germany, he escaped with another prisoner, "Jock" Whitney (who, before the war, had been an internationally known sportsman and ranking polo player), by jumping off the moving train.

September 10 *Drove twenty-five miles to the Third Division clearing station to have a filling in a tooth replaced. The* Beachhead News *is now using my daily column as its headline story.*

Moved into Besançon. Sleeping quarters for three of us are in the house of an FFI man.

The FFI were the French Forces of the Interior, part of the French resistance effort.

September 11 *Our CP is again in a large and beautiful old chateau. My quarters are in a room right next to the office and quite comfortable—too comfortable, I overslept.*

Drove back to Besançon and checked out a huge citadel, built in the time of Louis XIV, with walls 10 and 12 feet thick. It held up our advance several days and yet was only lightly defended.

Got a captured German stove, for heating a room, from Captain Snedal. Looks good.

Traded a package of pipe tobacco and a pack of Camels for a pipe, to replace the one I lost in the landings. The French have no tobacco and will pay a high price for it.

13

The V-1 and V-2,
Now the V-3 and V-4?

With the Führer constantly fulminating about his new secret weapons, we were a bit concerned that there might just be some truth midst the ballyhoo, and it behooved the interrogators and OB people to be on the watch for evidence of such weapons. One day I was told by an interrogator about a prisoner with sensational news. He turned out to be an emaciated young blond who claimed he was an inventor whose blueprints for a motor had been stolen by the Nazis and who had fled Germany in October 1942 when about to be drafted.

"Herr Oberleutnant," he said to me, "do you know about the V-3 and the V-4?"

I was startled. The V-1 and V-2 we knew about. They were terror weapons, rockets the Germans had fired across the channel and aimed mostly at London. Some were shot down by the British, while others penetrated the defenses and inflicted substantial damage. But of the V-3 and V-4 we knew nothing.

"I'll tell you," eagerly volunteered the German.

I shrugged, implying that we knew all about them except for a few details, and feigned nonchalance, but the man had won my attention.

According to the informant, the V-3 was a rocket bomb weighing twenty-seven tons and was designed to fly at an altitude of thirty to forty miles. It would be directed at the United States and would arrive there six or seven seconds after being launched.

A little quick mental arithmetic and I suspected I had a nut job on my hands. "Why isn't it being used now?" I asked.

The answer was that another three months were needed to complete development. All the experimental rockets launched thus far had defied the laws of gravity and gone off into space. But in three months the Germans would know how to bring them down.

V-4, it developed, was a huge bomb loaded with microbes. Only fifteen such bombs would be needed to kill 15 million Allies. They were being manufactured in an underground plant in Essen, Germany, with PW labor.

"Why isn't it being used now?" I asked.

The reply was that the microbes were ineffectual in warm weather. But they would be dropped November 10 or maybe November 30. If we would furnish a chemist to accompany him, he would return to Germany and steal the plans.

After further questioning and having him repeat his story several times, and each time with new inconsistencies, I concluded he was an unstable individual given to fantasizing on a grand scale. But in recent years, reading of germ warfare and evidence of Russian experimentation with microorganisms such as anthrax, I've wondered if my judgment about this man was correct.

Interrogators panning for gold had to be careful not to throw out the flakes with the silt. One had to be cautious not to lightly dismiss every bizarre story. Some months after this incident we had a deserter cross the lines with genuine information about the experimental rocketry and rocket building facilities at Peenemünde in north Germany on the Baltic coast. This man, I quickly determined, was not a kook but the real article. Not having the technical knowledge to question him in depth, I rushed him on to Air Corps Intelligence for exploitation. What, if any, prior knowledge Allied intelligence had of Peenemünde at the time, I did not know.

(Similarly, after the war's end, when I was interrogating specially held prisoners, one volunteered the whereabouts of all German research data concerned with the effort to develop an atomic bomb, a matter of interest to American scientists.)

At this time a note the G-2 of the Thirty-sixth Division sent me would have been a hot story, if true. The gist of it was that one of the men of his division, he believed, had killed Field Marshal Wilhelm List, the general credited with the training of the German army. I drove to the scene, thirty miles away, and found nothing. The civilians in the area knew nothing. I then drove to the regimental command post and had the S-2, a pleasant captain, get hold of the man, a sergeant named Dawson.

Dawson said he had shot up three vehicles, which burst into flames. He went over for souvenirs, found two cameras and a briefcase. The briefcase contained a picture of Field Marshal List and letters addressed to him. He took the photo but burned everything else for fear of being captured with it. The photo he hid. He and all the crew swore that one of the men in the vehicle closely resembled the field marshal, who looked a little older and was burned and shot and cut up, but they all recognized him by the picture. I questioned the sergeant closely and believed he was telling the truth. He offered to show me the scene.

When I told the story to Colonel Langevin and General Butler, the assistant chief of staff, they ordered me to investigate further.

September 15, 1944 *Moved our command post to a large farm. I've got a room together with Rieger.*

The colonel again wants me to write the armored paragraph for the G-2 Report.

This afternoon drove up to the front to the company headquarters of the sergeant I talked to yesterday. He was in line and it would have taken too long to wait for him, so I drove with Friedlander, who speaks French, to the scene of the crash. It was a long drive and I often had the jeep doing 70. But no luck. We found the vehicles and burned uniforms and parts of letters, but nothing involving the field marshal. Only other possibility is that he was buried in a cemetery by the Americans. But it was too late to investigate further.

While I was on duty in the war room General Butler and colonels Cassidy and Langevin asked me how I made out with the List investigation.

As time was later to prove, Sergeant Dawson was wrong. We captured Field Marshal List at Garmisch-Partenkirchen in the closing days of the war.

On these trips to the front, sometimes pretty bouncy despite efforts to skirt shell and mortar holes in the road, I kept a carbine in the jeep, anticipating sooner or later to be strafed by a German plane. My hope was to be able to dive into a ditch and get off that one-in-a-million shot that would get the pilot. It was not a duel I expected to win. Luckily I was never put to the test.

September 16 *On night duty. Nothing special happened in the war room after midnight except that Seventh Army headquarters sent a French captain to pick up a woman, twenty-four-years-old, a spy. We had no such gal here that I could find.*

The French were vigilant in their hunt for countrymen who had cooperated with the Nazi occupiers. The word *mercy* was not in their lexicon when they uncovered one. The time of day or night mattered little if they thought they had found the scent of one.

To the French there were no gray areas. Passions ran high. Cases were black or white. Retribution was quick. No lengthy trials, no appeals, no consideration of extenuating circumstances. The operating policy seemed to be "execute first, question later." As we moved up France I became increasingly chary of turning over questionable cases to Gallic justice.

Sixth Corps moved rapidly northward as evinced by my story for the *Beachhead News*—in the more subdued form insisted on by Colonel Langevin:

CORPS FREES FIVE CITIES
Vet Divisions Push Forward

The advance of the VI Corps troops yesterday was again greatest on the left flank.

The lights went on again in Baudoncourt, Quers, Velorcey, Villers and Faverney and other towns fortunate enough to be freed from their Teuton masters.

In this sector of biggest advance, enemy resistance was sporadic, consisting predominantly of delaying actions. To the south, northwest and southeast of Villersexel, the Krauts proved tougher customers. Here they employed tanks to bolster their infantry defenses and fought with much greater tenacity than in the north.

To the west of the Saone River the 2nd French Corps captured Jussy and rounded up large masses of prisoners throughout the sector, little resistance being encountered. On the VI Corps right flank the French repulsed a strong German counterattack at Goux.

In the 2nd French Corps sector an entire battalion of enslaved Ukrainians deserted from the Nazis, joined the Maquis and are now commanded by two FFI officers and a Navy lieutenant.

A study of a KO'd Panther tank, a Nazi-propagandized indestructible tank, revealed that it was destroyed by a rifle grenade fired by a member of the 3rd Battalion of the 179th Infantry Regiment.

The total number of PWs taken by VI Corps in southern France was swelled yesterday to almost 33,000. From interrogation of prisoners and from captured documents the gravity of the Kraut losses can be appreciated. Regiments have had as many as four commanders since "D" day.

Fighter-bomber operations were limited throughout the day by poor flying conditions and a low ceiling. The few missions that were flown attacked train convoys in Western Germany on the northeast of the Corps front. Three locomotives were definitely destroyed and many RR cars strafed, but results, for the most part, were unobserved.

Just how pessimistic the higher ranking German officers are of the outcome of the war, can be gleaned from an extract of a letter of an artillery colonel of the 19th Army. He writes to his daughter: "The war situation troubles me very much. How can we win the war when our enemies are already at our borders? How with our most important sources of raw material gone? Where do we have even one friend left in the world? So far Adolf always had an ace up his sleeve, but does he have one now? What good are all his grandiloquent speeches? The people don't believe them anymore anyhow."

It had become increasingly clear that, genius though he had been politically, the demon-driven, self-anointed Great Warlord was no longer capable of galvanizing his subjects. His histrionics had worn thin. For the *Herrenvolk*, oratory was no longer a match for despondency born of experience.

September 17 *General Truscott got his third star a couple days ago. He deserves it, and in my opinion is qualified to command an army, which he'll probably get. I'll hate to see him go.*

Lieutenant Colonel Conway got his eagles today from General

*Truscott and he had a party to which he invited me. It was in the mess
tent. The tables were laid with flowers and sandwiches and every
imaginable kind of choice liquor. The two generals, Truscott and the
Forty-fifth Division commander Eagles, sat at one end and all the staff
officers sat around. There was much loud singing of the old stand-by
army songs, plenty of drinking, jokes, and laughter. And suddenly,
among all the ribaldry, I felt very bad. I had a feeling of guilt. Here we
were raising a rumpus with all the comforts and luxuries, including a
string trio, in a heated tent, and outside in the chill rain, only 12–15
miles to the north, northeast and northwest, the GIs, soaked and tired
and hungry, were dying and being wounded and having their lives
shattered. I couldn't help remembering the words of a private, in a letter to his mother, given to me by a French civilian the day before, the
soldier having left it in the house. It wasn't censored, so I censored it
rather than go through the red tape of sending it back to his unit for
censoring. It said, "Mom, when you wrote that you think I'm mad at
you because I didn't write, it made me cry. I just couldn't write. We
were on the move all the time."*

*And it was true. He was a boy from a frontline outfit, Company A
of the 142nd Infantry Regiment.*

Letters like this, whether by an American boy or a German boy, had
a way of transporting me into a black contemplative mood. When these
moods struck, I could not join in the conviviality around me and would
retreat, unobtrusively, to my quarters, take a nip from the bottle in the
pocket of my bedding roll, stare into space, and agonize over the young
lives being lost up the road or, at best, squirreled in a hole for the night.
"Eat, drink, and be merry, for tomorrow you may die," was a rationale
that afforded me little consolation.

Lost in subjective reflection, my conscience, my inquisitor, would
ask, "Why can't fate at least be fair and distribute the burdens and sorrows of war evenhandedly? Why do some soldiers never leave the
States and others, like interrogator Webb, get killed within a week of
being overseas? Why isn't suffering distributed equally among the combatant nations? Why are the civilians of some countries spared the carnage on their soil while the civilians of others get caught in the meat
grinder of war and suffer starvation, destruction of their homes, and the
death of their families?"

There were times when I was obsessed for hours with a sense of mankind's savagery, with the costs of war—the horror and terror, the tremendous waste.

September 18   *Moved this morning to another elaborate estate. This one has been well kept up, except for the grounds. For sleeping quarters I'm in a house about 100 yards from the main building.*

En route to the new CP we stopped to buy eggs—or rather exchange captured German canned meat and lard. At the first few houses the story was always the same: "We gave our eggs to your comrades already." Though my French is miserably poor, that much I could always understand. Later though, as we got farther off the main road, we had less and less trouble and wound up with a batch. So almost every morning now I give the waiter two eggs to have fried for me.

While in one town, a man came up to me and told me about some German mines planted nearby. I notified the engineers.

In the afternoon General Truscott (now lieutenant general) had a reception for the staff at his trailer. It was a nice sunny afternoon, and when I congratulated him he thanked me and waved me over to the liquor his aides were mixing and pouring. Several photographers took pictures, and all in all it was pleasant. I didn't feel nearly as bad as I did at the party for Colonel Conway.

The colorful Truscott was not a blatant publicity seeker. Knowledge of his abilities and achievements was largely limited to those best placed to judge him, and among such judges he was ranked very high in all phases of command, from training and planning to vigorous execution. To his staff at the Sixth Corps it did not seem incongruous that, though not a West Pointer, he was to be the only American general in World War II to command a regiment, a division, a corps, and a field army in combat.

The next day I went to the Third Division PW cage in Faucogney to see Alex Shayne. It had been a while since we had last been together, so the reunion was a joyous one. We briefed each other on what was going on in our units, what the latest scuttlebutt was, and how things were going with the other OB and PWI men with whom we had gone to school. We swapped souvenirs, among them German medals, Nazi armbands, insignia, compasses, and swastika flags—still good for palm greasing when one wanted a favor, and especially effective with the motor pool mechanics when our jeeps needed quick repairs or servicing.

While I was at the cage, there was the rattling of machine gun fire in the near distance and the blast of cannons. The Germans were shelling the bridge over the river running through the town. A 170-mm shell landed a hundred yards from the cage.

"I don't mind if the Krauts knock off their own men," said Alex, "but not two nice guys like us with the war just about over."

I, too, thought the war was almost over. In the east the Russians had reached Warsaw, and in the west the Allies were pushing ahead on the northern front and we on the southern. German manpower was running low, the civilians were nearing starvation, and the Luftwaffe was virtually extinguished. Little did we dream that the Führer was determined to fight to the last man, that there was still much war ahead.

As we advanced northward along the main roads, the same ones on which the Wehrmacht was retreating, a frequent sight was destroyed German vehicles. If they haphazardly littered the landscape, that meant they had been destroyed by our artillery and machine gun fire. If they were in an evenly spaced column, they were the victims of our marauding fighter-bombers who had caught the column on the march. Driving along, one often had the impression of being in a linear junk yard.

The frontline troops usually had little time to forage among these wrecks, but the support troops, close behind, made forays to these treasure lands of automotive litter in search of seat cushions undamaged by fire or bullet holes, electric windshield wipers, powerful horns, and other accouterments that could be dismantled and transplanted in their jeeps and three-quarter-ton trucks. The aim was to increase their comfort or, perhaps more accurately phrased, decrease their discomfort.

September 21 *Moved to a new command post location in the woods near Miremont. It's a poor place for a corps CP, because machine gun fighting is still going on for the town, and our artillery is booming away all around us.*

En route we saw the usual graves of German soldiers along the road, sometimes one, sometimes two or three together. Each was marked with a cross and the man's dog tag number, the cross topped by his helmet.

Saw only one dead horse. The civilians get rid of horses fast because they stink so badly and are a health hazard.

The French landscape continues to impress me. The country is like

*one big garden, or rather a park. Even the woods are cultivated, no
brush between trees and all trees standing in straight lines no matter
from which angle you look.*

We spent three days in Miremont, and then it was on to Plombières,
a pleasant resort town with excellent cognac, far better to my taste
than the cognac in Italy. While here I received a note from Tally-Ho
(Carleton, now a general) directing me in my *Beachhead News* writ-
ings to credit smaller units—battalions and companies—not just the
divisions and regiments to which I had restricted myself.

I received the note with dismay, for it was the second time I was
given this order. If I obeyed, I feared Colonel Langevin would raise hell.

There was a constant difference of opinion and interests between the
division generals, who wanted the successes of their units publicized
because they felt it boosted their morale, and Langevin, the corps G-2,
who did not want his German counterpart to figure out how our forces
were deployed. While primarily responsible for intelligence, his secondary responsibility was censorship.

The first article I wrote based on Tally-Ho's directive had immediate consequences. I was away at the front for a few hours. On returning, Joe Haines told me the colonel wanted to see me.

"Any idea why?" I asked.

"No," said Joe, "but from his expression, I think the shit's gonna hit
the fan."

It was a harbinger of what lay ahead.

The colonel was not at his desk, so I went to his van, knocked at the
door, and was told to come in. Poring over the situation map, he slowly
raised his eyes, turned to me, and rasped, "Marshall, whose side are you
on in this war?"

Rattled, I stood there benumbed. In truth, I could have fallen through
the floor, although I was sure the question was meant rhetorically. Finally I swallowed deeply and said, "Colonel, what's the problem?"

"The problem," he roared, "is these companies and battalions of
ours you're mentioning in the *Beachhead News!* It's giving away some
of our order of battle! Of all people, you certainly know that! You know
these papers get captured!"

I sighed. "Colonel," I said, "I've been writing for the paper since
Anzio. I'd like to be relieved of this duty."

For several moments there was silence. Looking impenetrably grave, he stared into space, tapping the desk with a grease pencil and apparently considering my request.

Edgy with the silence, I tried to bolster my plea. "General Carleton and the division generals are displeased when I don't single out the companies and battalions. If I do, sir, you're unhappy."

No sooner had the words left my mouth than I realized I had slit my own throat, for slowly a forgiving grin suffused his face, followed by an absolving chuckle, "That makes you perfect for the job then, doesn't it? Stay with it!"

And stay with it I did, the conflict between the colonel and the generals unresolved. Till the day the war ended, I teetered on a tightrope above a bed of quicksand, trying to mention enough small units to keep Tally-Ho happy and few enough to prevent Langevin's ire.

Although I was annoyed by the incident, I had a tremendous respect that bordered on affection for the old buzzard. That the *Beachhead News* fell into enemy hands we knew, because it periodically turned up in the documents we captured, this in spite of the cautionary words at the top of the publication—"This paper must not fall into enemy hands"—plus periodic advisories within the paper telling frontline troops to destroy every copy by burning it.

September 25 *The Forty-fifth Division captured the Gestapo headquarters in Epinal. Colonel wants me to go up tomorrow and look over the documents.*

September 26 *Epinal was hardly damaged. We seem to go pretty easy on shooting up French towns. Compared to southern Italy, this area of France seems to have suffered little.*

The fighting in this part of France was not nearly as fierce as that I had experienced in Italy. There, some burned-out villages with their roofless houses were so shell-damaged that only rarely was there an intact pane of glass. Here, on friendly territory, we tried to destroy as little as possible. Towns the enemy did not defend were passed through in pristine condition.

Because of the many facets of my job and our rapid advance—entailing constant packing and unpacking—there was little time for the conventional chores. To write a letter, mail a package, send a money order, shine shoes, or do laundry was a major undertaking. There were periods when I was grateful for any respite, as when our two draftsmen, sergeants Edwards and Lucas, both talented artists, asked me to pose for a few minutes while one drew a sketch of me and the other a caricature.

As I sat for them, I thought about the fighting. How much longer could Germany go on before acknowledging its hopeless plight and suing for peace? A calamitous disintegration of its forces was in progress. Enemy deserters popped up in every engagement. A Polish deserter told me he fought only because he was given no choice but to fight or starve. All the opposition could field to reinforce defenders of a quarry at Cleury that denied us use of an important road was an emergency company formed from butchers, bakers, cooks, and other limited service personnel.

Increasingly the Germans were resorting to cobbling together the remnants of battered units into *Kampfgruppen* (battle groups). So beleaguered were they that after some engagements they were not taking the time to bury their dead. After a particularly savage clash in a pine forest, Third Division troops found a pile of enemy dead with only a few pine boughs thrown over them.

From a German army newspaper, *Die Wacht* (The Watch), we had learned that the High Command was so pressed that it was using fourteen- and fifteen-year-old boys to build defenses on the border.

A document captured by the Forty-fifth Division was a message sent by a sergeant to his company commander. It read, "I cannot assume further responsibility for my platoon. The men abandon their positions. They are completely bereft of morale. Except for a few, they are unable to take orders. I therefore ask that my platoon be relieved, because it is no longer capable of combat."

Morale was so low that SS men were being interspersed for surveillance in many units to forestall desertion and mutiny. Forthrightness made a man a prime target for suspicion and enhanced the vitriolic feeling that existed between the army and the SS.

Yet, contradictorily, one German youngster I talked to wouldn't admit his country was licked, only that things looked bad.

September 28   *Went to Plombières, popular resort town, for a steam bath and shower in the same bath the old Roman discoverers had* *built and used. In the bath was virtually the whole corps staff, including the G-3 and General Truscott's aide. War: Staff officers take steam baths, while a few kilometers up front the GIs die.*

The ironies of life during war! I never got over them and was often discomfited by them, even though logic told me I shouldn't be, that we all had to play the cards we were dealt.

The experienced, battle-wise divisions, I long ago noticed, never turned down the luxury of having their headquarters in buildings, if available, rather than tents. The green divisions coming into line, you could bet, would set up their headquarters by the book—in tents. But they quickly learned.

September 29–30 *On night duty in the War Room. We have moved to a new command post, again a little too close to the front for comfort. Our own artillery is still firing over our heads. It is in a factory. Officers' quarters are in an adjoining building, the one that used to be the offices for the factory.*

Was told an ego-boosting thing today by Major Dixon. He says General Truscott told Colonel Conway that the Beachhead News *story I write gives him a better, clearer picture of what happened than the official G-3 Report.*

October 1 *Just a day. Awakened at six o'clock by our Long Toms, which were shooting over our heads. A moderately light sleeper, I don't need 155-mm guns as an alarm clock.*

Wrote the Armored paragraph for the G-2 Report and the Beachhead News *story, tried to mail my glasses, with no luck, no APO [Army Post Office] near.*

Eyeglasses could be a problem. The steel-rimmed spectacles issued by the army were sturdy, but I preferred my own lighter but more fragile rimless ones. However, when they broke, they had to be sent home for repair.

For those of us with cameras, getting film processed could be troublesome. For me this was solved by my friends in the Photo Interpretation Unit. They developed mine, fresh eggs the quid pro quo.

Mail deliveries were irregular, mostly feast or famine; not one letter for a week or two, and then a batch of ten or twenty. One never knew if the letter that didn't arrive had been sent to the bottom by one of Hitler's U-boats.

These and similar irritations were of no great moment, since we considered the war to be close to an end. To any rational observer, the German plight in the air, on the sea, and on all land fronts was hopeless. And the domestic situation was no better. The Allied naval blockade was doing much to bring the master race to its knees. A surfeit of Goebbels's propaganda was no longer a substitute for food. Starvation was rampant, and what the hungry populace called "blockade mutton" came into fashion. This was the soubriquet the Germans gave to dog meat. Its sale was legal, and it could be found in butcher shops. Dachshunds were reputedly the most toothsome.

With the Reich's collapse apparently imminent, Allied discussions were taking place concerning treaty demands and Germany's future. This came dramatically to our attention on October 3 when *Stars and Stripes* ran an article detailing Secretary of the Treasury Morgenthau's plan, seemingly approved by President Roosevelt, to take away much of Germany's territory, shipping out much of her machinery and destroying the rest, sending Russia labor battalions of German workers, and making the Fatherland an agricultural country under occupation.

Reading the article, I became incensed. *The publication of this will result in wide German republication,* I wrote in my diary, *causing the Germans to fight on much longer. Such articles prolong the war and cost thousands of lives. You can't blame the Germans now for continuing the fight.* Uncolored by afterknowledge, this was how I felt at the time. Today I still feel Goebbels, the Nazi propaganda minister, had been stupidly dealt an ace. Like Hitler, a master practitioner of Mark Twain's dictum that "a lie can travel halfway around the world while the truth is putting on its shoes," Goebbels was not about to overlook this Washington gaffe, a mistake that was not even immediately disavowed. Even his fertile mind could not have concocted a better means to stiffen the spine of a Germany reeling under a disastrous summer of defeats, and at a time when the Führer's exhortations were falling on increasingly deaf ears.

My assessment proved correct. A few days later we saw from captured newspapers that the Propaganda Ministry was playing up Morgenthau's proposed plan and warning soldiers and civilians of what Germany's future would be if it lost the war. It urged greater sacrifice on the part of every man, woman, and child for the Fatherland and the Führer.

Roosevelt's apparent approval of the Morganthau plan dismayed us. Scrubbing my hands at noontime in the wash tent with other officers, trying as always to get rid of the stench, real or imaginary, that lingered after examining blood-stained documents, I was struck by the freedom of expression we exercised in talking about our country's leader, whereas our German counterparts would have been at great risk in making disparaging comments about Hitler. Criticizing the Morgenthau plan, I said, "I think Roosevelt's crazy."

Said one, "I don't think that Dewey would have made a good president, so I voted for Roosevelt. But I sometimes think Roosevelt is a horse's ass."

To which another replied, "In my family we weren't allowed to swear, but if we were talking about Roosevelt, we were allowed to say 'goddamn.'"

When I first came in contact with PWs in Italy, I was struck by how readily interrogators' questions were answered, even when the questions were such that a moron could understand the replies would be detrimental to his comrades still fighting. To determine the strength and condition of an enemy unit, the questioner might ask how many men were in the unit. How were they armed? How many machine guns did the unit have and where were they positioned? How many tanks were operable and what kind were they? Where were their antitank guns positioned? Was there a shortage of food? Of ammunition? Of gasoline? Where was the command post located? How many non-Germans were in the unit? What was their nationality? How was morale? And so on.

In France the German soldier was no different in his free responses; if anything, he was even more forthcoming, since morale was heading south at an ever accelerating rate. Information, unarguably devastating to his comrades, could be elicited with unbelievable ease from most men, especially one seeking to ingratiate himself.

Going down to the Third Division PW cage, where Alex worked, I took along a British friend, Captain Paul Whiston, one of the corps photo reconnaissance interpreters. Fluent in German, he had also been trained as an interrogator, but had been switched to photo interpretation. As we watched the milking of the captives, many too young, many too old, and one who appeared imbecilic, Whiston marveled at the ease with which the interrogators extracted information. In the British army, as in the American, it had been drummed into the soldier that, if captured, he was to give no information other than his name, rank, and serial number.

In a high-level document we were to capture in December, when we would be fighting in the Vosges Mountains, the writer, a German war correspondent, commented on the refusal of American PWs to give information, their "serene confidence in ultimate victory, and their blind faith in the truth of their newspapers." It was to that truth, he felt, that the American serviceman owed his ability to weather with equanimity the storms of capture and prisonership. He further noted that German men and officers no longer believed their newspapers and suggested a switch to the truth.

Unless I was on night duty in the war room, my last job of the day, aside from censoring my men's mail, was to write the *Beachhead News* story. This involved sifting through the action reports and coordinating the information with that on the war room map. It further involved scanning the pilots' reports, the interrogators' reports, and my notes of what we had extracted from captured documents that I thought would be of GI interest. When I felt I had the complete picture, I wrote a truthful uncensored story—perhaps, at rare times, inhibited by reasons of security, not the whole truth. And this was why the German war correspondent, in watching captured GIs being interrogated, noted that they believed their papers in contrast to the *Landser* who did not believe his.

German officers, it must be said, particularly in the higher ranks, were better educated, better trained, and aware of their rights under the Geneva Convention rules. It was almost a given that the higher a man's rank, the higher his level of information, but also the greater his resistance to disclosing it. Rarely would he reveal anything of tactical value to the battle then ensuing, but sometimes there were disclosures of long-range value.

We had supper with Alex, and later in the evening drove in blackout back to headquarters under a moon so bright I was able to drive at 50 miles per hour.

In the seven weeks since we had come ashore on the Riviera, the hard-driving corps had punched its way 350 miles up into France and was nearing Alsace. There had been little break in the fighting. Relaxation consisted of an occasional movie, reading the small tissue paper issue of *Time*, reading and writing of letters, and when one of the officers acquired a bottle of cognac there was a "birthday" party. Paris had been liberated by the Allied forces to the west, but since it was off limits, no leaves had yet been authorized. Once they were, Gay Paree would be the Mecca to which enlisted men and officers alike would make their first pilgrimage.

October 7   *In some things you can't beat the British. They have an officer with us, part of whose job it is to get into towns we liberate with the first troops and hand out British flags to be put up, although we have no British units fighting with us.*
   Letters from brothers Frank and Steve.

According to a rumor that had circulated a couple weeks earlier, the Fourteenth Armored Division would be leaving the States and entering the fray under Sixth Corps's command. The rumor proved to have substance. When a Lieutenant Phillips of its G-2 section appeared for a briefing and an introduction to our staff, he informed us that the Fourteenth was landing at Marseilles and was indeed slated to come under our command.

I was delighted. After being commissioned, I was posted to the Fourteenth Armored and was there for six months, until I was transferred to the intelligence school. I now looked forward to seeing old friends, the officers with whom I had served at Camp Chaffee in Arkansas, and especially good buddy and roommate Pete LeDoux.

14

The Big Brass Visits

An announcement that generals Marshall, Eisenhower, and Devers were expected for a visit caused a frenzied scurrying about. Everything in sight was policed up, and boots that had not seen polish in months suddenly sported blinding shines. The generals did not appear on the scheduled day, but on the following one Marshall and Devers arrived. Sixth Corps, under Seventh Army, was a part of Sixth Army Group, of which Devers was the commander. I had not seen him since he addressed the graduates at the Armored Force Officer Candidate School at Fort Knox, Kentucky, in 1942.

October 9, 1944 *General Marshall and General Devers came today, plus a flock of three- and two-star generals, and colonels.*

Everybody was in a dither. All the G-2 officers were loath to be in the war room lest General Marshall ask a few questions. So on one pretext or another they got out, and the executive officer told me to take over. And I, the lowest-ranking officer in the Section! But just before the VIPs arrived, Colonel Langevin entered and asked why one of the senior officers wasn't present and promptly called up Major Dixon.

I was sorry he did, because I had a complete picture of the situation and complete confidence in my ability to answer any question. Also,

I was anticipating the peculiar introduction, "General Marshall, this is Lieutenant Marshall."

We had now taken sixty thousand prisoners and, needless to say, the greater the number of PWs, the wider were opened the floodgates to information we sought. The Germans were trapped in a vicious circle. The more prisoners we bagged, the more information was vacuumed out of them. The increased information enabled us to fight them better, which in turn yielded still more PWs, which in turn brought about faster and bigger victories and still greater numbers of prisoners.

October 12 *Among the captured documents today is a picture of two Russians hanged by the Germans. I'm having the PRU boys make a copy for me before I send the original on to Seventh Army and the Atrocity Committee.*

Germans, we already see from captured newspapers, are playing up Morgenthau's proposed plan to de-industrialize Germany. It makes excellent propaganda, as though especially written for the German propaganda bureau. Those horses' asses in Washington!

While the French were our allies, I was not always happy with them, as I indicated earlier, faulting their summary system of justice. Another officer had a different complaint about our Gallic friends:

October 13 *Rieger showed me a letter written to him by Lieutenant Rothschild, who is on duty with the French Army. Disgusted with the French, he writes, "For the French war starts at 9:00 A.M. and ends at 5:00 P.M., and no war on Saturday afternoons and Sundays."*

With the Allied forces grinding irresistibly onward, the fighting would soon be on German soil. This moved the army and State Department to produce a directive outlining the policy to be followed by the occupation troops. Skimming it, and knowing something of the German mind, I felt that the attitude expressed was firm and that the populace would understand and respect it. However, when I came to the nonfraternization clause, I had serious doubts. Where had such a shunning ever succeeded before? With what army? And in what country? The male-female attraction dooms it to failure. And so it would in Germany. Like prohibition, the law would at first be covertly disobeyed, then overtly, and then so openly it would finally have to be repealed.

October 14   *Pundt borrowed my jeep "for a few hours," and at 11:00 P.M. we got a call that he had had "a vehicular accident."*

October 15   *This morning Pundt was in the office when I arrived and told me they broke the front wheel, leaf spring, and shock absorber. Later Sergeant Greiner, who was driving, said, in addition, that the front tire was blown and the windshield cracked. By the time the complete story is out, it will probably be even worse.*

Pundt paid me $10 today. I had bet him in the early Anzio days that the war would not be over by October 15th. Also now bet him another $10 that it will not be over by December 31st. And I would surely like to lose the money.

Bumped my nose against a building tonight in the blackout while walking to the war room.

October 16   *Had the draftsman make up a sign and post it on the bulletin board. It reads:*

> *Hereafter*
> *Hard Hearted*
> *Lt. Marshall*
> *Will not lend*
> *His jeep to*
> *ANYBODY!*

I had now been in grade as a first lieutenant for five months and was still resentful of having been a second lieutenant for what seemed like an eternity. When Rieger and Haines both told me that Major Dixon, who was now the executive officer, was pushing the colonel to have me promoted again, I thought my luck was changing. And when I got a call from the adjutant general's office wanting to know my date of rank, I was sure this was the case, only to have my hopes dashed when the AG later informed me that by AFHQ ruling an order-of-battle officer had to be in grade eleven months before being eligible for promotion to captain.

Afterward I was to learn Colonel Langevin was starting to get the ball rolling to get me promoted as quickly as possible. He and Dixon felt I deserved higher rank and that my long time in grade as a second lieutenant had been an injustice.

At one of our CP locations I noticed that a number of men were laying down gravel in the slightly rutted driveway of the house General Truscott was occupying, even though the speed of our advance mandated that we move every few days. A commanding general, I thought, is fawned over like a king. Any little wish expressed by him or his aides and people fall all over themselves to fulfill it. I doubted, though, that it was Truscott who was concerned about the ruts in the driveway.

With the Allied juggernaut rolling on, and the Red Army already in Budapest, the handwriting was clearly on the wall for the Reich. Still there was no sign of a formal German surrender. Deciding to try to get a fix on morale, I drove to the Forty-fifth Division PW cage to find a mixed bag of dispirited field-gray-clad men: old, young, starved, crippled, Germans, Austrians, Poles, Czechs, privates, corporals, sergeants, and a sprinkling of officers.

"What do the German people think of Hitler now?" I asked one German PW standing stiffly before me across the table.

The man, who had talked freely up to this point, looked at me silently and blushed, and then looked at the floor, and finally said, "What can I say?"

One told me that of the half million population Hanover had before the war, there was now less than a third of that, and they were mostly foreign workers. He could not see how Germany could go on much longer.

Another, a Swabian, swore that virtually all Germans in the Black Forest were anti-Nazi. "Early in the war," he said, "Göring had boasted that if one bomb ever fell on Germany, his name would be Meyer. Now we call the air raid sirens 'Meyer's hunting horns.'" Göring's prewar hunting parties had been much publicized, and I smiled at the picture evoked.

The PW smiled too, but ruefully. "When you're a German, Herr Oberleutnant," he said, "it's not so funny."

Yet there were a few swaggerers to whom Hitler was still God, and who still believed in his fatuous promises.

Having talked to men captured in battle, I decided after lunch to concentrate on the deserters, of whom there were many. Leaving my pistol outside, I entered the compound and strolled about as though I was just killing time. Assuming an "Aw shucks, I'm just another human, let's talk" manner, I engaged one in conversation. Soon another, his interest piqued, inched toward us to overhear what this friendly, German-speaking American officer was talking about. Then a third and fourth approached, and soon I had a group swarming about me as though I were Santa Claus dispensing gifts.

Turning from one man to another, I solicitously asked about his family, was he married, if so did he have children, were they boys or girls, and other friendly innocuous questions, such as what kind of work had he done before being called up. Then I offhandedly asked why he had deserted. The tactic quickly drew forth a plethora of information as man after man chimed in with his reasons. By this means I was able to quickly and accurately assess the morale situation, much quicker than if I had had the men before me individually in a formal setting. My evaluation appeared in the next day's G-2 Report:

Morale. Since the start of the present operation a marked increase in desertion has been noted. Being in line for too long a period, bad food or lack of food, poor supply, unbearable artillery fire—the usual reasons for desertion in the past—are given as justification by only a few deserters. The German soldier has been confronted with new factors deteriorative to his morale.

Führerbefehl, orders issued in the name of Hitler, to hold to the last man, are one factor. The German now finds that when he is unable to halt our advance he cannot retreat to another position without a specific order. If he does, he will be shot. And he has seen or knows of men who have received the death penalty for retreating from an untenable position. So faced with death if he leaves his position and faced with probable death by our fire if he does not, the only alternative left him is desertion.

Poorer discipline due to a shortage of officers is a second factor. Few companies today have more than two officers, many only one. Platoons are poorly officered, battlefield promotions of noncoms being extremely rare. Consequently the close "iron rule" of the German officer is less frequently found in the front lines. Noncom platoon leaders "talked it over with the men and we decided it was the only thing left to do."

Other deserters have made their decision before the fighting even starts. These are cripples, convalescents, and 40-year-olds who invariably resent being committed.

Still others are recently arrived from rear areas where they have supervised the construction of defenses by young boys and girls, and by elderly men and women, some 65 years of age. This strenuous labor is beyond the abilities of most of the workers and many collapse. The soldier cannot help but reflect that his own wife, mother, sister, and grandmother may also be digging somewhere—and collapsing. Then when he, up to now classified as limited service, is sent to the front, he is convinced "the jig is up."

Behind the big stories of the war was a plethora of little stories. It was not uncommon for small villages in the mountains to be bypassed by the conflict, the inhabitants knowing only from the sound of gunfire in the distance that warring was in progress. A corporal I picked up told me he could speak a little French and had driven into such a hamlet in search of eggs. When the villagers, alerted by their barking dogs, heard the jeep approaching, they poured out of their houses, saw he was an American, and considered themselves officially liberated. With flags, flowers, fruit, and wine they paid him homage. The women insisted he kiss their babies, and the children covered the jeep with blossoms. To top it all off, the mayor made a speech of official welcome and bussed him on both cheeks.

"Great!" I laughed, "You must have gotten a bushel of eggs!"

"No, sir," he said. "After all that fuss, I couldn't confess I had just come looking for eggs."

Document exploitation had its frustrating moments. Periodically we would capture an important paper but couldn't exploit it. One such episode took place on October 22 when we found the code of one of the enemy divisions, but couldn't make immediate use of it since we couldn't tell if it belonged to the Twenty-first Panzer or the Sixteenth Infantry. There was no identification on the document and no indication as to where it had been captured. Had we known at least the latter, we would have known which code we had because we knew in which sector each of the German divisions was operating.

After a recurrence of this situation with another important document a week later, I wrote a new S.O.P. (Standard Operating Procedure) for the handling of documents by the lower units and gave it to the colonel for his comments and hopefully approval and implementation.

October 25   *We heard there is a deal on to get experienced order-of-battle people for the Pacific. I drove with Pundt to army headquarters to get the lowdown, to find out if we were on the list, we being two of the most experienced officers in the game, but we got only a hazy answer.*

Every once in a while it is dramatically brought home to me how easy it still is for me to get killed. We were supposed to move into a new CP just behind the lines. We couldn't move yesterday morning because the Germans shelled all trucks crossing a bridge nearby. And lucky we didn't, because last night two shells fell into the middle of what was supposed to be the new war room. That, and being my turn for night duty, could have been my end.

General Truscott turned the corps over to a new general, Edward V. Brooks. Haven't met him yet, so no opinion.

General Patch's son was killed yesterday. He was captain of an infantry company.

Just as a son often follows in his father's career in civilian life, so too does this occur in the military, but sometimes with less luck. General Marshall lost a stepson in the Anzio breakout. Now here in France the commander of Seventh Army lost his son. Neither of these men had cushy jobs, and I strongly felt that it was men like them, and those who fought with them, who should have been decorated, not some of those whom I observed during a formation for decorations that took place while there was a pause in the fighting. Some awards with their overblown citations were little more than a mockery. One went to a doctor whose sole contribution was to treat sore throats, colds, cuts, and minor abrasions. Anything serious had to be referred to the hospital. Most of the day he was idle, bored out of his gourd, and half drunk. When I went to see him about a minor problem, he bitterly complained about the restrictions under which he worked. Nevertheless, he was awarded the Legion of Merit. It brought back to mind Colonel Weber's remark on Anzio that if he were president, he would wipe out the decorations for all but the combat men.

October 26   *Yesterday we got some dope on an enemy attack north of Les Rouges Eaux by 70–100 Germans in American uniforms. I sensed a good story in it, and wrote it up for the main headline. But now everybody up and down the line is in a dither. Army headquarters wants a verification of the story.*

Since my writing was not censored, and since the deviancy was a serious breach of the Geneva rules of warfare, I was on the spot. If the story was not true, I would have been an irresponsible dolt, and there would have been unpleasant repercussions. Fortunately for me, if not for the GIs faced with the problem of distinguishing friend from foe, the story was true. The next day, my diary notes, *Story of the Germans in American uniforms corroborated, plus more reports of similar instances.*

The enemy was again to resort to this deception in the Ardennes during the Battle of the Bulge.

October 28   *Last night helped Hugenin celebrate his captain's bars with my rationed bottle of Scotch.*

My 29th birthday today, but I've reached the age where I'd just as soon they stopped. Mom's birthday card arrived last night.

We moved to a little, badly shot up town called Grandvillers. Our offices are in a beautiful chateau, a little damaged but otherwise fine.

For living quarters we have tents, but most of us are living in whatever houses and barns we can find. My own place is a big barn with a hay loft and chickens running around. My trailer is also in it and my jeep is in another barn nearby. The place belongs to an old woman who goes around in wooden shoes. The roads are muddy and the place is run down. Reminds me of a scene from a movie of the First World War. Chickens and ducks cross the roads and you must be careful not to run them over when you drive.

I'm not sleeping in the hay. Afraid of lice. Using my cot. But I feel a barn day in and day out in this damp weather is better than a tent.

Heard today that a rug bought for the general's van cost $125. And *that signs made with radium buttons identifying the different offices cost as much as $200 apiece. You'd think war would be expensive enough without these ridiculous frills.*

Too close to the front lines again. Machine guns are firing close by.

October 29   *On night duty tonight.*

We have an interesting thing going on right now. A few kilometers to the east one of our battalions has been surrounded after being cut off by the Germans. They have been surrounded for six days now. Yet this is not as bad as it used to be. We have air superiority, so we were able to drop medical supplies, ammunition and food, although we lost two planes. A day later bad weather prevented further air drops, so we shot in medical supplies and chocolate bars by stuffing them into chemical shells.

Each chocolate bar, known as a D ration, was specially fortified and contained the nutritional equivalent of a single meal.

October 30   *The surrounded battalion was freed today. Another battalion finally fought its way to it.*

A letter from Mom tells me cousin Steve's mother hasn't heard from him in over a month. Something is funny.

Letters from the home folks were avidly received but were sometimes mixed blessings. After the news of the death of my tail gunner cousin Henry, I did not open letters with unalloyed joy, but rather with a bit of trepidation. They might contain sad tidings of a friend or relative, as Bill Guest's letter a few weeks earlier had informed me of the British intelligence officer Rus's death. So when my mother informed me that my cousin Steve, my childhood camping, fishing, and golfing partner, and now a telephone linesman, had not been heard from in over a month, I feared the worst. Happily I soon after received a letter from him, obviously still among the living.

But not all follow-up news was good. A letter from a girl I had dated at Camp Chaffee informed me that her brother was reported missing in action; a later letter said that he had been killed.

15

Temporary Duty
with Green Divisions

October 31, 1944 *Dixon told me the colonel was tickled with the new S.O.P I wrote for the guidance of the divisions in their handling of documents.*

November 1 *Going on temporary duty for a week to the Hundredth Infantry Division, one of two new divisions coming into line, to set up their order-of-battle system, show the green men what the score is, and how OB works in practice. A Lieutenant Colonel Reinicke is the G-2 there.*

November 2 *Like it very well at this place, although, as you might expect with a new division, they are set up in tents on a farm and the mud is ankle-deep. These people are grass green and call on me for the answers to all kinds of routine G-2 questions. I feel at this point I can do the army more good here than I can at corps.*
    Introduced to General Withers A. Burress, the division's commander, and briefed him on what kind of enemy he will be facing.

Burress had red hair and a florid complexion. To other generals he was known as "Pinky," obviously a West Point nickname. Although

higher headquarters' phones were equipped with scrambler devices to
guard against enemy eavesdropping, when discussing attack plans the
generals often used nicknames which, probably unintentionally, added
a security factor should the enemy somehow tap and unscramble the
phone conversations.

November 3   *I think I'll request a transfer to this division. Life here
would be more rugged. Meals and accommodations poorer, danger
greater. But I think the hours would be shorter, and less strain, and I
could probably get back to corps occasionally for a bath.*

*I took Rothschild with me. He's the sharpest enlisted OB man in
the section. Maybe later I can also wangle Lowensberg.*

*We have a room in a small village, Padoux. It is a poor one with
holes in the floor, walls, and ceiling. We could do with less fresh air on
these brisk November days.*

During the next few days I helped Colonel Reinicke organize his section so as to be a smaller replica of the corps section, duplicating many
of the forms and procedures so they would mesh with those of corps
and thereby benefit both. The work gave me a chance to get to know
the staff. They would not be faceless voices to me in future phone calls
when I returned to corps.

In the dawn, walking from the room to the officers' mess some distance away, I was beguiled by the blissful setting and reminded of the
summer I had spent in Benschek, the birthplace of my mother. Peopled
by descendents of settlers from the Black Forest, it was a little farming
village in Hungary before the area was ceded to Rumania at the end of
the First World War. There, and here now, the birds chirped, flapped,
and twittered in the trees. In the near distance a creek gurgled over a
dam as the chickens clucked and the church bells chimed the hour—
an aural feast defiled only by the distant sounds of battle. Ducks and
geese waddled along the puddly paths as dogs scampered about and
cows placidly ambled out to pasture. From ingrained habit, all, oblivious of the importance of the interloper's time, claimed their right of
prior passage. It was a lovely bucolic scene, and in this morning tranquility, among these farmhouses nestled in the hills, war was obscenely
out of place.

November 5   *To Epinal to pick up a new field jacket and try to get the cracked windshield replaced. No luck with the windshield.*

November 6   *Briefed the colonel of the 399th Regiment this morning and the G-2 this evening.*
   Later to corps to pick up a few things.

For the next few days it was more of the same, basically teaching the staff how to do their jobs and coordinate their activities with those of corps. Lieutenant Colonel Reinicke and I got along so well he asked me if I was agreeable to a transfer to the Hundredth. He swore he and General Burress would do everything possible to have me promoted immediately. I knew they could not be more effective than Colonel Langevin, but I was tired of the long daily grind at corps and the nightly story for the *Beachhead News*. I liked Reinicke and would have welcomed a transfer even without a promotion.

November 10   *Colonel Langevin called me in response to a letter Colonel Reinicke wrote him requesting my transfer to the Hundredth Division.*
   The gist of the call was that I was to set up the order-of-battle sections of each of the new divisions and then he will "consider" a transfer to one of them. In other words, no transfer. Proves that if you do a good job, they don't want to lose you.
   One of the new OB teams came up to the front and I turned our system over to them, lock, stock, and barrel. They are enthusiastic about it, and accepted it wholeheartedly.
   We moved to a forward command post as the Hundredth took over a sector of the battle front. Our map was actually more accurate than that of the division we relieved—eloquent testimony to the value of our system. Then tonight, on the 10th, Rothschild and I returned to corps.

The next day we went to the other new division, the 103rd Infantry, and here again I showed their order-of-battle men the ropes, explained certain matters to their PW interrogators, and instructed the MP officer on the routine of handling prisoners.

In the Vosges Mountains now, with the winter setting in, it was cold. Part of the first morning was spent trying to get a stove going in the shelled building in which G-2 operated. It smoked furiously, the carbonaceous particles in the air making seeing and breathing almost impossible. We finally stopped the smoking by plugging the pipe joints with mud. Then we nailed paper across the shattered windows. The roof leaked—it was raining, had been for days—and although technically indoors, to keep from getting soaked one needed a raincoat. "If I'm going to sleep dry tonight," I thought, "I'll have to pitch a tent over my cot."

To make matters worse, we were just a couple of kilometers behind the front and a battery of Long Toms outside the building fired its salvos every few minutes, each simultaneous discharge of the guns shaking the structure like a bowl of Jell-O. In the morning the litter of shell casings gave mute evidence for our poor night's sleep. Even my usual elixir for bringing on Morpheus, a swig from the whisky bottle in the pocket of my bedding roll, had failed.

November 12   *Spent another day at the 103rd.*

November 13   *Returned to corps in the evening.*

It was during this period, while I was setting up the order-of-battle sections for the new divisions coming into line and then checking on how well they were following through, that I received the highest compliment of my army career, although an indirect one. During my absence from corps headquarters, Colonel Langevin had called a meeting of the officers in the G-2 section. He asked them to discourage me from seeking a transfer.

According to Joe Haines and Doc Pundt, who separately told me of the meeting, he called me the most versatile officer in the section, one who could handle any job in it. That was the tenor of the meeting, and its only purpose. The colonel said he was doing all in his power to have me promoted again, but he was hamstrung by the Military Intelligence Service (MIS) rule that a first lieutenant had to be in grade a minimum of eleven months before he could be promoted to captain. (The colonel's constant pressure on my behalf had its effect eventually. Two weeks short of the required eleven months I was promoted to captain.)

The report of the meeting had a salutary effect on me psychologically. The colonel was not a practitioner of positive reinforcement, so to be bathed in praise, even though indirectly, had the effect of assuaging my sense of outrage, under which I was still suffering, at my long time in grade as a second lieutenant. It helped to dampen the embers of resentment that still smoldered within me. Despite my mother's oft-cautioning German proverb *Eigenlob stinkt* (self-praise stinks), I was good, I knew it, and I wanted it appreciated. While not one to blow my own horn, I was not short on self-esteem. In civilian life I would have demanded a raise, and failing that, looked for another job. In the army I did not have this option.

To keep matters in perspective, not everyone always thought of me so highly. Three weeks before the colonel's meeting, General Truscott, shortly after receiving his third star, had turned over command of the Sixth Corps to Major General Edward V. Brooks. Brooks's chief of staff was Brigadier General Charles Palmer. Among the staff, Brooks called him "Charlie."

The first meeting I had with "Charlie" Palmer was one that Charlie Marshall was not soon to forget. Scheduled for war room duty, I had gone there to relieve Joe Haines. As Joe and I stood at the map, he filled me in on the latest intelligence from the field. Through showing me the score, we walked toward one of the two doors of the room. "Oh, one thing more," said Joe, as he left. "On the desk is one of those cock-eyed Maquis reports. Just came in. I haven't had a chance to check it out, but it's nutty. Some of these Maquis don't know a squad from a division."

In France a certain amount of enemy information came to us from the Maquis. These were underground resistance fighters from all walks of life. They were loosely organized ragtag bands that harassed the Nazi units and sabotaged their installations and communications. They helped captured Allied soldiers to escape, hid downed pilots, and furnished intelligence information. I frequently interrogated them with the help of a French interpreter.

Going to the desk, I read the Maquis report. It said three German divisions were marching down a certain small road behind our front lines. The report was ridiculous on the face of it. The enemy had no such divisions available, and if they had had, they would not have been deployed that way. Our air recon people would have reported such a large incursion. Maquis intelligence was often considerable, especially in areas heavily infested by these partisan bands, but the quality of the information was erratic, with a proclivity for exaggeration.

As I reached for the phone to check out the report, General Palmer came in the other door and headed for the map. "What's new, Lieutenant?" he asked.

Putting the phone down, I joined him at the map and pointed out the latest developments. When I finished I made the big mistake of casually saying, "And we just got this wacky Maquis report that three German divisions are coming down this road. It's ridiculous."

"Have you checked this out?" cried Palmer, excited.

I said, "Sir, I just came on duty. I was just going to—"

Before I could finish the sentence, Palmer roared, "Why haven't you checked this out?"

I started again. "General," I said, "I just a minute ago relieved Captain Haines and—"

Again he interrupted. "Damn it! You should have checked this out!"

I said, "Sir, I just—"

Again he interrupted. As we went around in circles, he got louder and I, angered that my competence was being attacked and oblivious to the fact that a flash point was approaching, got louder also. The contretemps came to an abrupt end when he bellowed, "Lieutenant, if you don't shut up, I'll have you court-martialed!"

At that point I hastily raised the white flag. "Yes, sir," I said, "I'll check it immediately."

To me, experienced with the erratic nature of Maquis intelligence, the report was a blatant "no-brainer," just a matter to be routinely checked, but not worth the general's tizzy. However, in any confrontation between an obdurate first lieutenant, even though his obdurateness was buttressed by a superior knowledge of the situation, and a mulish brigadier general new to the area, it would be little short of miraculous for the vulnerable junior to come out on top, and no miracle occurred here.

I called the division in whose sector these supposed three enemy divisions were penetrating. In a few minutes the G-2 section called me back, told me they had checked with their units and there was nothing to it. "Was that one of those screwy Maquis reports?"

"Yeah," I said, "and I just got my ass chewed out on account of it."

I called Palmer and told him I had checked and there was no substance to the report. There was no apology or concession of any kind, but also thereafter no questioning of my competence.

Palmer, in comparison with General Frederick and other generals with whom I came into contact, was not a general with whom junior officers were comfortable and felt a sense of comradeship.

November 14 *Drove out to the Hundredth Division to check on how they were getting along. Command post is about twenty-five miles away. Drive back was miserable: rain, snow, fog, wind, and cold. Roads wet, muddy, and narrow. Big trucks with headlights blind you and crowd you off the road. The windshield was cracked and the wipers didn't work. A nightmarish drive.*

November 15 *The colonel wants me to go help out the 103rd order-of-battle people when we attack tomorrow morning.*

November 16 *On night duty last night. Then on to 103rd.*

November 18 *Still at 103rd. Today a PW gave us a target of 1,200 Russians who are fighting with the Germans. I notified corps artillery and they poured it on.*

The Germans are apparently following a "scorched earth" policy. There are now few towns between us and the German frontier. To make the winter tougher on us here in the mountains, they are burning all towns as they relinquish them. They have burned St. Marguerite and half of the city of St. Die. Consequently towns now afford us no shelter and the Germans force the refugee problem on us. We must feed, clothe, and evacuate the civilians—which we wouldn't have to do if they let the towns stand. Christ, what an awful, horrible mess war is!

The next day sixteen more of the enemy were put in the fold, mostly deserters, and a couple who still equated the Führer with God. After watching the disintegration of the Wehrmacht for months now, I could not fathom that there still remained men who had not lost their faith.

Also among the catch was a Gestapo agent, a Frenchman who, perhaps in remorse and resigned to his fate, blandly admitted his spying and gave us an immense amount of valuable information about the German agents' methods. (The Gestapo were the German internal security police as organized under the Nazi regime. The term was short for *Ge*heime *Sta*atspolizei, secret state police.) He was turned over to the French, and that was the last I saw of him. I had not the faintest doubt that after his countrymen had finished milking him further, he would be quickly and unceremoniously expunged. In his case I had little sympathy. My tolerance for traitors was small.

November 23   *On night duty. CP moves tomorrow to St. Die.*

The sight of St. Die seared the memory and was not to be forgotten. Formerly a beautiful city, it had been torched with characteristic Teutonic thoroughness and was now a vast expanse of charred houses, a skeleton of a once thriving community. It straddled the Meurthe River. Every house on the north side of the stream had been razed to the ground. Houses that had been spanking white were now flame-blackened relics and stood there in silent rebuke to the ghastliness of war. General Eisenhower happened to be visiting us that day. "It's one of the most appalling sights of wanton destruction I've ever seen," he remarked angrily.

Surveying the ruins I could now understand how ethnic groups could pass down hatred from one generation to another. The inhabitants I talked to swore they would "never forgive the Boche for this" and vowed when they got into Germany to burn two houses for every one French. It fueled for them, and surely for generations to come, a yearning for vengeance.

16

Battle of the Mind Warriors

In China, as early as six centuries before Christ, when war was not sporadic but endemic as warlords contested to expand their empires, military theorists discussed the subtleties of war. They pondered in their
essays the various aspects of battle—the importance of surprise, infiltration, the unpredictability of success—and concluded that the best
battle is the one won without being fought. Sun Tzu, the wily strate-
gist of deception, said: "Attacking does not merely consist of assailing
walled cities or striking an army in battle disarray; it must include the
act of assaulting the enemy's mental equilibrium. . . . To fight and con-
quer in all your battles is not supreme excellence. Supreme excellence
is breaking the enemy's resistance without fighting."

Most of the weapons used by armies are designed to maim and kill,
but one, propaganda, is designed to capture the mind, to encourage the
enemy to surrender or desert. It can inflict an insidious psychological
cost on the enemy, vast though not easily evaluated. The pitch may be
directed at the civilian or at the serviceman. If the opposing soldier can
be won over by persuading him to lay down his weapon and surrender,
you win in several ways. One, he won't shoot at you any more. Two,
he may also bring over a wavering comrade or two, or even a platoon.
And three, desertion has a demoralizing effect on those left behind.
Hence the constant proselytizing of the Ezra Pounds and the Axis
Sallys was not taken lightly by army psychologists.

One night at Anzio, Nazi propaganda leaflets based on a *Chicago Tribune* cartoon fluttered to the ground. The cartoon portrayed our Russian allies as subhumans. At about the same time, other leaflets were directed at British troops. The Nazi mind-warriors, aware of the Tommies' lament that the American soldiers in Britain were "overpaid, oversexed, and over here," tried to mine this vein by sending over leaflets claiming the GIs were sleeping with the Brits' wives and sweethearts. Sally, a specialist in seductive suggestion, would supplement this with, "What are those smart GIs doing to your English women while you are fighting and getting killed over here? Easy to guess, eh?"

This theme was hit hard with the British. Many variations were employed. One leaflet said, "Yanks are lease-lending your women. The Yanks are putting up their tents in Merry Old England. They've got lots of money and loads of time to chase after your women." The back side pictured a half-nude girl in bed about to be embraced by a Yankee sergeant. Nude pictures were a constant in the German propaganda output, and the men used them as pin-ups.

Another theme employed at Anzio was to remind the Tommies of the Dunkirk disaster and advise surrender before a similar fate befell them.

A third theme was an effort to weaken British-American unity by professing to show that the American command assigned the tough fighting to the British.

Subtlety was not a strong point of German propaganda, although one of sultry-voiced Axis Sally's phrases caught on and was widely repeated to the discomfiture of the officers. It was, "Go easy, boys. There's danger ahead."

American propaganda was handled by the Psychological Warfare Branch, which prepared leaflets and set up radio transmitters for broadcasting to the enemy forces. The leaflets were dropped by plane or delivered by mortar and artillery shells.

Now, here in Alsace, poring through a batch of documents, I came upon a copy of our propaganda booklet "Krankheit rettet" (Sickness saves). It taught the German how to fake the symptoms of various diseases and so stay home from work and dangerous factory areas, which might come under attack. It told him what to tell the doctor, how to talk to him, and advised him not to volunteer information. I thought it was one of our cleverest pieces of propaganda.

The new command post was a large factory on the south side, the untorched side, of the river. It was so spacious that each officer had a private room. Inspecting the new premises with Pundt and Haines, we came on a German propaganda leaflet that had been left by one of our frontline troops who had earlier been in the building. It featured a caricature of Roosevelt with his trademark cigarette holder sticking jauntily out of the corner of his mouth.

It was now November 1944 and too much had transpired for German psychological warfare to score effectively. Hitler's brutal invasions of country after country; his ruthless repression of all internal political opposition; the harassment of the Catholic church; the destruction of the trade unions; the pogroms of Jews; and above all, the emerging revelations that the dehumanizing concentration camps, originally the repository for "socially disruptive elements," had devolved into genocidal killing grounds had combined to harden the GI's determination to end Nazi rule.

Other propaganda leaflets found their way into my journal as we moved on. Slogging their way through the Vosges Mountains of eastern France now, the doughboys not only had to contend with German fire, but also with rain, snow, and cold. To capitalize on their discomfort, the enemy used a GI cartoon character popular at the time, Private Breger, warning him of the "grim damp PRUSSIAN WINTER" ahead. Another leaflet read "Safety First!" on one side, while the other, under a picture of a smiling young woman, touted the security of life as a PW. Still another piece had a large gold star on a black background on one side and, on the reverse, a picture of a mother at graveside mourning her GI son.

The effectiveness of propaganda is difficult to gauge. The mind warriors of both sides never gave up hope. Even as Seventh Army forces were crossing the Rhine over the Remagen bridge, the enemy's "Berlin Midge" was interspersing her malevolent overtures between Glenn Miller songs, still trying to persuade GIs to desert by insinuating that their girlfriends at home were being unfaithful.

Interrogation taught me soldiers desert for different reasons and different combinations of reasons. For many, fear of death looms large; for others, a prolonged period of physical suffering eventually becomes unendurable. Some feel they have been unjustly kept in line too long and become disillusioned with their noncoms or officers. Others have lost

'Personally, I don't think it's gonna influence the Germans to surrender to us!"

Hello, Pte. Breger!

'have always been a clever boy. Havn't yer got now a nice foretaste of what a grim damp PRUSSIAN WINTER will mean to you?

In winter over here you won't have the fine crisp cold of an American winter. The rainy days of last week were only a beginning! Lousy prospects for the days to come! Your uniform will always be damp and cold, just like last week; and no place to dry it!

Pte. Breger knows that, for he has always been a clever guy, and he thinks it might be a damn sight better to pass Christmas time in the warm barracks of a German PW's camp, than in the damp cold trenches of Lorraine.

THE MAN WHO PROMISED THAT NO AMERICAN WOULD BE SENT TO FIGHT OUTSIDE THE U.S.

THE MAN WHO SAID THAT U.S. SOLDIERS WOULD BE DEMOBILIZED WITHIN A FEW WEEKS

THE MAN WHO WILL BE RE-ELECTED

REMEMBER HIM! HE PROMISED THE SAME THINGS AND HE, TOO, BROKE HIS PROMISE

5

THE PoW LIFE ASSURANCE CO.
No Premiums to Pay

Insurance statistics show that the
average American reaches an age of . . . . 60,5 years
The average GI Joe in combat
reaches an age of . . . . 23,2 years
Therefore PoWs live longer by . . . . 37,3 years

All German PoW Camps are run on the
Geneva Convention plan

Congress has voted a law entitling

Gold Star Mothers

to a free trip to Europe after the War.

IS THIS
TO BE
YOUR MOTHER?

faith in their cause or may have a hatred of killing. Still others are moved to desert by a combination of homesickness, weariness, a general despondency, and a futility of outlook. This is particularly true on the losing side, and a bombardment of propaganda, when morale is low, may be enough to tilt the decision in favor of easy surrender, or even desertion.

To the Wehrmacht desertion was the unforgivable sin, and during the course of the war over 25,000 deserters on the German side were executed. Those were the unfortunates who failed to desert successfully. The successful deserters numbered many more.

The 103rd had been in battle for about ten days when I paid them a visit to make sure no bugs were developing in the OB system we had helped install. While there, I met with one of the interrogators, Lieutenant Heide, who told me of an incident that occurred a few days earlier. A PW, a fanatical Nazi, had refused to talk and was so determined to escape and get back into the war that he had made two attempts— one earlier at the regimental cage and one at the division cage—to grab a gun from the guarding MPs.

To the very end of the war there remained a few soldiers who possessed an inborn toughness, as opposed to that which might be instilled by military discipline, who were able to carry on no matter how dark the situation. Only days before the formal surrender I interrogated a young, supercilious Austrian lieutenant, a rabid knucklehead, with results no better than Heide's.

Seasoned interrogators rarely spent much time with close-mouthed doctrinaire Nazis when their time could be better spent extracting information from soldiers who freely talked and often volunteered information. There were some interrogators, though, who considered a difficult case to be a challenge. At one cage I heard about, interrogation was carried on in two tents. A captured major proved difficult, so at a signal from the interrogator one of the guarding MPs went into the adjoining tent, fired into the ground, lay down on a cot, was covered by a blanket, and carried out past the other tent. The major was shown "the results of not talking." Shaken, he now talked, but when he reached the army headquarters cage for further interrogation, he lodged a complaint about the violation of the Geneva Convention rules on the treatment of prisoners.

There was a quick investigation, all hell broke loose, and a "cease-

and-desist" order came down to all interrogators. Such overly persua-
sive methods were not looked on favorably by higher headquarters.

November 27, 1944   *Sick all day long, a bad cold or flu or stomach
virus. I don't know. In the morning we moved to St. Blaise—another
factory. Hit the sack in the afternoon for a couple of hours. At night,
after I went to bed again, Sergeant Morgridge awakened me: "General
Eagles is on the phone. He wants to talk to you."*

   *I was too ill to talk to anybody, general or private. I said, "Tell the
General I'm sick in bed. I'll call him first thing in the morning."*

   *But I went anyhow and answered the phone. It concerned the day's
story in the* Beachhead News. *I reported a wrong regiment taking a
town.*

The general's call came after midnight, and I had been vomiting repeatedly. I could not remember a time when I had felt so bad, and I
would not have answered the phone. The sergeant, however, became
extremely nervous, hemmed and hawed, didn't know how to tell a two-
star general that a first lieutenant wouldn't talk to him. I took pity on
the sergeant.

17

The Fight for Alsace

November 28, 1944   *Today the man who keeps my jeep asked me to "sell" him some gas. He said, "A young man needs money." I declined.*

Still sick, I spent the morning in bed. In the afternoon I drove to the 103rd CP and then searched the office of the mayor of Urbeis for documents. Found a few training films and got the location of a minefield and some unplanted mines from him. Also the location of a dead American soldier.

The 103rd cage had 350 prisoners in front of it. Stopped a few minutes to see Heide.

We're in Alsace now. Everybody speaks German. But I don't quite trust these people. They've been part of both sides too long.

For two thousand years ethnically riven Alsace had been a land pulled back and forth by the peoples and governments on both sides of the Rhine.

November 29   *Found out from PWs that the 2,000 German Army Russians we were shooting at a few days ago were really only 700–800, but our artillery got a number of them.*

November 30   *Spent morning in war room, afternoon doping out a dozen important captured maps.*

December 1   *Hot fight going on between 200 Germans in a fort on a hill overlooking this town, Mutzig, and our boys. Our planes have bombed them twice now. We open the windows to prevent the blasts from breaking the glass.*

December 2   *On duty last night. Little sleep. Major West, G-2 of the 103rd, came in at 11:00 P.M. and we shot the breeze till 1:00 A.M. Then a special messenger brought a supposedly valuable batch of captured maps and field orders. Spent two hours studying the stuff to find only a few items of value, one a map coordinate code.*

Some of the clerical staff got hold of a couple of large swastika flags and waved them flauntingly before the OB people. "Hell," said Doc, "we can get all of those we want in no time."

"No way," challenged the clerks.

At lunch time Pundt and I went out and got seven of them in less than twenty minutes. We asked a townsman where we could get some Nazi flags. He eyed us suspiciously and professed not to know. The second man we approached directed us to some stores. We entered the nearest one and the shopkeeper, uneasy, claimed he had no flags. We told him we had been informed otherwise and assured him there would be no trouble, that we wanted them simply as souvenirs. Still leery, he nevertheless brought out the swastika flags, but refused to be paid for them.

When we got back to the office we found to our amusement that our little venture had resulted in quick civilian reports to headquarters that "two German spies dressed as American officers were roaming the town."

Our push toward Germany continued unabated. Since the landings on the Côte d'Azur, we had taken 64,437 PWs while the Germans were known to have taken 127 of ours. Another 3,561 of our men were missing, some of whom were doubtless prisoners.

The recent battling had culminated in our capture of the city of Strasbourg, the commercial and cultural capital of Alsace. It had big brewing and tanning industries and was said to be the source of the best pâté de foie gras in all the world. Situated on the Rhine, it had been ceded to the French at the close of the First World War, and then reoccupied by the Germans in 1940 after the fall of France. Although everyone spoke German, 90 percent of the people professed to be sympathetic to the French.

Forts had been part of Strasbourg's defenses. I went to inspect one, a colossal stronghold extending underground for a vast distance. Still stored there were thousands of hand grenades, rifles, and a large assortment of munitions and supplies. I found the commander's office and rummaged through it, uncovering little of value on our level but considerable on a higher level.

Not having the time on my first visit to go through the immense fort, I returned for a second inspection. It yielded no further documents of value, merely information for a more detailed description of the stronghold and a collection of souvenirs for the whole G-2 section, including complete German uniforms. One of these I kept for myself and mailed, together with a helmet, bayonet, dress cap, and signal flag, to the teenage son of a cousin in New Jersey. After the war, when I returned to the States, I learned that his father, as a gag, had dressed himself in the uniform for a Sunday picnic in a public park only to have the entire police force of the small town descend on him for a proud capture.

Our headquarters had been established outside the city in a municipal building in a suburb named Dettweiler. The command post functions were carried out in the large rooms, and the smaller rooms became the sleeping quarters for the officers. In light of the situation at the front, it was expected that our stay here would last for a while. I decided to see if I could find more comfortable quarters for myself.

Knocking on the door of a house across the street, I asked the elderly couple, Hut by name, if they could put me up for a few days. They assured me warmly that it would be an honor, they would be delighted, and showed me to a room with a featherbed, no small luxury in this damp wintry weather, and a big improvement over a cot in an unheated brick building.

One evening I gave a cigar to Mr. Hut. It was gratefully received, but noticing he wasn't lighting up, I asked why. "Oh," he said, "I must wait till Sunday when I will have time to really enjoy it."

I asked him what other luxuries he missed.

"Never mind the luxuries," he replied. "Even the necessities are unobtainable. When the Germans told us, 'We freed you Alsatians,' under our breath we muttered, 'Yes, from milk, eggs, and meat.'"

Alsace had now been in the hands of the Germans for four years, and I wondered how the educational system had been affected. A woman in Mutzig had earlier complained to me that big doses of propaganda had taken up much time that should have been devoted to the standard subjects. Living in the house with the Huts was a nineteen-year-old niece. Asked about the schools, she confirmed the complaints of the Mutzig woman. A subsequent talk I had with a Strasbourg teacher corroborated their grievances. "To avoid nazifying the children," he said, "many of us teachers, at considerable personal risk, used various techniques to sidestep Nazi propagandistic infiltration of the teaching process. But one had to be careful. The techniques had to be subtle. All textbooks were rewritten in the Nazi spirit. I tried to defeat the system by ignoring the text books and teaching the principles by substituting examples devoid of propaganda."

Months later in Germany proper, I was to see how anti-Semitism was infused into even basic arithmetic.

Tipped off by Herr Hut that there was a metal fabricating plant in nearby Niederhofen, I sped off in search of the target. It turned out to be the Omefa Metallwaren Fabrik. Questions to the manager revealed that the plant made plane and gun parts for Junkers, BMW, Daimler-Benz, and other companies. He was cooperative, and I flipped through a mass of records. While the information was of no direct tactical use to the Sixth Corps headquarters, I notified Air Corps Intelligence of the plant. "Lieutenant," drawled the captain at the other end, "we'll have a look-see there real pronto."

The following afternoon the captain came in to see me. He and a team had inspected the plant and its records. The result, he said, would be many air targets, as well I knew. Not only were there the names and locations of the assembly plants, but also those of other parts-making factories. The bombing of these plants would make it increasingly difficult to move weapon components from point of production to point of assembly.

The nature of my job was such that I was often away from headquarters and thrown into situations conducive to the easy collecting of Nazi souvenirs. Visiting one of the PW cages, I returned with a beautiful Nazi dagger. Like so many soldiers of all ranks, including generals, one of our clerks, Sergeant Morgridge, was a collector of Nazi memorabilia. Seeing the weapon on my desk, he "went bananas" over it, pleading with me to give it to him in exchange for his Luger pistol, a much sought after souvenir. I already had a P38, the other official German army pistol, but yielding to his pleadings I swapped.

That night, what should come in a package for me from Alex Shayne but a duplicate dagger.

These daggers bore the inscription *Deutschland über Alles*, which translates as "Germany above all." This inscription and another, *Alles für Deutschland*, which translates as "Everything for Germany," were used in Allied propaganda to symbolize German fanaticism. Never mentioned was that above the entrance to Chequers, Prime Minister Winston Churchill's manor, there was chiseled in Latin: *Pro Patria Omnia*, which in English reads "Everything for the Fatherland."

December 12   *To Strasbourg to interview Herr Reibel, an engineer, of the International Rhine Navigation Commission. I found that documents and personal knowledge he has of the Rhine River will answer all our questions. Since we must soon break across the Rhine, I've let the Engineer Intelligence know about the man and they are rushing down to see him. We have a crying need for information of an engineering nature about the Rhine. I'm pretty sure my afternoon's work will save a lot of lives.*

No enemy had crossed the Rhine since Napoleon in 1805. To Hitler the Rhine was a thou-shalt-not-pass symbol of the steadfastness of the Third Reich. He had issued an order that any commander who surrendered a town or communications post on the east side of the Rhine was to be put to death. It specifically included bridges across the Rhine.

Stopped on the way back to see Alex Shayne. Found him in a blue funk. The French requisitioned the Mercedes limousine he had picked up and with which he had hoped to go to Paris for a few days.

I draped an arm around my friend's shoulder. "Geez, Alex," I said with ill-feigned sympathy, "fighting a war without a personal Mercedes is rough, isn't it?"

For a moment Alex eyed me dubiously. Then bursting into laughter, he cried, "You bastard! You got no compassion!"

December 13   *Our CP has been moved to a large hot sulphur springs sanatorium. John Rieger and I have a room together. Steam heat, but not too good.*

Hated to leave Dettweiler and the nice setup. The family regretted my leaving too, especially the 82-year-old father-in-law who lived with the Huts, a noble chap, typical of the best in the French Alsatians.

The last evening snack we had together was eaten off beautiful hand-painted plates, over 100 years old, and they broke out a special white wine as a send off.

My twelve-day stay with this family had spoiled me. Each night, when I came in from the chilly winter weather, I found the foot end of the bed, underneath the feather cover, heated by a hot stone wrapped in towels. When I crawled in, after chatting and snacking with the family for an hour or so, I truly felt as snug as a bug in the proverbial rug. After I told my fellow officers about my luxurious quarters and extended my phony commiseration for their cold and drafty cots, I became the subject of a lot of good-natured razzing about my decadence, a condition into which they too would have liked to have fallen.

December 14   *A long talk this morning with General Baehr, the artillery commander, about document retrieval and exploitation.*

The general was surprised at the voluminous amount of intelligence we were able to extract, and to all the uses to which we were able to put it. He thanked me for the enemy artillery codes we had sent him and the many targets we had given him. He could hardly believe it when I told him that during the past fighting at Anzio and now in France we almost always knew the enemy passwords, making easier the penetration of enemy territory by our reconnoitering patrols. I told him about the *Soldbuch* and how it helped us determine which divisions were being eliminated and which decimated divisions were being welded together to form new divisions. I mentioned the times we had had the complete plan of German withdrawal. I told him of the recent visit to the metal fabricating plant and how its records would enable the air force to locate and target assembly plants, and on and on. "I doubt," I said in conclusion, "that even one GI in a hundred has the faintest idea of what a large part document exploitation plays in war."

Baehr had listened in earnest, and as we parted he told me I had given him an education.

December 15 *Heard some details of the Schirmeck concentration camp. Almost impossible to believe. Butcher hooks, whole rows, for hanging dead humans while they await their turn to be cremated. Crematorium with rows of urns to hold the ashes. Torture chambers with things like alternating hot and cold showers, gallows, gun pits, etc.*

Yet, difficult as these stories were to believe, they confirmed those Mr. Yaselli had told me back in Rome.

December 16 *Colonel Dixon told me today that the 103rd Division had requested my transfer to them and Colonel Langevin had turned it down. A transfer would almost automatically mean a promotion.*

Dixon, the executive officer, had recently been promoted to lieutenant colonel. He was a staunch ally and friend, felt I deserved higher rank, and would periodically plug for my promotion. He felt it could be wangled if Colonel Holsten, my AFHQ boss, would release me for assignment (not attachment) to the 103rd Division where I could have been immediately promoted as assistant G-2 with captain's rank. I knew, however, that Holsten, a bureaucratic type officer, would not agree to such a precedent-setting step. It might lead to other transfers and diminish his turf.

I also knew that Langevin was trying to get me promoted through regular channels as quickly as possible, and the requests by the generals of the 100th and 103rd divisions gave greater weight to Langevin's efforts.

18

Straw Shoes for "Good" Soldiers

As we neared the small city of Haguenau, twenty-five miles from the Fatherland's border, the intensity of the fighting increased as German resistance stiffened. Driving into the town, I found it well shot up, but the inhabitants were in the streets greeting us joyfully. Many showered us with straw slippers, called *Schlappen*. I asked one four-year-old girl, *"Was hast du da, Liebchen?"* (What have you got there, sweetheart?) And she answered in the native dialect, *"Schühe für die guten Soldaten"* (Shoes for the good soldiers), emphasizing "good."

Coinciding with our imminent attack on the German border was a big, surprise counteroffensive going on up north in the Ardennes Forest. The U.S. Army held a seventy-five-kilometer front with three divisions, and the Wehrmacht attacked with over twenty.

Learning of it, I was disgusted. Such a big attack, I felt, must have made itself evident in the preparation. "This damned war is going to go on for another six months!" I shouted angrily to Doc. "How the hell could our intelligence have been that flawed?"

The answer to the question had several parts, future study was to show. During most of the war the messages transmitted by Hitler to his field commanders were sent out on the High Command's Enigma coding machines. These coded messages, considered by the Germans to be unbreakable, were intercepted and deciphered by British and

American cryptographers, who had successfully built a decoder, one of the Allies' most closely guarded secrets. Consequently, the Allies suffered few nasty surprises, the commanders being forewarned of the German plans in what were known as ULTRA messages, ULTRA being the generic term for Enigma-based communications intelligence. At the battle for El Alamein in North Africa, for example, the dashing Rommel did not know, and never discovered during his lifetime, that in addition to the overwhelming odds with which he had to fight Montgomery, the British commander was being supplied by ULTRA with vital intelligence about his strength, supply situation, and plans—akin in a poker game to knowing four of the five cards held by the opponent.

However, by the time of this attack in the wooded Ardennes plateau, later to be known as the Battle of the Bulge, Hitler had begun to suspect that the Western powers were reading his messages. He ceased using the Enigma machines, switching to more secure land lines for communication, and the High Command imposed radio silence, preventing Allied radio intercept from picking up and evaluating the normal wireless traffic between Wehrmacht units. Although there was some detection of German troop movements, their significance was not properly evaluated by Allied intelligence. Nor was proper significance attached to the report of the mistress of a German general, a British agent, who warned Allied intelligence of the coming offensive.

A run of luck further strengthened the Führer's hand. A long period of bad weather prevented the aerial reconnaissance that would have revealed the buildup along the front. And because of the nature of the terrain, hilly and wooded, with narrow roads, and bedded in snow, there was a mindset in the Allied camp that the enemy did not have the strength and competence to launch an offensive through the Ardennes. Much of the top brass, lulled by the wintry tranquility, went on leave.

After the war, German general Hasso von Manteufel disclosed that Stalin knew of this impending attack through a security leak in the High Command. Stalin, though, did not inform the Allies.

Nevertheless, considering the many overt and covert means used to gather information, I am still baffled to this day by the failure of American intelligence.

At this point in the war, Germany's navy and air force were defeated. Fate, once indulgent, was now increasingly unkind to Hitler's aspirations. The Russian front, the Balkan front, the north Italian front, and the two fronts in France were all crumbling; German armies, their supply streams having dwindled to a trickle, and getting little support from a Luftwaffe stretched too thin by all the demands made on it, were spent. The highly industrialized Ruhr region, together with the Saar and its vital coal mines and steel works, were threatened. City after city became for the Führer a fortress that had to be defended to the last man, no matter how this contradicted Clausewitz's dictum that in retreat the wise man holds the essentials; the fool tries to hold on to everything.

Although the flower of its youth had long fallen and Germany had lost the war, we had not yet won it. The end, though, seemed tantalizingly close.

As General Hans Speidel, Field Marshal Erwin Rommel's chief of staff in Normandy, was to tell me later, the High Command at this time no longer had a grand strategy, but was increasingly reduced to patching up unraveling situations. Hitler's "no withdrawal, stand or die" mentality had stultified German strategic thinking. "Yet," said Speidel, "the Führer was still driven by visions of *Endsieg* [final victory], even if the last German had to die for it."

(Speidel, one of the conspirators in the July 20, 1944, attempt to assassinate Hitler, was the man the Allies selected after the war to be the architect of the new German army. In 1957 he was named commander of the Allied Forces, Central Europe, one of the most important posts in the North Atlantic Treaty Organization, and served in that capacity until 1963.)

Since the Battle of Stalingrad, there had been titanic changes in the German fortunes. Yet, despite the profusion of reversals, the astronomical losses, and the obvious denouement in the offing, the Germans soldiered on. There was not a scintilla of an inkling that the Führer was ready to give up. How he hoped to win beggared the imagination.

When I interrogated high-ranking officers and asked why they continued to fight when they knew the war was lost, a common thread ran through their answers: honor, duty, and their oath to Hitler. A few months down the road, in April, when we were to capture Field Marshal Wilhelm List, and I acted as interpreter for General Brooks as he queried the marshal, List repeatedly emphasized the German tradition that the military hierarchy refrain from politics. The consequence, he said, was the political illiteracy and ineptitude of the generals, which permitted Hitler, a master of machinations, to achieve control of the country's armed forces.

From that consequence there followed another: The Führer's authority became unchallengeable and reduced the General Staff to an executive mechanism for carrying out his orders. This assessment was confirmed to me independently by two other field marshals we were to capture.

To further solidify Hitler's hold on the army, every soldier had been obliged to take an oath: "I swear by God this holy oath, that I shall render to Adolf Hitler, Führer of the German Reich and People, Supreme Commander of the Armed Forces, unconditional obedience, and that I am ready, as a brave soldier, to risk my life at any time for this oath."

Thus it happened that a substantial percentage of aristocrats, men of spotless honor and heretofore highly principled, had become submissive (though truculent) generals to a former Austro-German corporal with limited education and no command experience who had risen to head of state through spellbinding oratory and Machiavellian dissembling they could not match. To the highly schooled officer corps, this abrupt ascendancy to active head of the Wehrmacht was tantamount to a kindergarten child propelled overnight to the presidency of a university.

Furthermore, to the disgust of those who had originally considered National Socialism a solution to chaos and a bulwark against communism, they were now wedded to its increasingly questionable tenets. They were forced to accept the burgeoning power of the party's functionaries, too often zealots saturated with immorality and intent on achieving a sclerotic grip on the political life of the country.

At the start of the First World War, Speidel told me, the chief of the General Staff, as military adviser to the head of state, automatically became one of the most influential people in the Fatherland. At the start of the Second World War, to the dismay of the generals, the powers of this office were sharply limited as the Nazi dictator assumed the role of commander-in-chief of the armed forces. And after the fall of France in 1940, no one was allowed to detract from his aura of genius and omnipotence.

Whereas blind, unthinking obedience had never been a characteristic of the General Staff of the Imperial Army, said Speidel, it was now an essential. Formerly honor-bound to voice their objections to unwise or illegal orders and to resist their implementation, they were no longer permitted to be independent thinkers. The senior generals, cowed and humiliated, were shuffled about by the former corporal until he had a coterie of lackeys—mindless conduits for orders that came from Hitler himself. Said the Führer, "I do not ask my generals to agree with my orders, but only to carry them out."

The aggrieved officer corps, dismayed by the emasculation of the top generals in the OKW (High Command of the Armed Forces), bitterly jested that OKW stood for *Oben kein Widerstand* (no resistance at the top). They further joked that not a single private could be moved from door to window without the Führer's approval. In sum, the operational control of the Wehrmacht lay in the hands of an ungifted amateur war-lord possessed with an overblown sense of his own military acumen and allergic to all ideas but his own. For the Allies, it was an underappreciated blessing.

When, after the war, I asked Speidel to explain the defeat of the Wehrmacht by the Red armies, he began with a quip: "Too many Russians and one German too many."

That Hitler had been a brave soldier in the First World War was undeniable. He had been decorated with the Iron Cross First Class, an honor not often conferred on a corporal, and it may have accounted for his frequently expressed contempt for his generals' courage. The senior ranks of the officer corps, to our puzzlement, fought on even when collapse was taking on apocalyptic dimensions, causing us to wonder about their famed military acuity. While never able to reconcile their enslavement to Hitler, they faithfully served their deranged master with a subservience based on their belief in the ideal of "the soldier above politics." Oath-bound, their loyalty was implicit in their continuation of a resistance they knew was fruitless. Embittered, they were left with no recourse in desperate situations but to circumvent the Führer's orders at great risk to their own lives.

Commanded by Germany's senior field marshal, Gerd von Rundstedt, all available forces were marshaled for a grandiose attempt to break through the Allied lines, strike for Antwerp, and encircle the Allied troops. That Rundstedt would fail, he knew. In Russia he had commanded an army group until, in strenuous disagreement with Hitler, he had requested his own relief. Among senior officers he inveighed against the Führer, alluding to him as a vulgarian and military illiterate, holding him in such contempt that he referred to him as "the Bohemian corporal." Although by rank he had the privilege, Rundstedt never telephoned Hitler directly.

After the war the marshal strongly resented historians' references to this operation as "the Rundstedt offensive." He had nothing to do with its planning and considered the manpower, equipment, ammunition, and gasoline supplies inadequate for the mission's far-reaching goals, especially in light of the western enemies' control of the air. Further, he had no freedom of action in its execution. "It came down to me as an order complete to the last detail," he said. And in Hitler's own handwriting, consistent with the exalted opinion of his military genius, the Führer had written on the plan, "NOT TO BE ALTERED."

While not intended as a prophecy, my angry ejaculation to Doc Pundt that the war would now last another six months proved to be quite accurate.

December 18, 1944   *Joe Haines had a party tonight and Lieutenant Colonel Davison, assistant G-3, who had commanded a battalion for eight months, made a statement I found interesting. He said, "As a general rule, I found Nordics make good soldiers, Latins poor ones. And among the Nordics you can't predict from a man's looks or behavior how good he'll be in battle. It's impossible."*

Davison was a tall, thin, ramrod-straight West Pointer with a scarred lip. Knowledgeable, efficient, and determined, he did his job with a steely panache that discouraged opposition. When he barked an order, the officer at the other end of the line knew that if he protested it couldn't be done, Davison would appear at the front, personally direct the operation, and prove it could be done. After which the reluctant officer might find he had been relieved of his command. Like General Truscott, Davison was of the school: "Don't tell me it can't be done. Just do it!"

December 19   *Interrogated a German civilian today, the railroad traffic dispatcher for the whole Palatinate region. I found out the main lines being used by the Germans for military traffic. A copy of the report is being sped to army headquarters.*

The air force, needless to say, was tickled to get this information, blowing up trains being a favorite pilot sport. The Palatinate is the section of western Germany nestled between the Rhine and the areas of Alsace and Lorraine where American forces would soon be fighting. Prior to the First World War, the German General Staff's railway section had laid out many miles of the railroads according to its anticipated needs to speed troops and supplies in the event of war. With Hitler's ascendancy to power, the sprawling Autobahn superhighway system had further enhanced the military transport capabilities, over 1,000 miles of motorway being constructed between 1933 and 1937.

December 20 *Saddled with a new job. To help brief the colonel in the morning in the war room before the General Staff conference. The Old Man operates on the principle that if you want something done, give it to a busy man.*

We have a report the Germans are pulling their officer candidates out of school and throwing them into infantry battles. Another report states that men who have contracted venereal disease are entitled only to second-rate rations while hospitalized.

December 21 *Visited Fourteenth Armored Division to touch base with their G-2 section, especially with their OB people, and to look up old Camp Chaffee friends.*

December 22 *Take a sulphur bath every day or two. You can't work up a lather in that water, but at least you get wet with hot water. And a sulphur bath—we're in a resort hotel—may be good for you, who knows?*

December 23 *Had a little party in my room tonight. Joe Haines, John Rieger, Doc Pundt, and I drank up my bottle of rationed Schenley's rye with some cheese and crackers sent from home.*

December 24 *An air raid this morning. A German plane flew by the CP at tree top level, but our gunners popping away at him didn't get him.*

Our counterattack in the north against the German penetration is reported going well. If we're lucky it will shorten the war by months.

Christmas Eve was spent with small parties in every fifth room or so. Felt pretty blue. Didn't seem like much of a way to spend Christmas.

December 25 *On night duty. At 2:00 A.M. I got a scare call of "8 parachutists landing." Happens whenever we alert people to watch for them.*

The colonel asked me to write up his notes for the morning conference, which I did.

A slow day as far as work goes, so I had time to feel sorry for myself—and indeed I did.

The best part of Christmas Day had been the meal, of which I am reminded by a leaflet pasted in my journal. The cover is a drawing of a wintry pastoral scene and bears the words, "Christmas Dinner 1944, HQ. VI Corps, in the Vosges." Inside, surrounded by a drawing of bells, ribbons, and holly, is the menu: Fruit Cocktail, White Wine, Roast Iowa Turkey, Snowflake Potatoes, Sage Dressing, Giblet Gravy, Early June Peas and Diced Carrots, Chef's Salad, Cranberry Sauce, Pumpkin Pie, Marble Cake, Coffee, Fresh Fruit, Nuts and Xmas Candy and "Good Cheer"!

Had our meals always been of this caliber, instead of a seemingly endless diet of C rations, the war, too, might have been more palatable.

December 26 *Battle in the north not going too well. Could set us back for at least six months, if we don't succeed in cutting them off.*

The war room was always the focal point at headquarters, but now even moreso with officers from all sections dropping in repeatedly to learn the latest about the battle in the Ardennes. The situation was bleak. As the teletype machines clicked away, we weighed with excruciating concern each bit of information spewed out. Then came reports of the Germans using every imaginable weapon and knavery of a type not previously employed. There were reports of saboteurs, of Germans in American uniforms, of others carrying sulfuric acid to throw into captors' eyes, of paratroops and others with gimmicks to instill panic in the rear echelons, and of the dastardly SS killing PWs. The surprise attack by the Fifth and Sixth Panzer armies resulted in nineteen thousand Americans killed and fifteen thousand taken prisoner. They were nail-biting times.

My fears about our ability to counter the German offensive were dispelled when the weather cleared, allowing the Allied planes to effectively get into the game.

After several worrisome days, it became clear that the enemy was bogged down, the battle was going better, and the adversary's swift successes would be short-lived. On the ground the waist-deep snow was no longer a German ally, as the supply columns struggled in it while attacked from overhead. The Second Armored Division found the Second Panzer Division was out of gas and worked it over mercilessly, destroying its eighty-eight tanks and twenty-eight assault guns. Patton's Fourth Armored Division crashed through the southern front of the 'Bulge' and relieved the 101st Airborne Division surrounded in Bastogne, a thrilling epic in American military history.

In the succeeding days it became increasingly evident that the Führer, in pursuit of his *Endsieg* goal, had shot his wad and failed. Over 100,000 Germans had been killed, wounded, or captured in the Ardennes, gargantuan losses the High Command could ill afford. On the eastern front, the Germans were faring no better. Mile by hard-fought mile, the Soviet forces had encircled Budapest, severing all the rail lines, forcing the Germans to set fire to great stores of gasoline, ammunition, and ordnance materials, while two Red spearheads headed for Vienna.

December 30   *Lieutenant John Hammer came over yesterday. He's here for three days to study our order-of-battle methods before taking over the Twenty-first Corps's setup. Wants me to take it over. I don't want it, even if the colonel would let me go. I'm tired of these early morning till late at night jobs seven days a week and never any time off. There it would be even more hectic until I got things organized to my satisfaction.*

December 31   *Doc paid me the $10 I had bet him in October that the war would not be over by the end of the year. This was a bet I would rather have lost.*

The author examining a newly captured 72-ton German self-propelled gun. These heavily armed behemoths were formidable weapons.

No New Year's Eve celebration, partly because nobody felt like it, and partly because it wasn't allowed—an attack being expected tomorrow.

January 1, 1945   *The expected German attack developed. They jumped off shortly after midnight. By evening they had penetrated our line at several points, and the situation begins to look bad. In view of it, our rear echelon was ordered to leave for a new CP farther back, and we, the forward echelon, will move tomorrow morning—the first time the Sixth Corps has ever retreated.*

The exhilarating scent of approaching victory was replaced with a sharp drop in morale.

Our northward drive from the Riviera had been till now relentless and successful, but there would still be some bumps in the road ahead. For the past three days the Germans had been using captured American planes with American markings against us. The ruse prevented our antiaircraft from firing at them, the gunners uncertain whether they were aiming at friend or foe. In one of their raids they killed two men from my MIS company and wounded another, all interrogators at the Fourteenth Armored Division. One, Captain Andre, I knew. He was hit in the head by shrapnel and killed. His sergeant lost a leg and died. His corporal was wounded.

During the battle, I called one of the divisions, and the G-2 officer answered excitedly, "Okay, tell me, but I can't write it down! I'm under a table!" Their CP was being machine-gunned and had been bombed just shortly before.

That evening the Germans tried to panic our rear echelon. Several in American officers' uniforms and driving American jeeps would enter a rear area installation and yell, "Pack up and move! The Germans are coming!" These Germans in American uniforms, when captured, were summarily executed.

January 2   *Moved our CP back to Dellweiler. Got same room in same home. The Huts appear genuinely glad to see me again.*

As though the battle we were engaged in didn't give me enough problems, I now got a call from Captain Snedal, the adjutant of our Military Intelligence Service company, from the safety of army headquarters, to tell me he was classifying me as "military intelligence interpreter."

"So what?" I said irritably, snowed under with work and occupied with weightier matters, such as could we beat off the attacking Germans and, if not, would I still be alive the next morning. Later, still bristling, I called Snedal to learn that first lieutenant was the highest rank for that category. When I told Dixon about it, he exploded and told me he would see that I got promoted as soon as possible, Snedal or no Snedal.

Dixon's regard for Snedal, like mine, was as low as a snake's belly, and I know our feelings toward him came through to him. To me the combat infantryman is the army hero, the guy who does the heavy lifting, and when Snedal turned up one day sporting the Combat Infantry Badge, it raised my hackles. He had never served one day as an infantryman, and I let him know in terms not too well veiled how I felt about rear-echelon paper-shuffling heroes. (When Congress in 1961 voted that all holders of the Combat Infantry Badge automatically became Bronze Star recipients, I felt the award, by and large, had been well earned.) Snedal and Holsten occasionally visited us on "inspection tours," and always when things were quiet, never when all hell was breaking loose and the battle was up for grabs. Needless to say, my attitude toward them was not an asset when my name was forwarded to them for promotion.

January 4	*Dixon called Snedal. Told me I was again classified order of battle.*

January 5	*Germans crossed Rhine to south in small groups. A pain in our side, could get serious.*

January 6	*In the latrine this morning, I had a lengthy chat with General Townsend, in charge of the corps's antiaircraft, in the course of which he told me all the things he had done to make his trailer comfortable.*

Nothing levels a lieutenant and a general more than, pants down, sitting on adjoining holes of a six-holer. In the latrine all men are equal, rank has no place, and sociability just naturally sets in.

In addition to the trailers of the colonels who headed the G-1, G-2, G-3, and G-4 sections, the generals of course had their trailers with self-contained offices and living quarters.

Often I did not get back to the house of my Alsatian hosts until 11:00 P.M., but they insisted on waiting up for me. They further insisted that I drink their *Schnapps* and wine and eat their preserves and cookies. One evening Mrs. Hut brought out an eighty-year-old family album that had a miniature music box in the back cover and played two songs. I was intrigued by the little mechanical marvel. The hour before bedtime was invariably an enjoyable one. And when I was invited to have Sunday dinner to celebrate an anniversary, and described to my C-ration-eating compadres what I was told the menu would be, I got the expected good-natured, but envious, razzing and was solemnly warned that the decadence into which I had fallen was now so deep that I could never again be rescued into the ranks of normal humanity.

Came Sunday and what started out to be a lovely dinner was spoiled by the appearance of two Frenchmen from the FFI (French Forces of the Interior) in the middle of it and the taking of Herr Hut, the husband, to Saverne for questioning. He had been forced to join the Nazi Party after the Germans came in. He had owned a little shoe manufacturing plant that was shut down by the Germans. Only big plants were permitted to operate. To survive he had taken a job in the mayor's office as a clerk, and this he could hold only by nominally joining the party, a situation not unlike those found back home in the days of Boss Tweed and Huey Long when a political machine controlled governmental jobs.

I verified the Hut story the following day with neighbors. Later, when we got into Germany, I found this type of Nazi pressure was pervasive.

January 10 *When Hut will be released is questionable, although the chief of the section's FFI is personally intervening for him.*

Heard that Frank Roesch, the executive officer of my company back at Chaffee and a good friend, was killed the other day in the fighting.

The news of Roesch's death caused me to reflect on the quirks of fate. Or was it God's unseen hand directing our lives? Had I not fortuitously been born to parents who had emigrated to the States from German-speaking towns in Hungary before World War I, and had I not then fortuitously studied German in school, I would have remained a line officer in the Fourteenth Armored Division and might now be lying dead with Roesch. Yet, ironically, although not a frontline combatant, I had been in battle for a whole year now and Roesch for only two weeks.

I continued to open letters with apprehension. A letter from my cousin Charlie Maurath informed me that his brother Johnny was hospitalized in England—wounded in the legs, some of his teeth knocked out, and shrapnel in the forehead—a casualty of the Ardennes fighting. I would have liked to have visited him, but all I could do was send him a carton of cigarettes, my accumulated cigarette ration savings.

Humor, fortunately, lightens a little the grimness of battlefield life. Army communication takes many forms. One of the earliest, messenger pigeons, had been used in wars ever since the siege of Mutina in 43 B.C. But I thought their day had come and gone until I received a call from the Forty-fifth Division that they had captured a pigeon with a message showing the Germans were using raiding parties. "What are the rules of warfare concerning prisoner pigeons?" asked the officer jocularly. "Do we have to feed him?"

"You got me," I laughed. "I hear pigeon tastes good. Bon appetit!"

January 12 *The general of the Second French Corps came to the General Staff conference this morning. Made an eloquent speech, filled with beautiful imagery, about the rewards of unity—only to have it all messed up by his interpreter.*

With the advent of good flying weather, Allied air power came into play in a big way. On January 14 I counted close to a thousand planes flying overhead en route to dropping their cargoes on Germany, and not one Luftwaffe plane did I see rise to challenge their mission.

January 15 *A little party, if you can call it that. Played cards with Mrs. Hut, her father (Herr Willmes), and the niece. Then a few phonograph records. The niece, Suzanne, tried to teach me to dance their waltz—not much luck. Must be getting old.*

The Sixth Corps troops were now seeking to wrest control of several towns in the northeast corner of France's border with Germany, one of which was Sessenheim, home of the famous Goethe museum. The enemy, on the other hand, was successfully infiltrating across the Rhine on our right flank, seeking to cut us off, and I was afraid we would again be forced to retreat.

German infiltration, though, came at a high price. Poking through captured papers, I came on a form letter written by an *Oberleutnant* (first lieutenant). He had evidently lost many men and expected to lose many more. To ease his administrative burdens, he had drafted a form letter to notify the soldier's parents of his death, leaving only the man's name to be filled in and the date. According to the letter, the recipient's son was "killed by a bullet in the head and was buried in the cemetery at Gamshein with military honors."

Not far away, in the Reipertswiller area, Nazi casualties were so heavy, said a captured cook, "that my work was easy during the past week. There were so few left in the battle to feed."

The retreat that I feared came on January 22 when we moved to Saverne. It meant the end of my cozy featherbed and my pleasant evenings with old Herr Willmes and the Huts. They wept, embraced me, assured and reassured me I had not overtaxed their hospitality, and pressed pictures of Dettweiler on me, including an exterior view of the house with the window of the room I had occupied marked with an arrow.

We were hampered in our withdrawal by roads clogged with wretched, terrified refugees. Trickles of them rapidly swelled into streams. Some bore on their shoulders whatever belongings they could muster, mainly essential household items. Others trundled wheelbarrows and handcarts piled high with their possessions through the road's maze of potholes. Still others pulled and pushed carts meant to be horse-drawn, but now horseless because of earlier German requisitioning of the animals. Many of the carts hauled bedding and furniture with suitcases lashed to the sides. Rarely did I see any of the fripperies that commonly adorn Alsatian homes.

Of the countless sad by-products of war, the refugee ranks high. As a resident in an area about to be fought over, he has little choice but to flee, anticipating the destruction of his home and often his means of livelihood. Although he is an object of pity as an individual, in the mass he becomes to an army an encumbering nuisance who, in addition to spreading panic, imposes ruinous burdens on already strained civilian services in the area to which he is fleeing.

Not only were these Alsatians sick of the war weaving back and forth across their land, but now with the Germans about to come into

This captured German recruitment-propaganda postcard could have had little effect. The manpower barrel was empty.

control again, the older men, and the incapacitated, feared being drafted into the *Volkssturm* (People's Guard), which Hitler had activated in late September. This organization consisted primarily of boys from the age of fourteen up, men up to the age of sixty-five, and men previously exempted from the draft for physical reasons. The Wehrmacht, desperate for manpower, and no longer able to field units of able-bodied men, was calling on this combination of the young, the lame, and the old for salvation. An article in a newly captured newspaper instructed the new *Volkssturm* recruits on how to dye their civilian suits a "battle brown."

The Alsatian disappointment in our withdrawal, ordered by higher headquarters for strategic considerations, was matched by that of the men and officers of Sixth Corps. There was a temporary but noticeable plunge in morale. We had fought for this ground and we resented giving it back. The mood was, "We've got the Heinies on the run. Let's push on and get the damned war over with."

During the next days the front was stabilized and a protracted somnolence set in, which was disturbed only by the sporadic nighttime shelling by the enemy railway guns across the Rhine, an unsettling reminder of Hitler's determination to fight on.

At headquarters there was now time to distribute a liquor ration, booty captured from the Germans. Each officer was given two bottles of champagne and a bottle of cognac, for all of which he was charged 150 francs, the equivalent of $3. Why, I wondered, since the stuff was captured, did we have to pay for it at all?

19

Tales of Gay Paree

In the course of this lull in the fighting, Joe Haines was given a two-day leave to Paris. Mixed with my pleasure in seeing Joe get his leave was envy. When I was thirteen I had spent a couple of days in Paris with my mother and brothers en route to my mother's hometown in Rumania, but all I could remember of it was the Eiffel Tower, the railroad station, the pissoirs at street corners, and eating in a restaurant that charged extra for tablecloths. I was itching for a Paris leave, but I knew that as "attached" officers Doc Pundt and I would be far down on the list for passes. To boot, ours would then have to be approved by our nemeses Snedal and Holsten.

We celebrated Joe's coming leave by pooling our champagne allotments and throwing him a party. As we quaffed the bubbly wine, I commented that although it was eight years old, it didn't taste right when drunk out of the tin cups that were part of the mess kit. "It's too bad," I said, "that we can't drink this stuff out of decent glasses."

"Hey, look who's bitching!" cried Alex Shayne, who was visiting us and saw a chance to put the screws to me. "The same guy who didn't sympathize when I lost my Mercedes!"

"Yeah," chipped in Rieger, "war is hell without a Mercedes and champagne goblets. They ought to be GI issue."

Warming to the theme, Doc weighed in with, "All the finer things in life ought to be GI issue. For both sides. We'd be so busy enjoying them, there'd be no time to fight!"

We agreed that might be the way to end all wars.

"From champagne and good fellowship," orated Joe, hoisting his cup, "springeth forth a noble idea!"

As the level of risibility grew, the convivial wassailing group, in its alcoholic bonhomie, unanimously voted to present its solution to war at the next world peace conference.

Before Joe left for Paris, I asked him to bring me back some perfume I wanted to send to my mother and to Marian Schmidt, a girl with whom I was in love and would eventually marry. I had intended, and then forgot, to give him the money for it before he left, since he was afraid he would not have sufficient funds in light of the high Parisian prices.

Joe returned without my perfume but offered me a deal. He would give me his bottle if I would give him my new combat jacket in exchange for his old one. I rejected the offer. These jackets—warm, snug, and comfortable—were in my opinion the best garments ever turned out by the army and were now impossible to get. I had recently wangled a new one from my friend Bill Pate, the supply officer of my old outfit in the Fourteenth Armored. Meant for combat men, the item was too often shortstopped by the rear echelon who wanted to look like fighting men.

For forty years after the war, I still wore my jacket, insignia removed, for fall and winter outdoor jobs around the house. In it, I felt both comfortable and proud. Only after it fell apart seam by seam, after being repaired seam by seam, was it finally, and with heavy heart, discarded. And then only after repeated badgering by my wife that "the neighbors will take up a collection for you, if you don't get rid of that thing."

During this relatively tranquil interlude, John Rieger and I had a room in a vacated apartment house a short walking distance from headquarters, which was now located in a palace in Saverne that had once belonged to Napoleon. I was not especially impressed by it, I told Rieger jokingly, because I had been initiated into palace life at a higher level, recalling the magnificent marble palace in Caserta.

During this same period, several officers and noncoms from my old Fourteenth Armored went to the trouble of looking me up, which pleased me no end. One had been my reconnaissance sergeant, a small, bright, wiry boy named Howard, whom I had tried unsuccessfully to persuade to apply for officer candidate school. When he volunteered that I had been the most popular officer in the company, I was moved. "Why was that?" I asked. "Because, sir," he said, "you worked our asses off, but we knew it was for our own good. And you were always fair."

While not eloquently put, it was a comment I've treasured through the years.

January 29, 1945 *A few rounds of really big stuff fell in town last night, 380-mm shells from railroad guns across the Rhine. People excited and ran into cellars.*

The Wehrmacht was buckling in the east. The Red Army was tackling remnant forces in encircled Budapest. In Poland, Warsaw had fallen, as had Lodz, Poland's second largest city, and Cracow, the biggest German stronghold in that country. The Russian Bear had penetrated the Reich's border and was now less than a hundred miles from the German capital. The smell of victory was in the air, although tainted particularly by the high cost in Soviet blood. Twenty-eight million of Stalin's hordes had fallen or been captured since Hitler attacked in June 1941, a sacrifice that Russian officialdom would often remind the Western powers was not sufficiently appreciated. In my diary note of February 1, I remark, *Russians still plowing ahead like mad. A few more weeks of these kind of gains and the war with Germany should be over.*

A copy of an enemy division newspaper captured at this time sought to instruct its readers in proper deportment. It gave the G-2 section cause for a chuckle. The paper berated its readers for applauding a theatrical performance by whistling. "Only the ill-mannered American whistles to express his delight. The proper way for a German to applaud is by stamping his feet."

February 4 *Pundt got sick tonight. Has 103 fever. Going to hospital. Means I have to take over all his jobs, including his part of the briefing at the morning General Staff conference.*

For a considerable time Doc and I had been part of the briefing team at the morning conferences. His part of the order-of-battle briefing highlighted changes in the strength and ordnance of the troops facing us. My briefings consisted of the latest information derived from captured documents and PW interrogation. These briefings, condensed later by the colonel at the morning press conference, provided the basis for many of the stories by the war reporters.

When small groups of correspondents occasionally appeared outside the regular press conference time, the colonel would brief them. If he was too busy, or was going to be away from headquarters, the job might fall to me.

I quickly learned that dealing with the press had its frustrating moments. I presented some background material on the situation on our front to a group of Russian, French, Czech, and British reporters. When I was through, I found that the Czech reporter, whose English was poor, understood virtually nothing of what I had said. Fortunately he was fluent in German, so I repeated myself in that language, while wondering how many inaccurate stories were due to language difficulties.

At another briefing, when fighting was lackluster and the colonel had gone on leave, I casually remarked, as the newsmen were closing their notebooks and preparing to leave, that one of our officers had just returned from a mission with the air force and had told me of an ingenious gimmick being used by some of our night fighter-bombers. The bottom of the wings and fuselage were being painted black to make it difficult for the searchlights of the German flak batteries to pick up their targets against the night sky.

Immediately, to my astonishment and dismay, the reporters whipped out their pads again. "Wait a minute, fellows!" I cried. "That's off the record."

"Oh, no!" they groaned in unison.

It had not occurred to me that they would fail to see that this was obviously not information to be published. Just as German newspapers constantly fell into our hands, so our papers fell into theirs. We certainly did not want to call attention to our stratagem and have the enemy use it against us.

The problem of what to tell and what to withhold is one that has plagued relations between the press and the armed services in all recent wars. The newsmen, demanding freedom of the press in their quest for a good story, are too often insensitive to the military's requirements for secrecy. The military, on the other hand, while believing in freedom of the press, has a concern that that freedom be limited to publishing only information that will not be detrimental to its operations. Regrettably, reporters rarely have an intelligence background and are simply ignorant of what will be of harm. (The naïveté evident in some of the newsmen's questions to General Schwarzkopf during Desert Storm had me squirming in my chair as I watched on television.)

I could understand the reporters' disappointment in my not allowing them to print the story. Even though I was an intelligence officer, I was also acting as a reporter for the *Beachhead News* and could easily put myself in their shoes. The reporter in me would often have liked to tell more, but the intelligence officer in me cautioned against telling anything that might cost American lives.

It was Joe Haines who had told me about the airmen's gimmick. In the course of our campaigns, we in G-2 had frequently been critical of the accuracy of the air force reports detailing the damage their bombing runs had wrought. We would request that a certain installation be bombed, and the next day the air people would report it destroyed. A few hours later a photo reconnaissance plane would photograph the area attacked, and the Sixth Corps photo interpretation team, after studying the pictures, might report the installation still intact or only slightly damaged.

To get us to better understand their problems, the air force invited us to send an officer to fly a mission with them as an observer. This job fell to Joe.

When Joe returned, he explained to us that the pilots were trying to report honestly, that the mistakes were unintentional and unavoidable.

The mission Joe had flown on was to destroy a certain railroad bridge. "The problem," said he, "is that as we came down at it, the flak came up at us. So we drop the bombs on the bridge, we think, and shag ass out of there before we buy the farm. We look back and see a lot of smoke, and the pilot honestly thinks we hit the bridge. Maybe we did, and maybe we didn't. Maybe there's a little wishful thinking. It all happens so fast! But the flyboys are doing the best they can."

The night of February 4, to remind us that they were still a presence to be reckoned with, the Germans lobbed two 280-mm shells into

town. One slammed into some buildings not far from the one in which
Rieger and I were staying, reminding us that at this late stage in the
war we could still become casualties. Arriving at the office in the
morning, I found one of the windows broken and a piece of shrapnel in
the room near my desk. *Almost have the feeling*, reads my diary, *the
Germans are gunning for me personally.*

There were other ways to be killed. At night, as we walked from our
palace office through the black and deserted street to our room in the
empty apartment building, we sometimes speculated on how easily we
could be stabbed in the back. We knew from captured documents that
the Germans were infiltrating men with such missions.

Back in America there were cautionary slogans such as "Loose lips
sink ships." The Germans had similar slogans. One of the most graphic
was the shadow of a sombrero-hatted man painted on walls in public
places. Beneath the figure was the inscription "Feind hört mit" (The
enemy is listening too). What it did not warn was that we were also
reading. Among papers taken from a dead soldier was a letter from his
girlfriend in a women's auxiliary unit similar to our WACs. In it she
said that she was presently working in a high headquarters in Bad
Kreuznach and that it had never suffered bombing. And that letter, of
course, was all it took to end that German headquarters' virginal state.
We sent the target to the air force.

It was now deep winter, the fighting went into a desultory phase, and
there was time for inspections and ceremonies. So it was no surprise
when General Brooks, the new corps commander, popped into our office on a tour of inspection. After asking what I had been doing in civilian life, he asked me some questions about the knitting business, of
which he was somewhat knowledgeable, having a friend in the business in New Hampshire. A tall, energetic man in his fifties, I got to like
him as I came to know him. A story circulated that soon after he took
command, he was returning from the front on a rainy, blustery evening
and was saluted by the two MPs guarding the headquarters entrance.
Noticing that one of the men was not wearing galoshes, he asked the
reason why.

"I don't have any, sir," said the guard.

"Why not?" asked Brooks.

"None issued to me, sir."

"Put your foot out," said Brooks.

The general placed his foot alongside and saw they were about the same size. "Here," he said, "take these," and stripped off his own galoshes and handed them to the MP.

Little stories such as this spread rapidly and did much to give the GIs the feeling that the general cared about his troops.

With the ceremony season in swing, the Seventh Army commander, General Patch, inspected corps headquarters, stepping into our office for a few minutes before going out to the palace grounds. There, in a most appropriate setting, in elaborate, colorful ceremonies conducted with Gallic flair, General Charles de Gaulle decorated him and General Devers, commander of the Sixth Army Group. Tunisian, British, American, and foreign legion troops in "spit and polish" condition stood stiffly at attention as bands played and banners flew. Amplified oratory, larded with phrases the speakers hoped would go down in history, swept over the captive audience.

As I took in all the razzle-dazzle and overblown rhetoric, some of it little more than eloquent vacuity, I reflected once again on who the true heroes were: the thousands of unbemedaled young men moldering in graves along the battle routes. No flowery blather would return them to life.

February 13   *Reading Ernie Pyle's book,* Here Is Your War. *Quite good. He catches the spirit. Nothing phony in it anywhere.*

The front continued quiet, so inactive that when I called the G-2 section of the division that had captured the carrier pigeon, the officer said, "It's so dead here even the pigeons are coming in with their motors off." And this suited us all. Leaves to Paris were being granted liberally. The last extended period of relaxation had been in Naples six months earlier, so the passes were highly valued by the hordes of youthful libidinous soldiers, who were less intent on acquiring a patina of European culture than experiencing the fleshpots of gay Paree.

On their return, the lucky recipients of these passes complained about the high cost of Paris, but all had stories of their adventures, many having to do with female conquests, as was to be expected. How many were true, and how many were the products of fertile imaginations, was hard to tell.

One, though, had the unquestioned ring of truth. A noncom in the operations section told me he had wandered into a nightclub, but found no girl to dance with. All were taken. But at one table a pretty girl sat with two civilians, the men deep in conversation and ignoring the girl. "So, Lieutenant," he said, "when the band began another number, I figured what the hell, what have I got to lose?"

He crossed the floor and in his deplorable French asked the girl to dance, expecting protests from the men. The men, however, paid no attention, and the girl, who spoke a bit of English, rose and joined him on the dance floor. They danced away the entire evening number after number. To the soldier's puzzlement, the men never objected.

Eventually he got around to, "Voulez-vous couchez avec moi?" "And what happened?" I asked.

"You won't believe it, sir," he said, in deep disgust. "She points to one of the guys at the table and says, 'I dunt zink my husband would like eet.'"

"Yeah, Sarge," I commiserated, trying to check my laughter, "some married women can be tough."

"Sure," he replied indignantly, "but how was I to know she was married? She wasn't wearing a ring. That friggin' Frenchy should have spoke up instead of letting me waste the whole goddamn night. I only had a two-day pass!"

February 14 *Had my first real exercise in a year. Hiked with Captain Paul Whiston, the British photo interpretation officer, to the Hohbarr, a chapel and local point of interest overlooking the surrounding country, about five kilometers away.*

Played volleyball in afternoon, G-2 against G-3. Even Colonel Langevin played. Everybody is relaxing now. Both we and the Germans are doing nothing.

Because the G-2 and G-3 sections worked so closely together, there was considerable camaraderie and somewhat frequent late night "birthday" parties, at several of which an officer named Shorty was the host. Sometimes he had two or three "birthdays" in a month.

Shorty, who came by his nickname for the obvious reason, was a hard-working, conscientious major in the operations section and was a whisky taster by profession in civilian life. At parties, though, he drank little, fearing it would affect his nose and palate and harm his civilian work once he returned home.

February 15 *We opened an officers' club in town with a dance. About 20 Alsatian girls came, in addition to a few nurses, a few Red Cross gals, and the French mistress of one of the majors. He has somehow carted her along for a couple months. All the generals attended. Quite successful.*

February 16 *The Germans shelled Saverne with one of their biggest guns, a 380-mm railroad cannon. They were aiming at our headquarters, the main installation in town, and shot 13 shells in between 4:15 and 5:15 A.M. Five hit the CP grounds, wounding two MPs. None hit the building itself, although windows in the CP and all over town were shattered by the blasts. Elsewhere in town nine people were killed.*
   Rieger and I roomed together. I slept through the first few shells. He awoke, got dressed, awakened me, and told me of the shelling and claimed I was crazy when I refused to get out of bed and run with him to a shelter. He claims I have no nerves.

I was snugly ensconced in the down sleeping bag my parents had sent me, its warmth further captured by being kept within the regular officer's bedding roll. The thought of forsaking this cocoon of comfort for a cold cellar in midwinter was prohibitive. But not to head for the cellar was stupid. Railroad cannon firing 380-mm shells are not peashooters.

February 17 *Colonel Dixon told Captain Snedal to try to arrange with army headquarters to get me a few days leave in Paris. The colonel also told me he would like to recommend my promotion, but since I am assigned to MIS and since I fall under their "must be eleven months in grade" restriction, he sees no way to do it. He suggests I take up the matter with MIS headquarters in Paris.*

February 18 *Army headquarters called. My leave was approved.*
   Drove to Paris with one of my sergeants, Rothschild. When we got to army headquarters to pick up the orders, we found we had a flat.

Changing to the spare and getting the flat fixed cost us half an hour. Then, after driving for two hours, we developed electrical troubles, a short circuit that cost us three hours. There was no ordnance outfit around, the nearest one 20 miles away. I stopped the first army truck that came along and got dropped off at Ordnance. It was near an airport, so I made inquiries about hitching plane rides to Paris and leaving the jeep. But they were willing to take only me, not Rothschild. So that was out. Went back to the jeep with a mechanic, and he couldn't find the trouble until he pulled a few wires and she suddenly started up. We drove on and got to within 35 miles of Paris at 8:30 in the evening and put up at a small hotel for the night. By that time I was dead tired, and having had little sleep the night before when I was on night duty and the Germans threw four 380-mm shells at the CP— which kept General Palmer in the War Room half the night. I felt like saying, "Damn it, General, go to bed so I can get some sleep!"

When the fighting was light, as it was at this time, the G-2 and G-3 duty officers, each with his desk and phone at opposite ends of the large detailed map, would alternately take catnaps under the map while the one stayed on watch, waking the sleeper if his phone rang and he didn't hear it.

February 19   *After a typical French breakfast consisting of black ersatz coffee and a roll, arrived in Paris at 10:00 A.M. Dropped off Rothschild, then drove to the American-Russian Liaison Officers School to see Alex Shayne, who is studying there. We laughed together for a couple hours as we reminisced. The girls in Paris use makeup to an extreme, but all in all quite pretty, quite chic in spite of wartime deprivations.*

Got billeted in a hotel near the center of town, the Hotel Haussmann. Room was cold. No coal in Paris. Seems ironic that for the comforts of heat and hot water you have to go into the field.

Got my meals in a Red Cross officers' club—a converted gambling house—very pretty. Shopping prices terrifically high—inflation.

In Paris the subway is excellent. Much more practical than the New York lines. Service is good, the subway crowd greater but more cheerful. Heard no gripes about pushing.

In evening I went to a dance in the Red Cross Club. Felt good to be

dressed formally. First time in fifteen months that I have worn my
blouse and pinks.

("Pinks" refers to the officers' formal gray trousers, which had a
pinkish cast.)

After the dance, which ended at 11:00 P.M.—the time the Metro
stops running—I went to the world-renowned Montmartre section. It's
an artistic and amusement center, much as Greenwich Village in New
York—and went to the famous Moulin Rouge. It was similar to a large
American nightclub. A good orchestra and big dance floor, no food but
liquor, and many women around waiting to be picked up. I ordered a
glass of cognac. Cost 95 francs ($1.90) and at that moment I had the
whimsical thought that Sergeant Allen's spending $190 in two days
was skimping.

The American serviceman, and particularly the private with his
salary of twenty-one dollars a month before deductions, did not have
to be profligate before running out of money.

The next day I headed for MIS Headquarters where I talked to
Colonel Harper, the big boy there, about my situation and asked what
could be done about it. He assured me a reorganization was in process,
but for the moment nothing could be done.

That evening I went with Alex to the Folies-Bergère. It was a beautiful show, much like the Ziegfeld Follies in New York, although better, characterized by beautiful girls and breathtaking sets. But we felt
we had seen much of it before in a *folies* in Algiers.

Since I had spent one day driving to Paris, and had to allow one day
for driving the 250 miles back, I spent most of the fourth morning and
afternoon visiting the usual tourist spots. While crossing the Seine
River over the Pont Alexandre to where my jeep was parked at Les In-
valides, I noticed two magnificent buildings on either side of the street.
I consulted my city map. They were the Grand-Palais and the Petit-
Palais. In the main entrance of the Petit-Palais was a sign: PRO STA-
TION. I looked at it in disbelief. "The American mark on Paris!" I muttered.

PRO stations, where the soldier could get condoms and postcoital
prophylaxis, were strategically placed in areas where GIs went for entertainment.

On the ride back to headquarters, I was haunted by what I felt was the impropriety of having a PRO station in what I believed must be a historic building. Despite all efforts to banish from my mind the jingling phrases and pictures evoked, I could not. By the time we pulled into headquarters I had committed a little doggerel to memory.

A Tale of Paris
As I wandered thru the streets of gay Paree,
Just to gawk and see what I could see,
My questing gaze did fall in startled observation
Upon an edifice of breathless ostentation,
A monarch's gift no doubt to the lady of his adoration.
And in a burst of happy inspiration
I searched my map for some elucidation.
"Petit Palais" it read in silent explanation.
"Petit Palais!" I hoarsely whispered, rapt in contemplation.
For this petit palais was beaucoup grand in any nation.
And thoughts historical came to mind in quick rotation:
I saw dukes and earls at brilliant balls
Dancing pirouettes in gilded halls,
And beauteous queens and their romances
With roues dressed in fancy pantses.
I saw pretty painted paramours with powdered pearly breasts
And princes whispering perfumed words apropos of lovers' nests,
Apropos of silks and satins, gems and gold—
All the ladies' fickle loves to hold.
But dungeons dark there were for those who met the King's displeasure,
Plus other tortures such as stock and guillotine in all good measure,
All these for those who fell afoul the kingly hates,
(More oft than not they were the Queen's playmates.)
Yes, this and more I saw in yonder palace,
Scene of love, intrigue and malice,
Champagne and heated passions,
And fancy dishes, no "C" rations.
And as these thoughts ground through my mental mastication
I advanced with steady steps and little trepidation
And crossed the boulevard for close exact examination.
And thru its flowing fountained gardens I strode in dreamy meditation

Until it lay before me, this edifice of stirring fascination,
And searched for some inscription to improve my education.
But in the massive palace portals I found instead a big notation,
Explanation of the Yankee use of the "Petit Palais" of famous reputation.
In letters large and bold and black there stood a lurid invitation.
It read, in candid revelation,
Much to my consternation:
PRO STATION

Some day, I thought, as we pulled into headquarters, I'll have to polish the meter.

On a recent trip to Paris I was sadly disillusioned to learn that the Petit-Palais was a relatively modern structure. It was built in 1900 as an exhibition hall.

The Paris leave had been an enjoyable distancing from the war, a distraction from its horrors, although belied by the speed with which we returned to it, often at seventy miles per hour over roads that were badly cut up by the heavy military traffic to and from the battle zones.

During the lull in the fighting I often went for solitary walks along the canal in Saverne or in the bordering woods, exchanging pleasantries with the natives I met. Notes my diary, *On the stroll I met a refugee girl and her mother from Drusenheim. Same story of suffering and brothers forcibly drafted into the German Army. In time one becomes inured to these poignant stories in spite of one's self. To how much misery can the human heart and mind give refuge?*

Throughout my fifteen months in the war zones, I had heard untold numbers of such stories of suffering and of sons dragooned into the Wehrmacht, stories often punctuated with copious weeping. Perhaps the sympathetic ear of an American officer offered some solace to the sufferers who seemed to want to beg forgiveness for their men's being on the other side in the conflict. Often I felt like a priest in confession giving absolution when I assured them that we understood their dilemma. At times I was able to be of a little help, such as when I was given the name and address of a brother or sister in America and asked to write a note telling the relative that the sufferer was alive. This I could do and did, since there was no international mail for civilians.

February 26   *Visited the Fourteenth Armored and my old Trains Headquarters Company. Everybody as delighted to see me as I was to see them. First sergeant told me all his troubles, but philosophically. Good boy.*

Captain Paul Whiston, in charge of our aerial photo interpretation team, and one of the finest British officers I had met, now got orders transferring him to the fighting going on in northern Italy. We had a party for him at the club, and he left with his ears ringing with the age-old bawdy American army songs and the knowledge that he would always be welcomed back to the Sixth Corps.

March 4   *I leave for a Top Secret school tomorrow on sudden orders.*

March 5   *The Forty-second Infantry, the legendary "Rainbow Division" of World War I, is coming under our command.*
Left for school near the city of Nancy.

The school proved to be a beautiful chateau in large manicured grounds on the outskirts of the city. Each of the dozen or so officers had his own room. The meals were prepared by a French chef, who accomplished gastronomic miracles with the army rations, and champagne and other liquor flowed freely.

Instruction was conducted in a most informal manner by a lieutenant colonel whose sole purpose was to devote as little time to it as possible. Dissolute in appearance, it was said he was the son of a wealthy plantation owner in Cuba, a ladies' man and reputedly a West Point graduate. In the morning he handed us mimeographed sheets, after which we were free to leave. We could study or ignore the sheets since there were no tests to find out what, if anything, we had absorbed. To a fellow student I said, "If this guy is a West Pointer, I hope this isn't indicative of how the academy is run."

"Don't worry," he responded. "If it were, we'd still be on the boats coming over."

Basically the school, or rather the sheets, explained the organization of T forces, similar to the Rome S Force of which I had been a part.

When I returned to corps, Colonel Langevin asked me about the school. I told him it was a complete waste.

March 12   *Pundt left for Paris on a 60-hour leave. I took over his part*

of the briefing at the morning General Staff conference. Went ex-
tremely well.

Doc Pundt, with an owlish look behind his steel-rimmed army-issue
glasses, had some laudable qualities and overall I liked him. Many of
his fellow officers, however, disliked his pomposity, with which I had
no trouble, having learned early in our association to cut him down to
size with an impatient, "Oh, lighten up, Doc!"

In addition to his penchant for pontificating, he was addicted to long
esoteric words. He seemed to think polysyllabic wordage guaranteed
the essence of what he was saying.

As a teacher of European history, his erudite briefings, into which
he often worked information about areas through which we were moving, were impressive. (When I once asked him why he had studied European history in Germany for his doctorate, he said that the best his-
tories of European countries were usually written by German scholars,
not by the native historians.)

Some, like me, admired the informational aspects of Pundt's schol-
arly dissertations while despairing of his pretension. At one General
Staff conference, when we had so much visiting brass that all officers
below the rank of colonel were forced to stand in the back of the room,
Pundt launched into his imposing spiel. One of the less impressionable,
standing officers, unable to resist pricking the pomposity, passed an
index card to another, who handed it to another, who in turn passed it
on until it had gone to all the standees. In large letters the card read:
BBB (over).

The other side said: Bullshit Baffles Brains!

As each man in turn received the card, he burst into laughter that
he hastily tried to control. The successive snickerings, quickly camouflaged behind coughing spells, caused the seated generals and other
high brass to turn around to seek the cause of the commotion, as the
junior officers desperately strove to smother their glee and reconstruct
their features into appropriately serious miens.

For the rest of the war, behind Pundt's back, the jibe "BBB" became
a code term among many of the Sixth Corps staff officers.

Doc's love of big words also carried over into his paragraph for the
G-2 Report. Once Joe Haines, reading the paragraph, said to me testily,
"Charlie, what the hell does this mean?"

The paragraph contained eighty-three words. Taking a thick lead pencil, I blacked out forty-two words of excess verbiage, substituted a few unpretentious synonyms, and handed it back to Joe. "Oh," he said, "that's what he's trying to say!"

Another time, when Doc was ill and I had taken over his work, I dictated his daily paragraph for the G-2 Report to one of the stenographers, a fine New England boy with a somewhat effeminate manner. When I was through, he said, thrilled, "Why, Lieutenant Marshall, this is the first time I've ever understood what this is all about!"

In all our time together I was never able to convince Pundt that the purpose of army speech and writing was to convey one's thoughts as clearly, simply, and briefly as possible. Yet, among the daily conference attendees were some, including Colonel Langevin, who were bedazzled by his performances.

Doc suffered blinding migraine headaches from time to time, yet to his credit he never let them interfere with his work, even when the pain turned his face ashen white.

He had strong competitive instincts and was not above a little backstabbing or resorting to the politics of academia. Once, during our breakout from Anzio, I was called by Colonel Langevin to interview a captured German general. Pundt, who was aching for the assignment, was later overheard by one of my sergeants telling the colonel that he thought "Marshall's German was not up to the job."

The sergeant, a native-born German who knew well my capacity for the language, was aghast, so outraged by the disparaging remark that he informed the more-approachable executive officer of it. Dixon, a man with strong likes and dislikes, had early taken a shine to me but had little tolerance for Pundt the Pundit, as he sometimes privately referred to him, and thereupon pointedly anointed me in the presence of the entire staff as the interrogator of all future captured high-ranking officers.

Doc's occasional chicanery did not always serve him well. All in all, though, I enjoyed working with him despite having to be on guard against his slipping a shiv into my ribs.

March 13 *I'm laughingly told that lately at the conclusion of my briefing I look at the general and growl, "That's all I have, sir." I claim I don't growl, just say it in an ordinary tone.*

March 15 *Just a busy day yesterday. This morning we launched our big attack. Expect to reach the Rhine. Going well.*

In the middle of the conference, somewhat before my turn to speak, four-star General Devers entered the War Room. It took startled Brigadier General Baehr [chief of the Corps artillery] a few seconds to get into stride again.

As for my talk, I did a good job, especially on a study of Mindanao for which Sergeant Edwards had made a map for me. Old Jake [General Jacob L. Devers] even smiled his approval at the conclusion of my presentation.

Mindanao was not in France, of course, but is part of the Philippines. Pundt's conference duty at this time, which I had taken over due to his illness, was to give a brief summary of the fighting in the Pacific. My own briefings still concerned what we had learned from PWs and newly captured documents.

With spring approaching and the snows melting, it was time to get back to the gruesome business of killing. Large-scale fighting resumed. With French units making up a part of the Sixth Corps forces, and with French and American generals having awarded each other decorations in the interim, I was given lengthy instructions on how to write the day's news story. In a nutshell, I was to be cautious of French sensibilities, and to be lavish in my praise of their fighting, even when it wasn't particularly meritorious.

Two days into the fighting we moved our CP to our old location in Morsbronn, from which we had retreated in December. Then a pretty town, it was now a mass of rubble, shot to pieces like any town over which the war had passed back and forth.

March 18 *On Dixon's reminder, Colonel Langevin again recommended my promotion to captain. With our messed up MIS outfit, it will probably take five months before it comes through, instead of two weeks.*

Told by Dixon of Langevin's latest recommendation, Joe Haines came to me and said, "Charlie, bet you ten bucks you make captain within a month."

Feeling it would be immodest to agree, I said, "I doubt it."

"Okay," said Joe, "bet you ten bucks you *don't* make captain within a month. Take any side of the bet you want."

"Okay," I said, feeling I would win either way, "Ten bucks I don't make it."

Joe liked to spice up the war with little wagers.

On March 20 I searched the command post of the Forty-seventh Volksgrenadier Division. We had bombed it a few days earlier, scored direct hits, and killed twenty-one members of the staff. The debris was so bad that I had to call on the engineers to help me get at the load of Secret and Top Secret documents, some of immense value. One was a map showing every defensive construction and its number in the section of the Siegfried Line we would soon be attacking. After translation, Langevin hightailed with it to General Brooks.

Since the men killed in the command post had been buried, I wondered what had happened to the papers in their pockets. On a hunch I sought out the local *Bürgermeister*. Sure enough, he had all the papers. Our business over, we engaged in a little small talk. I swapped him five packs of cigarettes for a bottle of thirty-five-year-old cognac, and that evening I had a "birthday" party. Everyone brought his own glass and smoked Joe's fifty-cent Corona cigars. The cognac went over big.

In February Goebbels's own newspaper, *Der Angriff* (The Attack) had ceased publication, and for some time now in the Führer's increasingly shrill speeches there had been no references to the existing military situation or to any concrete factor on which the hopes of *Endsieg* could be based. Devoid of compassion for the suffering citizenry at home and the young men doing the bleeding and dying on the battlefronts, Hitler appeared determined to race into the maw of total destruction. Most of his units had suffered a series of defeats, lacked reserves, were afflicted by a persistent shortage of equipment and casualty replacements, and had taken refuge in the philosophy of every man for himself.

Hopelessness had become the overarching mood of the German soldier. To even the lowliest *Landser* it was becoming crystal clear that the end was near. Five deserters from the Sixth SS Mountain Division, once considered one of the Wehrmacht's best, and now severely mauled by our troops, raised the white flag despite rumors that their division was about to be relieved. A battalion commander of the Thirty-sixth

Volksgrenadier Division, a veteran of twenty years service, was relieved
of his command, he told us, when he refused to attack our positions.

Too, there were some humorous aspects of this demoralization. A
battalion surgeon of our 103rd Division found a German pistol and decided to try it out. He fired a few shots at a hill, whereupon five Germans came running out of a nearby woods with their hands up.

For one, surrender was painful. He was a Don Juan in whose possession was found a notebook with the addresses of eighty-five girls, all
of whom he had known personally since 1941, numbered from one to
eighty-five, with dates as to when he had last written each. "He hated
to give up that notebook," said the interrogator.

"Maybe he was afraid you'd look them up," I laughed.

"Maybe I will, sir," grinned the sergeant.

Our PW count had now risen to 98,000 as we stood within sight of
the Fatherland. The Third Reich, which Hitler on coming to power in
1933 had boasted would last a thousand years, was now coming to an
end in twelve. His vision of a vassal Germanic empire, which would
encompass from far and wide all the *Volksdeutsche* (racial Germans
from outside the original boundaries of the Reich), was rapidly fading
into an impossible dream. But with the death of millions in the military, plus millions of civilians, and the infliction of misery and suffering on a scale heretofore unknown, plus the perversion of thought and
spirit, the Führer had indeed won a permanent place in history: the
damnation by decent Germans for centuries to come.

We were now nearing the demarcation line between France and Germany. However, to get into the Reich we first had to pass through the
much vaunted Maginot Line. This was a barrier of defensive installations stretching along the French border from Switzerland to Belgium.
Supposedly impenetrable, it had proved to be no great deterrent at the
start of Franco-German hostilities. The Wehrmacht had outflanked the
line by attacking through the Ardennes of Belgium. When then attacked from the rear, many of the big French guns could not be swung
around to fire in that direction.

Hopping into the jeep with Pundt and Haines, I went to look it over,
and found the Nazis had made a thorough job of blowing the defenses.

With the Germans in full retreat, at times in disarray, unable to position themselves for effective defense, and their will to fight flagging,
our advance was accordingly swift. We moved our headquarters to Wis-

sembourg, a small town on the border, almost literally within spitting distance of the Reich. After the eleventh day of our offensive all organized resistance west of the Rhine had collapsed.

The Siegfried Line was the next barrier to our advance. A counterpart of the Maginot Line, it too stretched from Switzerland to Belgium, and in many places was nine miles deep. It would have been formidable had the Führer had suitable forces for its defense. By now, though, the villages in it had been bombed and shot up worse than any I had seen in France or Alsace. With the defenses softened up by our preponderance of artillery and air power, we breezed through.

It had been a long haul, but now we were in Germany.

Doc, Joe, and I wandered through Landau and inspected some of the flattened buildings. Once a fine, substantial, middle-class city, it was a gigantic heap of brick and mortar, vivid testimony to the routine trashing of war. We speculated on how many millions of man hours it would take to restore it to its original condition.

March 25 *On night duty. Liaison officer of the Fourteenth Armored came in at 2:00 A.M.—battered and dirty. Took a wrong turn and went over a bridge that wasn't there. Driver in hospital.*

My promotion recommendation bounced back. A technicality. Bet Joe Haines an additional $5 that my promotion would not come through before we had an armistice.

With our incursion into Germany, multitudes of non-Germans, most of them forced Russian, Pole, Czech, and Italian laborers, plus a good sprinkling of German soldiers in civilian clothes, came under U.S. jurisdiction. They were rounded up and temporarily lodged in a Displaced Persons Center, and it fell to John Rieger to supervise the interrogation there and sort out these people for future repatriation or disposition.

March 29 *Examined a library of industrial films. Would have been interesting and educational to have seen them projected.*

Colonel Miller, G-2 of the Fourteenth Armored came in today. In the course of the conversation, he told me one of his reasons for coming was to request Colonel Langevin for my services, and Langevin turned him down. I'm very flatteringly in demand. The G-2s of the

Hundredth and 103rd infantry divisions and now the Fourteenth armored have each requested me.

Joe Haines had a solution: "Charlie, put yourself up for auction and you'll be a light colonel (lieutenant colonel) in ten seconds."

Drank some captured beer, but it's no longer the famous German brew. Now just water flavored like beer.

At one of our command post sites, the mess was set up across the street in an inn. Some of the officers thought it would be nice to have beer with our meal, so I asked the owner if he had any. "Yes," he said, deprecatingly, placing a stein under a tap, "if you can call this stuff beer."

On March 30 at midnight we crossed the Rhine on a pontoon bridge as we headed to our new CP. Ludwigshaven and Mannheim, sister cities on opposite sides of the river, were the most war-smashed large cities I had seen. Block after block, street after rubble-strewn street, every building was a razed shell. The detritus from the collapsed buildings made many of the streets impassable. We were driving blackout, and I came near decapitation when my jeep hit a downed trolley wire. Luckily the windshield was up and deflected it.

Lit up by the momentarily turned-on lights of a truck was a warehouse wall on which was painted an oft-repeated prewar quote of the Führer: "In 10 years you will not recognize Germany."

"Yes, Adolf," I thought, "the Germans already don't recognize it. Your much-proclaimed thousand-year Reich is coming to a rapid end."

March 31 *Heard two T Force officers in Mannheim were killed in bed, knifed while asleep. I knew one from the school near Nancy.*

The CIC sent me a bottle of good champagne. They found several cases.

Again I was dumbfounded by the dubious justice with which many decorations and citations are awarded. A major in the G-1 section remarked to me that the general told him to write up a citation for the deputy chief of staff so that the deputy could be awarded a Bronze Star or Legion of Merit. The major can't find anything to write. We've never

seen the deputy do anything except bawl people out for not carrying
their gas masks.

From Mannheim we moved on to Heidelberg. Dead horses lined the
road. In one area there were said to be over a thousand lying within a
few miles and another two thousand were reported roaming around
loose in the valley. As I have remarked earlier, much of the German
army was horse-drawn.

20

Heidelberg of Song and Story

As we approached Heidelberg, I was struck by the number of white surrender flags flying from the houses. The town itself, built along the
Neckar River and the heights that overlook it, was undamaged, pristine, and strikingly beautiful. For the soldier with a camera there was
a surfeit of views to choose from, including sumptuous estates, a medieval castle, and the famous Heidelberg University. Some months later
I was to be reminded of its saber-dueling tradition, famed in song and
story, when I was introduced to one of its alumni, a man with a scarred
cheek as the result of a duel. These dueling scars were considered a
mark of honor and a distinction greater than our Phi Beta Kappa key.

With the Sixth Corps barreling ahead, the enemy's forces continued
crumbling all around us and the Wehrmacht's combat ability declined
at an exponential rate. The German army increasingly was manned by
dispirited *Volkssturm* conscripts and suffered widespread desertions
and the surrender of demoralized veteran units. No longer did we have
to besiege village after village. In a state of near-paralysis, the German
High Command watched its power withering to near zero as town after
town fell into our hands.

One day I rummaged through a hundred bags of mail taken from a
post office. The search provided an insight like no other into the food
situation in Teutondom. Being sent by the soldiers to their folks were

their post exchange rations: cigarettes, candy, soap and razor blades, their only amenities, to lighten the burden at home. Going the other way, to the soldier at the front, was food, often just a piece of bread or two. Since "an army travels on its stomach," it was clear the Wehrmacht would not be traveling much longer.

In the distribution of foodstuffs, it was German practice to feed their frontline troops best, according lesser rations to the rear echelon. Numerous times PWs told me they had been in rear echelon jobs, but so limited were the rations that they had volunteered for frontline service for the better food.

Not only was all Germany starving, but because of the Allied blockade, Holland too was on the verge of starvation. However, an agreement between the Americans and Germans permitted U.S. planes to drop food to the Dutch.

No longer having the means for an effective defense, nor even any rational plan of defense, the desperate enemy raced around in captured American ambulances and attempted to blow up our dumps and cut our telephone lines.

On a visit to our Hundredth Division I was told that the division's medical officers had found four hundred civilians in a hospital who had been driven insane by our bombings of Mannheim. Recalling the endless rows of buildings smashed into smithereens that I had seen, this was understandable. *I hate to think of the total number of lives wrecked in all our bombings*, notes my diary.

April 4, 1945 *Our headquarters now in Mosbach, forty or fifty kilometers east of Heidelberg.*

Found a sword in the house we're using for officers' quarters. There is a regulation against looting, but looting is going on all around.

We're in a nice room in an upper middle class home, Pundt and I. It is in fact the master bedroom.

We "found" a radio for our office. Everybody is "finding" radios.

Another radio came into our hands as a result of a captured letter. It was addressed to a family in Heidelberg. Seeing the handwriting on the wall, the soldier had written a sister telling her where he had hidden the family's belongings and valuables. Among the items mentioned was a compact radio. Though compact, the radio of 1945 with its vacuum tubes was monstrous in comparison with today's wallet-size transistor sets. Nevertheless, though cumbersome, it was portable, and Doc badly wanted a radio for our quarters so he could listen to the army station and to BBC. Writing out a requisition, he went, bull's eye, to the hidden location and picked it up.

It was over this radio that we learned that President Roosevelt had died. We all had the same reaction—even those of us who had voted against him—that it was an unfortunate time. Some felt, as did I, that in the coming peace negotiations, President Truman, inexperienced in foreign affairs, would be outfoxed by our Allied statesmen, and that a kind of peace would be fashioned that in some future year would involve the U.S. again in a European war. It would be said that Roosevelt won the war and Truman lost the peace.

With complete German collapse inexorably nearing, Goebbels's propaganda machine, to bolster what little was left of German morale, increasingly churned out reports of the imminent introduction of secret weapons that would bring the Fatherland victory. To all but the fanatics among the German soldiery, this hyperbole only served to highlight the desperation of the High Command.

We discounted these reports, but one day one of these miracle weapons did materialize. It was a jet plane. As I was walking from the office to my jeep, and carrying a carbine because I was headed for the front, the jet suddenly whizzed by overhead at such low altitude that I could easily see the markings. Before I could lift the carbine to take aim, it was out of range. I could hardly believe the speed at which it flew.

April 6 *Walked around town, pleasant place in valley between mountains. Beautiful and restful.*

Listened to General Brooks talk to General Patch over the phone. They were using a scrambling device that prevents interception on the line. All an interceptor would hear is unintelligible noises.

Ferguson, a friend of mine, a major, was telling me at noon about the Mercedes-Benz he requisitioned for General Brooks from a home in Heidelberg.

What use Brooks could have had for the Mercedes was beyond me. Three-star generals, which Brooks now was, having been promoted, had

Packards, a car no longer manufactured today, but then the equivalent of a Cadillac.

With German soldiers being captured in enormous numbers, and simultaneously large numbers of foreign forced laborers being freed, the interrogation people were stretched thin, and the heads of interrogation teams all screamed to corps headquarters for more men. In an attempt to allocate interrogators to the spots where they were most needed, Colonel Dixon asked me to inspect the different facilities and make recommendations to him.

One of my stops was the Displaced Persons Screening Center, where John Rieger had charge. It was an old SS Punishment Camp and contained the barracks in which the foreign workers were housed. Rieger showed me through the place. In one building was a warren of "solitary" cells into which the Germans had put particularly tough customers. The cells had nothing but a triple decker bunk in them, and were no bigger than five feet wide and six feet long.

All kinds of people were now here: The Germans were gloomy; the Russians, Poles, Italians, Serbs, Czechs, and Belgians were in high spirits. In one room I inspected, a group of Russians were playing an accordion and dancing polkas. There were dramatic scenes of frenzied joy, and I regretted not having a movie camera to record them.

On my report, Rieger was sent a couple new interrogators. One of the men was Larry Armour, a sergeant and scion of the Armour meatpacking family. Unpretentious, efficient, and likeable, he came under my command briefly later when I was working in Innsbruck, Austria. He had learned his German in Germany, he told me, where his family had summered for years.

When Rieger's army career came to an end and he was searching for a job, he contacted Armour, who had worked for him for a considerable time, and asked him to recommend him to his father. Rieger went to Chicago for a meeting with the father and was offered a job in the stockyards, but shoving cattle around and shoveling offal was not John's idea of a new career. He eventually found a job with the State Department.

April 8   *Some soldier in Heidelberg found a letter in German at the statue of Bismarck addressed to "General Eisenhower, U.S.A." and signed "The Women of Heidelberg." In an impassioned plea, but in* *contorted English, it professed to express the opinion of the women of the town on what they expected in the way of a peace. It was full of lofty phrases and confusion. So, knowing the German mind, I doctored it up to read in more polished English the way I knew the writer would have liked it to read, and we published it in the G-2 Report. Then this evening the correspondents called up and wanted to know if they could send it to their papers in the States and England, Canada, etc. So, ironically, I have become an accessory spokesman for "The Women of Heidelberg."*

April 11 *For a walk into the hills. Beautiful country.*
  G-4 sent over some fancy scarf cloth.

General Truscott, while commanding the Sixth Corps, was always seen with a white silk scarf and, back during the Anzio campaign, had authorized the headquarters staff officers to wear blue scarves as part of our uniform. The insignia of the Sixth Corps was a white "6" in a blue ball. Originally made of parachute silk, the scarf remained a part of our uniform and we liked to think lent a certain élan, not to mention that it helped prevent "ring around the collar."

Receiving a call that our troops had captured an underground airplane motor plant, I went to inspect it. Dug into the side of a mountain, the cavern extended for 600,000 square feet. Contained in its immensity were vast quantities of equipment and supplies worth millions of dollars. Even though the army and the air force had no immediate use for the plant, it was disheartening to witness the vandalism and looting in progress.

It was mid-April and outside there was sunshine and warmth. Inside this bomb-proof factory, the temperature was fifty or fifty-five degrees. This in itself must have been a considerable challenge to the machinists as they forged the raw steel into precision engine parts. A further deterrence was the constant dripping of water from the ceiling. Lathes, grinders, drills, boring machines, and other equipment stood in puddles. Did the workers, I wondered, wear rain gear while tending their machines? Across the ocean, American labor leaders would have had apoplexy, even in wartime and with the country at stake, if their men had had to labor under such conditions. I could recall strikes for increased wages by American unions that were bitterly resented by servicemen whose lives were on the line. Walking about this plant, I had to give credit, if grudgingly, to the Germans for the limits to which they had gone to continue their war effort and protect this vital plant from air attack.

April 14   *Today a friend of mine, Lieutenant Bogart, was killed while looking for a site for our next CP. Sniper got him.*

Rieger gave me two bottles of the best cognac (Martell) and a bottle of rare Cointreau. The Forty-fifth Division captured a warehouse full. In one sense the German looting of France plays into our hands. In France we would have had to pay for the liquor, but capturing the looted French stuff from the Germans, we get it for free.

The provost marshal was telling me today about the "gangsterism" taking form on the part of some GIs. He deplored their looting and bullying of civilians. "We even caught some digging up a medieval grave looking for jewels," he said.

In some units a certain amount of hooliganism developed, not to mention other reprehensible activities. And though looting was strictly forbidden, the rule was honored more in the breach than the observance. Since the GI knew that the Germans had looted the countries they had invaded, and since he had been taught to hate the Germans, he could see nothing wrong in looting from them. When I commented to Dixon about all the pillaging I heard was going on, he was not overly distraught and took refuge in an earthy response. "Look, Marshall," he said, "if we have a disaster back home—an earthquake, a flood or a tornado—there are people who come from far away to loot. The National Guard has to be called out, right?"

"Right," I said.

"Disasters," he continued, "draw looters like shit draws flies. In war all armies loot, some more, some less. Trying to stop it completely is like pissing against the wind."

In France we had come as liberators. Here in Germany we had come as conquerors. In France we were guests, even though we had to shoot our way into the country and take our hosts' feelings and customs into account. German sensibilities, on the other hand, were of no importance, and in no way was this more evident than in the manner in which soldiers were billeted. Whereas in France and Alsace we could not requisition a house for quarters, in Germany the use of private homes was militarily acceptable and swift. If the occupants of a house had not fled, they were given an hour or two to move out, sometimes fifteen minutes, or simply booted out. The house and its contents became, for practical purposes, the property of the servicemen. Looting, vandalism, and some rape were inevitable consequences, especially in the early stages of the occupation. The same was true, I was told, of our British and Canadian fellow fighters. Kindliness toward Germans and their property was not the overriding mood with them either. Looting was considered a less despicable offense on enemy territory than on liberated territory. It was so widespread at the start as to be considered a soldierly sport.

In going to our next command post, we passed through towns that were completely destroyed and others that were still burning. The blistering pace of our advance necessitated the frequent relocations of our headquarters. To reduce the frequency, the newest location was Ohringen, right behind the front lines. In the near distance the lethal chattering of machine guns could be heard. There was the crackle of enemy bullets and the hissing of shells overhead. Our own light artillery was firing over us. It was about the right distance from the front for a battalion CP, all right for a regiment in an emergency, ridiculously close for a division, and for a corps headquarters little short of foolhardy. I could see why my friend Lieutenant Bogart was killed finding the place. A few snipers left behind could also have picked off some of us.

As I maneuvered our jeep with its trailer through the areas of indescribable destruction, sometimes on roads spotted by potholes made by shell fire, Sergeant Rothschild repeatedly expressed his joy in seeing the sights of German misery and desolation. His hatred of the Germans was awesome, but understandable. I thought then, as I had thought so often before, how fitting it was that the Jews Hitler was so anxious to get rid of were so significantly instrumental in contributing to his defeat. A substantial percentage of the intelligence personnel, both officers and enlisted men, were of the Jewish faith.

After supper one evening, I went for a walk through Ohringen with Joe Haines and Doc Pundt. The town was well shot up. In one section, all rubble, an elderly woman was beating out a rug in front of her half destroyed house. "She must be a nut for cleanliness," said Joe.

"I don't think it's that," said Doc. "I think she's in such shock that she doesn't know what she's doing."

On April 20, much to my surprise in light of past disappointments, my promotion to captain came through. Two other officers and Captain Grimes, editor of the *Beachhead News*, were promoted as well. We rounded up a couple dozen bottles of liquor and a box of cigars and threw a party that lasted into the early morning hours. The best drink was the punch bowl we mixed, about five gallons of assorted liquors flavored with grape juice. The concoction tasted really good and, above all, killed no one.

As Colonel Langevin removed the captain's bars from editor Grimes's shoulders and with a big smile and hearty handshake pinned them on mine, he told Grimes to give me a by-line and write me up in the *Beachhead News*.

Joe Haines promptly claimed his bet. There was no armistice yet and I had made captain. Never had I so cheerfully parted with fifteen dollars.

April 21   *Moved to Welzheim. Very beautiful scenery en route. Southern Germany is getting more and more beautiful. On the way saw 30 dead horses just on the one road.*

April 22   *On night duty. Chaotic. Generals calling up all hours of the night and even pulling rank on each other to use the phone first. General Devers called up and told me to get General Harrison out of bed.*

The French took Stuttgart tonight and boundaries and everything were changed.

By "boundaries and everything" I meant the sectors, directions of attack, and target cities of the different corps divisions.

April 24   *Issued 10 bottles of rum, free. Can't drink the stuff fast enough unless I want to become an alcoholic.*

April 25   *Got a call from the antiaircraft people. While looking for a CP location they found the widow of Field Marshal Erwin Rommel, the famous German general. Did we want to do anything about it?*

I certainly did! Rommel was lionized in Germany and held in respect and awe by the British, French, and American generals he had defeated. I yearned to know more about this legend.

21

Field Marshal Rommel's Widow

Field Marshal General Erwin Rommel, admired for his skill and chivalry and, unlike some of Hitler's commanders, never tainted by war crimes charges, was considered by many eminent military authorities to have been the most brilliant general on either side during World War II. The youngest of Germany's nineteen field marshals, Rommel had raised havoc in North Africa as commander of the Afrika Korps in 1942 and 1943. The korps's sweep across the desert to within sight of the Pyramids caused deep despair among the Allies. For his wily unorthodox tactics, he became known as the "Desert Fox." Although they were his opponents, admiring British veterans soon came to call any ingenious tactical move "pulling a Rommel." Decades later General H. Norman Schwarzkopf was to say, "Rommel had a feel for the battlefield like no other man."

Eventually, short of gas and ammunition, the Luftwaffe swept from the skies by the Allied air forces, and outmatched by the far superior numbers of men and weapons under Montgomery, Rommel was defeated at El Alamein. He was forced into a long retreat in the course of which his tired veterans administered a severe drubbing to the green American troops closing in on him from the west. Kassarine Pass would be long remembered in American military history. Though defeated, the German had captured the imagination of the world. Starting from scratch, lacking even maps of North Africa that the High Command could not supply, he had built his Afrika Korps out of troops sent from the frigid German winter to the fiery desert heat with no desert training and without proper uniforms and equipment.

Rommel returned to Europe and, after a period of recuperation from the malaria, desert sores, and stomach problems he had contracted in Africa, served for a time in northern Italy. Then, after inspections of the Danish coastal defenses, he was put in charge of reinforcing those on the French coast and rejuvenating the defending divisions that Eisenhower's forces would have to overcome in their invasion of France.

When the Allies learned that Rommel was in charge of defending the French coast, they concocted a plot, under the code name Operation Gaff, to either kill or kidnap him, so highly feared were his talents.

Since neither of my sergeants was in the office when the call informing us of the whereabouts of Rommel's widow came, I took along Thomas Greiner, one of Doc Pundt's sergeants, and we drove out to the address, which was in Herrlingen, an undamaged village a few kilometers from the badly shattered city of Ulm.

Before driving up to the house, I said to Greiner, "I will pretend not to speak German and you are my interpreter. That will give me more time to think about the answer and to frame the next question."

I wrote a story of the two-hour interrogation for the *Beachhead News*. It was picked up by other army newspapers and was widely reproduced in the press in America and around the world. It read as follows:

> The widow of Field Marshal Erwin Rommel, the "Desert Fox" who commanded the famous Afrika Korps and later the anti-invasion forces on the western front, was yesterday discovered by men of the 216th AA Battalion.
>
> Mrs. Lucie Marie Rommel, 50, lives in a simple but exquisitely furnished villa in the little Swabian town of Herrlingen, suburb of the recently captured city of Ulm. She is the daughter of a school teacher from Danzig where she was born and raised. An intelligent woman who feels strongly about the cause and fate of her people, Frau Rommel talked freely about

Two views of Ulm, like many other German cities almost totally demolished by air force bombs. *Photos by author*

her husband's life and his death, of Germany and the war in a two-hour interview with Captain Charles Marshall and T/3 Thomas S. Greiner, both of Sixth Corps Headquarters and New York City, although carefully evading all efforts to draw her into a discussion of leading Nazi Party and Wehrmacht personalities. "I have a 16-year-old son in the labor service," she said. "Therefore you will understand." She disclosed, however, that the field marshal got along only poorly with Göring and Himmler.

To clear up the question of how her husband actually died, the question was put to her. "He was wounded by shrapnel at the front in France on 17 July 1944 when his car was attacked by a fighter bomber. The left side of his head was pushed in and the base of his skull fractured. The wound healed nicely but left the field marshal with a paralysis of the left side of the face and loss of sight in one eye. After a period in a hospital in France and despite the remonstrations of his doctors, he returned home to re- cuperate under the care of his personal physician, Professor Albrecht. 'I have always told my students,' the Professor said, 'that a man with such a wound could not live.' 'That just proves one thing,' said my husband, 'what a Swabian blockhead I am.' Day by day he went through painful exercises trying to raise the eyelid, but on 14 October 1944, while ap- parently on the road to recovery, his heart gave out and the field marshal died at home in bed."

At this point Frau Rommel asked if the interviewers would care to see the Field Marshal's death mask. It was brought into the marshal's office by her niece and lay in a wooden cabinet with glass doors. The plaster mask clearly showed where Rommel's head had been bashed in. The face was that of a stern, cold, intelligent man.

"He was a man," said his widow, "who drove himself and his staff mer- cilessly. During all the war he never attended one concert or took time out for other relaxation. He worked feverishly and lived for nothing but the war. When he returned from Africa, he knew he had lost a battle and the Army had lost the war, and he was a broken man. He knew that fur- ther sacrifice was senseless, but he was a soldier and he had his orders."

Asked what she had done when war was declared on America on 7 De- cember 1941, Frau Rommel answered, "I read a geographical treatise on the distribution of raw materials throughout the world," she said. "What more do you want for an answer?"

In the fall of 1943, when thousand-plane Allied raids were penetrating the German air defenses, the field marshal worried about the proximity of his home in Wiener Neustadt to the Messerschmitt aircraft plants. He moved to this modest villa in the sleepy village of Herrlingen, a suburb of Ulm. It was here that I first interviewed his widow. *Photo from Mrs. Rommel*

Her husband, she continued, disagreed with the strategy employed in the defense of France and was not permitted to dispose his forces as he wished. Furthermore, the widow continued, Rommel, contrary to all reports, was not a protégé of the Nazi Party. He was a professional soldier and a good one. He was no politician. He made many enemies as do all men with power. He was willing to place his services at the disposal of whoever governed Germany. It was his book *Infanterie Greift An* (The Infantry Attacks) that won him Hitler's attention. When he was appointed Commandant of the Military Academy at Wiener Neustadt, he had never met Hitler personally.

Asked why Rommel had carried on when he knew the war was lost, she replied in a shaking voice, "A soldier cannot ask questions, even if he is a field marshal and commander of an army group. If he had—well, you read the papers—you see what happens to those who oppose. His fight in Africa was hopeless and he knew it. He could not get supplies and sufficient reinforcements after the American landing. But he had orders to hold. When it was over and he had seen the best of his men fall or be captured, he begged Hitler to allow him to stay and share the fate of all his troops. But Hitler ordered him to save himself. My husband also believed that if the Allies were able to land and establish a firm bridgehead in France, the war was definitely lost for Germany. Events have proved him right."

What did she think of the continuation of the war?

"It is insanity! The best are dying and only the disabled and cowardly remain. All German youth has been killed off. It will be felt for generations."

What did Rommel think of the American as a soldier?

"He had, unfortunately, deservedly, only the highest respect. Also for the English. My husband said, just before he died, that your matériel superiority makes our fighting seem like that of primitive man."

As the visitors left, they noticed on a table a German translation of British Field Marshal Wavell's book on Rommel.

There was much more that I wanted to know, but because of my other duties I didn't have time then to linger in conversation. At the conclusion of our talk I asked Mrs. Rommel for her husband's papers. She said the German High Command had taken them, that she had only personal papers. I asked to see them. She led me into the cellar and pointed out a suitcase and wooden box. The combined weight was about sixty pounds. There were about a thousand letters to her from the marshal and vice versa, and to the marshal from military and political personages.

Thinking that I might find papers of high-level importance, I told her that we would have to take the box and suitcase with us, but that I would return whatever we had no interest in.

In several lengthy interviews I was to have alone with Mrs. Rommel in the months ahead, she never failed to rib me about my need for an interpreter. "For someone who does not speak German," she would say, "for someone who needs an interpreter, you do very very well, Captain Marshall. Did you learn the language yesterday?" When I laughed, she joined in heartily. We were to develop a great rapport.

In fact, not only did I speak German, but after four months of German studies at the intelligence school and a year and a half's immersion in German documents and interrogating and conversing with German prisoners and civilians, I thought in German and translated my thinking back into English. This habit took root so deeply that it was not until I was back in the States for four or five months that I once again found myself thinking in English.

April 26, 1945   *I am having the sergeants translate the Rommel letters while I edit and excerpt them for a Rommel diary. It will be widely reproduced and the original letters should wind up in the Library of Congress for future study by historians.*

According to the latest interrogation reports, German officers are now often telling their men to go home, the war is over.

I don't believe the war will last many more weeks.

Just as I was ready to go to my quarters for the night, one of our OSS agents came in. A week before he had jumped from a plane over the Austrian Alps.

I pasted into my diary a copy of the report of my debriefing of this agent because it showed dramatically the German deterioration and the frantic measures the Nazis were taking to stave off complete and final collapse:

Landed vic [vicinity] ZELT (50 mi SE of MUNICH). Took road WORGL, YENBACH, SCHWAZ, INNSBRUCK, SCHARNITZ, PARTEN-KIRCHEN, RUETTE, KEMPTEN to a point S of MEMMINGEN where he entered our lines.

Roads from ST JOHANN to INNSBRUCK crowded with refugees. Party members riding in cars. Many Russians, Poles, etc. among refugees. Also many deserters who are living in the woods and mountains. Italians are heading for the BRENNER PASS and ITALY.

Barracks in WORGL full of soldiers. The 4 barracks in INNSBRUCK crowded with soldiers, Hitler SS troops. No troops coming through the BRENNER PASS which is bombed out. 10 km W of INNSBRUCK is the

Hq of Regimentsführungsstab [regimental transport staff] closely guarded by Gestapo.

RR bridge vic RUETTE bombed out.

Vic SCHARNITZ there are tank ditches and btry [battery] positions under construction. An SS Lt. Col. is in charge of the defense in area SCHARNITZ-PARTENKIRCHEN. There are many soldiers in PAR-TENKIRCHEN. Also many hospitals. 200–300 men from Div VIKING in PARTENKIRCHEN. All approaches to PARTENKIRCHEN are blocked. The small towns vic PARTENKIRCHEN contain all the govt adminis-trative offices. Protected by tank ditches, road blocks, field positions.

Road from WILSO-NESSELBAANG, and from WILSO-FÜSSEN, fortified across width of valley.

KEMPTEN has about 8,000–10,000 soldiers, withdrawing from MEM-MINGEN. Part belong to the VLASOV Russian Army. The Russian troops are not motorized. South of KEMPTEN, W of ILLE River are 12 88-mm Flak guns, which have received supplies of the new type rocket ammunition. Agent saw ammo train S of KEMPTEN which had been bombed by our Air Force—exploded for three hours. Troops are poorly equipped. Armed mostly with Panzerfaust [anti-tank grenade]. No divi-sional organizations—only scattered units.

Small air field W of INNSBRUCK, which used to have 40–50 planes for missions in ITALY, had only 2 planes. Agent saw the field several times and never saw more than these 2 planes.

Morale of troops and civilians alike is very low. The Austrian people re-alize 100% that the war is lost.

In MEMMINGEN agent saw 3,000 assorted vehicles, loaded with troops. Sent E to MUNICH and S to KEMPTEN with no attempt to separate units. Bridges prepared for demolition. 10–11 SS men guard each bridge and the troops there. No desertions allowed, and if bridge doesn't blow up, soldiers are shot by SS. SS has orders to stay behind after Americans have taken a town, and if the civilians have shown the white flag, the SS has been instructed to burn the town to the ground. SS also ordered to shoot troops who retreat against orders.

Rail lines E of RUETTE bombed out. No repairs under way.

Factories and railroads generally not operative due to lack of coal. RR runs from RUETTE to KEMPTEN Tu, Thu and Sat mornings, and returns in the afternoon. No coal for further trips. Food supplies are very bad, particularly in the army. It is the agent's opinion that the enemy will not be able to defend very long in the Redoubt area.

Capt Charles Marshall Dist: Col Langevin, Duty Officer,

T/Sgt F. W. Luck G-2 Report, G-2 Journal, Order of Battle

The "redoubt area" mentioned in the last line of the report, and through which the agent had wound his way, was supposedly a last-ditch Alpine stronghold from which the Führer would direct the resurrection of a beaten Germany. Somewhere along the line, high-level Allied intelligence thought it had learned that Hitler had established such a place, its plausibility doubtlessly enhanced by the fact that it encompassed Hitler's mountain retreat at Berchtesgaden. This apprehension apparently affected Eisenhower's strategy. Some weeks before, he had ordered a sudden change in the direction of the Sixth Corps advance, sending us southeast to take on the Germans supposedly entrenched here.

Conjured up by the fevered brain of some high-level armchair intelligence officer, the redoubt was described in fanciful terms: "Here, defended by nature and the most efficient secret weapons invented, the powers that have hitherto guided Germany will survive to reorganize her resurrection; here armaments will be manufactured in bombproof factories, food and equipment will be stored in vast underground caverns and a specially selected corps of young men will be trained in guerrilla warfare, so that a whole underground army can be fitted and directed to liberate Germany from the occupying forces."

Now that we were occupying the area, and encountering no evidence of such last-ditch endeavors, it was apparent that the redoubt existed only in the imaginations of a few fanatical Nazis and some gullible interrogators who had swallowed their stories and passed them up the chain of command to the highest levels.

April 27 *Our new CP is across the Danube in Austria in a monastery built in 1493. . . . Many German officers now committing suicide. Men often told to go home. Many generals surrendering.*

All in all, in the course of the war, 81 generals took their own lives, 253 were killed in action, another 44 subsequently died of their wounds, 23 were executed by Hitler (most by hanging), and 326 died of other causes.

April 28   *A report, authentic, that Himmler had offered to surrender Germany unconditionally to the Americans and British. Offer turned down.*

Our corps now corralling 15,000 PWs per day.

It gives me the willies to think of the value of the hundreds of letters Rommel wrote to his wife and vice versa, and letters of the son and other generals to Rommel. Talked to Colonel Langevin about my keeping the Rommel papers and letters and publishing them as a book. He said no, couldn't be done, the letters belonged to the army. So I suggested that when we were through with the letters they be immediately and directly flown to Washington without going through regular channels where, I felt, most would be purloined as souvenirs. He agreed and went to see General Devers, who was present at corps just then, and said he would ask Devers to include a note to the effect that I be given first chance at exploitation after the war.

During the course of the hour-long conversation, the colonel placed a value of one million dollars on the letters, "a gold mine."

April 29   *A call from army headquarters press office. Wanted me to interview Prince Hohenzollern and do a story on him, as I had done on Rommel. He had already been evacuated, however.*

Late that same afternoon General "Charlie" Palmer, who upon first meeting had questioned my competence, but had apparently since revised his opinion of me, called to tell me that an emissary from the other side was coming to headquarters, and I was to stand by to interpret.

22

An Emissary and
More Field Marshals

During the week following our visit to Mrs. Rommel, the German army lapsed into its death throes. High-ranking officers were surrendering left and right. I could find little time to work on the Rommel letters. To complicate matters, General Charles Palmer, the corps's chief of staff, received a call late one afternoon from our Forty-fourth Division informing him that an emissary of General Andrei A. Vlasov, commander of the renegade Russian troops fighting with the Germans against Russia, had crossed the lines to negotiate a surrender.

Vlasov was a Soviet lieutenant general who had been sent by the Soviets to offer military advice to Chiang Kai-shek in China in 1938–1939. In 1942 he was one of the heroes in the defense of Moscow against the Germans who were hammering at its outskirts. He later headed an army in the defense of Leningrad, but as the battle progressed Stalin refused to allow him to retreat to a more defensible position, causing the annihilation of his army and his own capture.

Feeling deeply that communism was worse than nazism, and hoping to set up a free Russia after the defeat of Stalin, Vlasov offered his services to the Wehrmacht. He was given command of all Russians under German control, a unit called the Russian Army of Liberation.

This consisted of 100,000 Ukrainians, Cossacks, and other anti-Stalinists, and he now fought against the Red Army. The sending of his emissary was an important development, and I knew we would be called to interrogate him.

Indeed, General Palmer asked me to stand by for his arrival. A half hour passed and a jeep pulled up containing Colonel Snyder, G-2 of the Forty-fourth, and the emissary, a Major Jung, a man about forty, a little short of six feet, effortlessly graceful, who wore a black overcoat over a black uniform.

Colonel Snyder spoke German, so, outranked, I had to let him do the interpreting between the emissary, Palmer, and my boss, Colonel Langevin. The talk concerned the 100,000 Russians in the German army who wanted to surrender to the Americans and fight with the allies against the Germans, or failing that, surrender as PWs with the condition that they would not be returned to Russia at the end of the war. On completion of the talk, I was told to take the emissary to Seventh Army headquarters with the expectation that I would be inter-

Major Jung and the author en route to Seventh Army headquarters on April 19, 1945.

preting between him and General Patch, the Seventh Army commander.

Colonel Langevin ordered a sedan for me, and with a driver and an MP I took the emissary to Seventh Army headquarters, which, since we had been advancing so rapidly, was now a long drive behind us.

Standard Operating Procedure for a situation like this was to blindfold the man while he was being brought to corps headquarters. On leaving corps headquarters to go to army headquarters, he was again to be blindfolded. Since Germany was now in the last stages of collapse, however, I considered the blindfold unnecessary and removed it after a few miles, for which Major Jung was appreciative. After two hours on the road, I had the driver stop so that we could stretch our legs, and I handed him my camera for a picture of the emissary and me.

We arrived at Seventh Army headquarters a few minutes before midnight, only to learn that two other emissaries of General Vlasov had crossed the lines and all three were to be interrogated in detail by the Combined Services Detailed Interrogation Center (CSDIC). My services were not needed; instead I served merely as an officer-courier on a 120-mile trip.

During the drive, I discovered the Russian major to be friendly, intelligent, informative, objective, and as it turned out, prescient. "What," I had asked, "will happen to Vlasov's men if the terms of his surrender offer are rejected?"

"If we are returned to Stalin," he said, drawing his hand across his throat, "that will be it."

And that was the fate that befell Vlasov and his men. Unknown to us at the time, a secret agreement made at the Yalta Conference in February 1945 condemned Soviet citizens who fell into American custody to repatriation, even against their will. And the Allied media, playing into Stalin's hands, castigated them as traitors. I returned, dog-tired, to Sixth Corps headquarters at 4:30 A.M. Not only was the hour late, but for the past days I had been working feverishly on a catch-as-can basis editing Rommel's letters, working late into the night and sometimes into the early morning hours, devoting every moment to them that I could steal from my myriad other duties. I needed a good night's sleep, but instead I had time for only a two-hour nap before we packed up and moved to our new command post in Steingaden.

There the command post was located in a cheese factory and my quarters were in the vacated home of a *Generalleutnant,* the equivalent of a major general in the U.S. Army. In the late afternoon, when I was counting the hours before I could get away to bed in my fine quarters, we were notified that our rapidly onrushing forces had captured a colonel, a major general, and the famous Field Marshal List, whom our Thirty-sixth Division had thought they had killed in France the previous September and whose death I had tried unsuccessfully to confirm at the time.

List was the longtime chief of the Wehrmacht's training section and was widely credited with the development of the German powerhouse. He had been a planner and chief executor of the blitz of France. Disagreeing with Hitler's strategy in the Russian campaign, he had been relieved of his command and was now at home on inactive duty.

While I enjoyed interrogating high-ranking officers, all I wanted at this point was sleep. Instead, Langevin told me that when List arrived I was to take him to the quarters of General Brooks, the commander of the Sixth Corps, and interpret. Shortly a jeep arrived with a military police major and Field Marshal List. I introduced myself to the German, and we walked over to the general's quarters. And there it was that I committed the worst faux pas of my life: In my torpor I presented List to Brooks as Field Marshal Rommel.

The quizzical look that crossed the general's face alerted me to my error. Mortified beyond words, I corrected myself and apologized. Perhaps the misintroduction would not have occurred had I not been so tired and so engrossed in working on Rommel's letters. I still tell myself so.

Captain Wilson, the general's aide, served tea, and two hours quickly passed. The conversation proved fascinating inasmuch as Brooks was an excellent interviewer. His questions were incisive and precise, and List responded fully and freely, often expanding in some detail since Brooks at the start had promised to keep the interview confidential. And confidential it was kept. I mentioned the capture in the *Beachhead News* but said nothing of the interview with Brooks.

At the close of the talk, the general chivalrously asked if there was anything he could do for the marshal before he was sent to the rear for high-level interrogation and internment.

"Yes," said List. "Your troops took me away so quickly I had no chance to pack a bag. Could you let me return to pack and bid my wife and daughter good-bye?"

"Yes," responded Brooks, "you may spend the night and return in the morning, if you will give me your word as an officer that you will not try to escape."

The German agreed and asked another favor. "Can you spare the captain to accompany me? Your troops are occupying my house and I may have trouble."

"Yes," said Brooks, "Captain Marshall will go along as your guest, not as your guard, and he will see that no problems arise."

"How bizarre!" I thought. "I am surely the first American officer in history to be the overnight guest of a German field marshal while our countries are at war."

General Brooks put his Packard sedan and chauffeur at my disposal, a delightful treat after months of bouncing around in a jeep. After the three-star license plate was covered, since the general was not in the car, we took off for the marshal's home in the winter sports resort town of Garmisch-Partenkirchen, some forty or fifty miles away. The snow-covered winding Alps roads could only be negotiated slowly. Not only had night fallen, but our headlights were dimmed in observance of the blackout. It was going to be a long drive both in distance and in time.

List, I had discovered at the interview, was a brilliant man with a remarkable memory. Thinking that conversation would speed the trip, I ventured a comment about the weather and road conditions, but he appeared to prefer reticence, perhaps even complete silence. "Oh, Lord," I said to myself, "this is really going to be one long, long trip."

Tired from a series of short nights, I considered lying back in the car and going to sleep. But then I offered the comment that I sympathized with his plight of becoming a prisoner of war at his age. List softened. I had hit a vein. He was sixty-five, he told me. And for the next several hours, sitting in the back of the Packard, we discussed his swiftly successful operations in Poland and France and contrasted them to the German travail in Russia.

I told him that while we were in Naples preparing for the invasion of southern France I had been the briefing officer for the eastern front at the General Staff conference and had to rely for all my information on teletyped Allied Force Headquarters reports. "One of the things that puzzled me," I said, "was that the Germans would report the loss of a city or other stronghold a day or two before the Russians reported capturing it."

"Their press wasn't as efficient as their artillery," commented List dryly.

"Just why," I asked at one point, hoping for a more detailed answer than the one he had given Brooks during his interrogation, "were you relieved of your command?"

"That's a bit complicated," he said, "but put simply, I considered foolhardy Hitler's plan for an offensive through the Caucasus passes to attack Stalingrad and then establish a foothold on the Black Sea. When I told Hitler in a private conversation that Germany was mired down in Russia and did not have the resources to win the war, he had Keitel dismiss me."

"Keitel," I said, "the chief of the High Command."

"Yes," said List.

Field Marshal Wilhelm Keitel was one of Hitler's top confidants and military advisers, a constant presence, and instrumental in directing the German campaigns.

We continued to talk about our two armies, and he expressed surprise at my depth of knowledge about the German army until I told him my specialty was order of battle—the study and tracking of the enemy's organization and equipment.

About midnight we arrived at Garmisch-Partenkirchen and the marshal's house, stopping en route to pick up Mrs. List and their daughter, who were staying with friends.

List's wife was a charming, soft-spoken, gray-haired grandmother type, much different than the younger, dark-haired, vibrant, and militarily oriented Mrs. Rommel. In Rommel's letters to his wife, he informed her daily of the battle situation. I could not imagine List reporting the military situation to Mrs. List.

The List house was now the command post of a field artillery battery. After explaining my orders to a somewhat incredulous captain, we went to the master bedroom, which contained two beds. Smack in the center of one, still in his fatigues, lay a GI sound asleep, snoring gloriously. Awakened, he grumbled, "Jeez, sir, don't bagging a field marshal rate me a night's sleep in a real bed?"

I put him and the driver into another room, evicted a GI from a third

The author and Field Marshal Wilhelm List at List's home in Garmisch-Partenkirchen, April 30, 1945.

room and restored it to the daughter, and then settled myself in a fourth room, which adjoined the Lists' bedroom. I felt like an innkeeper assigning rooms to a group of skiers.

The List family and I then had a snack, and before retiring, Mrs. List brought me a bottle of wine, which I politely declined.

In the morning we had breakfast together and the marshal's wife told him that while he was away the American Military Government (AMG) people had issued a decree that all citizens had to turn in all guns and other weapons. List took me to his gun rack and asked me to take his hunting guns, all six or eight of them. I had the driver load them into the trunk of the car together with List's bag, and then had him take a picture of us.

The photograph, which now hangs in my study, shows a dour-faced contemplative List in knickers and overcoat, his hands thrust in its pockets.

On the return trip, made in daylight and much faster, I recounted to

List what I had heard a year earlier in Rome from a lawyer who had returned from Germany, and from reports that had crossed my desk
since, about what was going on in the concentration camps.

The marshal shook his head in disbelief. "Most Germans will never
believe it," he said. "Many, however, will because of the other sacrifices they have been forced to make."

As we neared headquarters he complained that a drawing and a
sword his father had given him had been taken by the public relations
officer of the Tenth Armored Division. I promised to look into the matter and I later did: I called up the officer, put the fear of God into him,
and told him to return the "liberated" items. ("Liberating" had become
the euphemism for "stealing" in the GI lexicon, perhaps to salve the
conscience.)

At headquarters as we prepared to part, the marshal gave me a photo
of himself and his official calling card and posed with me for another
picture. I then called the motor pool for two sedans and sent List and
some other high-ranking officers back to the Seventh Army headquarters interrogation center in care of an MP lieutenant. (At the Nuremberg War Crimes trials, List was sentenced to twenty years, but he was
released after five.)

I distributed List's guns among the officers in the section, keeping
for myself a .22 hunting rifle and two double-barrel shotguns, one a
side-by-side and the other an over-an-under.

May 3, 1945   *Two more field marshals captured. Interrogated both
Field Marshal von Leeb and Field Marshal von Weichs today.*

Field Marshal Baron Max von Weichs was sixty-four, a fairly tall
man with darkish gray hair and thick glasses. He was hoarse,
rheumatic, and I was to observe, a bit absentminded. A charming mixture of a rural Bavarian and a cosmopolite, he was dressed in a blue
leather coat and pants having a wide red stripe down the legs, indicative of membership in the General Staff. He wore the Oak Leaves to
the Knight's Cross, one of his country's highest military decorations.
He had headed the Thirteenth Corps in the Polish campaign, the Second Army in the French campaign, Army Group B on the Russian
front, and when captured, had been commander of the German troops
in the Balkans.

Early in my interrogating experience, I had found that I got the most information out of high-ranking German officers by immediately putting them at ease, offering them a cigarette and a chair, making sympathetic small talk about family and home, and only indirectly delving into the relevant matters. Talking in a relaxed manner, confidentially as man to man, rather than brusquely as victor to vanquished, invariably produced good results.

An expression that worked well when used with the right inflection was, "Oh, come now, just between two officers," implying that, after all, we were both members of an international fraternity and therefore brothers under the skin. And to some extent this was the case among professional officers, particularly those who served in diplomatic missions, such as military attachés and those who spoke each other's language. Deep friendships often developed, as I was to learn.

I set Weichs at ease by indicating a chair and offering him a cigarette. At the beginning of our talk, his aide, a major, kept interrupting what

Left to right: The author, Field Marshal Baron Maximilian von Weichs, his aide, and guarding officer Major Chews in Garmisch-Partenkirchen, May 3, 1945.

he considered were the marshal's indiscretions with "the Herr Feld-marschall cannot answer that."

Annoyed, I threatened to throw him out and make his life miserable. Thereupon Weichs threw him a cautionary glance and, with a shrug, said to him, "The game is up."

After that the interrogation went smoothly, especially when I learned he was a Bavarian and switched from high German to his native Swabian dialect, much to his delight.

"Tell me," said he after a while when all tension had subsided, "what is the difference between a 'Schwab' (high German for a Swabian native and pronounced Shwahb) and a 'Schwob'?" (Swabian dialect for a Swabian native and pronounced Shwobe).

I smiled. "I bite."

"A Schwob," he said, "is a Schwab who calls a Schwab a Schwob."

It never failed after the war to get a laugh from Germans when I told it as my own.

Like List, Weichs believed we would soon be at war with Russia and that Germany's salvation lay in our taking her as an ally in the fight against Bolshevism. He asserted that we would get along with the Soviets only as long as we acceded to Soviet demands.

He was amazed at all our motor transport and expressed admiration for our ability to move sufficient food across the ocean for our troops.

After our somewhat lengthy talk, I took Weichs and his aide to the nearby enlisted men's mess. The GIs had already eaten and the leftover food was cold. When I told the cook I wanted the two officers fed, he looked hatefully at the two "Krauts," slapped some cold canned beef and noodles on two plates, and hacked holes with his cleaver into two cans of orange juice. He was about to slam the dishes on the bare table when I ordered him, in spite of his painfully obvious reluctance, to spread out a cloth. To myself I said, with a mixture of horror and humor, "My God, what a meal for a field marshal accustomed to being indulged!"

To my surprise, Weichs ate every scrap with obvious relish and couldn't praise the food enough. Both Germans repeated that they couldn't understand how we got all that food overseas. The orange juice, to the marshal, was just out of this world.

Much of the conversation during the meal was small talk. Weichs was humorously philosophical about his capture until I asked him about charges that civilian hostages had been shot in some Balkan towns during his campaign. Then, quickly serious, he said to me, "A town has surrendered. You have troops in it, and at night some are shot or stabbed in the back. You take hostages and warn the populace that the next such occurrence will result in the hostages' lives being forfeited. Then, in spite of the warning—and remember, the town has surrendered—you have a repetition of the shootings and stabbings. What would you do?"

I thought a long moment, rubbing my tongue over my teeth. "They don't pay us captains enough for answers to knotty problems like that," I finally said.

"Yes," said von Weichs grimly, "field marshals are paid more, but they don't have the answers either."

As we were walking back to the house where the officers were being held, I asked Weichs to pose for a picture with me. This hangs in my study today.

I asked Weichs how he had been treated so far. "Fine," he said, "no complaints." And he meant it.

I was to see Weichs only once more, a year later in the War Crimes Camp in Stuttgart, when I was supervisor of interrogation at eight PW installations.

After leaving Weichs, I interrogated Field Marshal Wilhelm Ritter von Leeb. Nervous, watery-eyed, and unprepossessing, he did not look like a man who had commanded vast legions of invaders. It was now midafternoon, and I learned he also had not yet had lunch. I took him, too, to the enlisted men's mess. When the mess sergeant saw me coming again, the scowl on his face told me I was scoring no points with him this day. Getting me aside, he said, "I don't mind the work, Captain. It's just that I hate to feed good American food to these goddamn Krauts."

The chivalry that General Brooks had displayed toward the Germans was not found in all soldiers but tended to be the hallmark of the professional officer, traditionally dignified in defeat and gracious in victory. For many men, chivalry was a virtue that had died with King Arthur and the knights of old. At List's house, before retiring for the night, when I had told the officer on duty at what hour to wake me in the morning, he had grumbled about my "kicking a good American soldier out of bed to make room for a goddamn Kraut." For this officer, "goddamn Kraut" was one word.

Leeb ate his cold bully beef and noodles with a relish equal to that von Weichs had displayed. As we talked, he too expressed amazement at our ability to transport overseas the enormous food, fuel, ammunition, and supply requirements of our army. To a great extent the German army had lived off the occupied territory.

When I asked him why he was relieved of his command at Leningrad, he protested that he could not answer such a question.

When I cajoled, "Ach, es ist unter vier Augen" (Oh, it is under four eyes), a German idiom equivalent to "just between the two of us," he opened up and explained that he had commanded the Northern Army Group, and when the decision was made to resume the winter offensive, he regarded it as a futile effort doomed to failure. Aside from that, he was opposed to the Nazi regime and happy to have an excuse to resign, a fact I was later able to verify.

After involvement in the takeover of Czechoslovakia, Leeb had headed Army Group C in the invasion of France, where he successfully attacked the Maginot Line. "In France," he said, "I ran my command without any suggestions from Hitler and everything went like clockwork. In Russia it got to the point that every time I submitted a plan it came back to me for execution exactly in reverse. To make matters worse, Hitler interfered even to ordering the disposition and missions of battalions."

"And since you put such a direct question to me," said the marshal, "let me ask you one."

"Go ahead," I said.

"Why," he asked, "did you join in the war against us?"

I recited a litany of Hitler's invasions and crimes against humanity. When I finished, Leeb looked at me for a few moments in contemplative silence.

"Nevertheless," he said finally, "history will prove your alliance with the Russians to have been the greatest tragedy for the human race."

Like List, he could not believe my description of what went on in the concentration camps.

When I asked Leeb how he had been treated by the Americans so far, he replied, "Not too well. At two o'clock on Sunday two of your soldiers came into my house, and when they left, they took my marshal's baton!"

I pretended to be horrified and took out my notebook for details. Just what was a legitimate war souvenir was never to my knowledge clearly defined. I, too, would have liked a marshal's baton, but only if it were offered to me, not if I had to seize it over protest.

When I told Leeb that his book on defense had been translated into English and was highly thought of in America and that I had studied it in the intelligence school, he said, "Who put it out, the British or the Americans?"

I said I didn't know.

He said, "Don't you at least remember the publisher's name?"

"Regretfully," I said, "I don't."

He said, pensively, "The mark won't be worth much after the war. It would be nice to get some royalties in dollars or pounds."

Despite my effort to maintain a straight face, I couldn't avoid a little smile, although Leeb's grimace indicated this was to him no laughing matter.

In his civilian clothes, Field Marshal Leeb looked to me like a meek, harassed, retired grocer, at great variance with my conception of what the commander of Army Group North should have looked like. It was hard for me to believe that he was on the list of war criminals. Later, at Nuremberg, he was sentenced to three years' imprisonment, but since he had already been imprisoned three years by the time of the trials, he was released.

With the once formidable Wehrmacht falling apart as we spoke, there was no information that List, Weichs, or Leeb could have given us that would have had tactical or strategic value. Their interrogation had only historical import. After we had finished questioning them, they were sent to Seventh Army headquarters for further interrogation and then on to the detention and interrogation center for high-ranking Nazi and military leaders, a resort hotel outside Mondorf-les-Bains in Luxembourg, known by its code name of Ashcan. Here numerous General Staff officers were retained as prisoners of war and put to work under the former chief of the General Staff, Colonel General Franz Halder, writing studies of the operations in which they had been involved. The prisoners turned out hundreds of manuscripts for use by the U.S. Army historical program and in the training courses at service schools. The British also had such a detention center, code-named Dustbin.

The interrogation of prisoners was usually a fairly routine procedure when the captives were of the lower ranks. An interrogator could usually cow a reluctant private or corporal into responding by glowering, slamming a fist on the table, and bellowing, "Ich bin der Vorgesetzter hier! Sie werden meine Fragen antworten!" (I am the one in authority here! You will answer my questions!) The German, reared to mindlessly obey authority, usually capitulated.

Information extracted from an enlisted man was rarely as valuable to G-2 as information that officers, particularly high-ranking ones, could furnish if they would talk. Usually, and especially when in their eyes Germany still had a chance of winning, they were not persuadable. My interrogator friend Henry Heide told me of an incident that occurred in France. He was frustrated by a lieutenant, a sullen Nazi, who refused to talk and to whom Heide took an instant dislike. As a matter of pride he resolved to break the Teuton. He kept the lieutenant in a barn with his arms raised until he collapsed, then he forced the German to do this twice more. He still wouldn't talk. Next he took him to the nearby cemetery, held his pistol at the German's back and forced him to kneel. Then Heide told him to look at the moon—it was almost midnight—and asked him if he wanted to see more such moons. He gave him ten to talk and started counting. The Nazi was shaking like a leaf in a storm and begged Heide to pull the trigger. When Heide reached ten, the German still wouldn't talk. So Heide said, "You win."

Needless to say, this technique was not approved by higher headquarters. In fact, it was prohibited. A very different technique is mentioned in my diary entry of November 16, 1944:

On night duty last night.

In afternoon Petty picked me up—I took my jeep to Ordnance yesterday for overhauling—and we went to the 103rd. They had seventy-five PWs during the day and I showed the MPs how to search prisoners quickly and showed the interrogators and order-of-battle men how to interrogate them quickly and efficiently.

One of the PWs was an officer, a battalion commander, who refused to answer any of the interrogator's questions. After the interrogation, I sat down next to him in the big hall downstairs and we chatted for an hour. We talked about the American and German soldier, the differences and similarities, politics, discipline, prisoners, interrogation, and everything else. In spite of his original security-mindedness, I

*found out that the Meurthe River was to be the winter defense line
and that no defenses exist between the Meurthe and the Rhine.*

Obviously this was a valuable piece of information for G-3 and our
commanding general. It was not elicited through threat, but through
quiet discussion and some indirect questioning. I convinced the German that the war was lost and that any help he could give us toward
bringing it to a faster end would be of greater benefit to the Fatherland
than his silence, and therefore his true patriotic duty lay in helping us.

Interrogation was not always routine; sometimes it was dramatic
and at the end called for a difficult decision. One such episode occurred
when our 103rd Division first came into the battle area and I was ordered to report to their G-2 section to supervise the installation of the
order-of-battle system so that it would mesh with that of the Sixth
Corps system. The same Lieutenant Heide was a new interrogator at
the time, and I sought to help him with a few tips. That night some
prisoners were taken. As I stood by, together with a CIC officer, Heide's
questioning of one soldier revealed that he was from the Second Company of the Fifteenth Field Punishment Battalion. His identity was confirmed by his *Soldbuch.* The reason for his being in this unit, he said,
was that he had gone AWOL to see his girl and had been caught and
sentenced to eighteen months in the battalion.

By the rules of the Geneva Convention, however, his civilian clothes
branded him a spy. Worsening his plight, we caught him in a lie as to
where he had acquired the clothing. First he said it was given to him,
and then he said he had taken it from a bombed French house.

After two hours of grilling, during which we made him strip, he still
stuck to his story that he was a deserter and had used the civilian
clothes to help him escape. What made us doubt his story was a pair of
opera glasses we found on him. His military history, though, checked
out. I knew all about the field punishment battalion.

Heide and I sat on one side of the table, the German, a tall, twenty-
six-year-old blond, on the other. The blacked-out room, heated by a little stove in the adjoining room, was lit by two flickering candles that
shone on the prisoner. It was a dramatic scene that would call forth
some soul searching.

By 9:00 P.M. Heide had filled out a form that would turn the German
over to the French secret police. This meant that he would be merci-

lessly beaten and then shot, no matter what story he told. Based on my observations, French passions made no allowance for reasonable doubt. Turned over to our Gallic allies, this German was as good as dead. I couldn't sit by knowing this would be his fate and yet do nothing. I believed the essence of his story.

The German's defense for having the opera glasses was plausible. He said he had found them in the same house as the clothes and wanted to use them to help him pick his way to the American lines. The CIC man who was present at the grilling was all for turning him over to the French. I turned to Heide and explained my reasons for believing the German's story—mainly the accuracy of his military history. Fortunately for the German, Heide respected my opinion and acceded to my suggestion that he be classed as a bonafide deserter.

23

Rommel's Battlefield Letters

On returning from the interrogation of Field Marshal Rommel's widow, I skimmed the papers and letters we had brought back whenever my other duties permitted. I quickly realized we had struck it rich. The general's daily letters to his wife from the battlefield all began with "Dearest Lu" and were obviously meant for no eyes but hers. They described the military situation, his frictions with his Italian allies and other problems, his hopes and disappointments. They portrayed him in all his moods: exultant and optimistic in victory; angry and pessimistic but nevertheless ever-hopeful in defeat despite the broken promises of Hitler and the High Command. They were of historic importance and a primary source for current and future historians to draw on in their accounts of the battles in the North African deserts. I decided we should translate them and extract the sections dealing with his battlefield comments for a war diary. (Many of these extracts can be found in an earlier book I wrote, *Discovering the Rommel Murder: The Life and Death of the Desert Fox*, published by Stackpole, 1994. Others can be found in *The Rommel Papers*, edited by Liddell Hart.)

After sorting through the mass of papers, I sent Sergeant Greiner back the next day to return to Mrs. Rommel everything but the letters. I did not know it at the time, but it was on that occasion that Mrs. Rommel confided one of Hitler's great secrets to Greiner, a bespectacled, ascetic-appearing youngster who struck one as a harmless boy in need of mothering.

April 28, 1945 *Greiner, I've noticed for the past two days, has been trying to get something off his chest, and last night while we were both on night duty, he did. Told me that on his trip back to the Rommel house to return the documents we did not want, Mrs. Rommel confided to him that her husband had not died of a heart attack as she had first told us, but had been poisoned by two generals sent to Herrlingen by Hitler for that purpose. Since she still had a son in the army, she begged Greiner to say nothing until the boy was either killed or captured.*

I told Greiner to write up his notes for a story to be written once the Rommel boy's fate was known. Some time after midnight, when Greiner was not quite through with his notes, Major Murray of G-3 handed me a teletyped report from the French. The last line read, "Son of Field Marshal Erwin Rommel captured." I showed Greiner the French report and spent the remainder of the night using his notes to write the story of Rommel's murder. I am sending him back in the morning to tell Mrs. Rommel that her son has been captured and is well.

May 1 *The story on Rommel's murder, which I wrote from Greiner's notes in the early hours of the morning of April 28, was finally passed by army censorship and we are printing it in the morning.*

Colonel Langevin just called and told me the chief of staff had talked with General De Lattre today about the Rommel story and that the Rommel son had told the exact same story, adding that his father had been convicted in a secret session of the court in which it was decided who the guilty ones were in the attempt on Hitler's life, and that Rommel had been given the choice of taking poison or being hanged publicly.

As our advance continued with no cohesive resistance, mass surrenders now being the norm, corps moved its CP to beautiful Garmisch-Partenkirchen, Field Marshal List's home town and scene of the 1936 winter Olympics. The views were magnificent. On the way we passed through Oberammergau, and I took a few pictures of the Pas-

From the living room of Hitler's substantially destroyed retreat at Berchtesgaden, I had a fine view of the surrounding mountains.

sion Play theater. It was now May 2, well into spring by the calendar,
but it was cold and snowing heavily.

May 4 *Investigated a building, a hospital, which turned out to have
250 truckloads of the German military archives of all past wars. Don't
know what we intend to do with them. Maybe we ought to burn them
to keep the Germans from studying their military history.*

*Investigated a PW camp supposed to contain all the records of
American PWs in Germany. It didn't, but had other records, such as
prison conditions in Germany.*

*In the camp I found an American girl. A few questions soon re-
vealed she was Marian Tanzler Hertsch, had graduated from Newtown
High School in New York, and had lived in Flushing, a few houses
away from a girl I had once dated. Seems she came to Germany in
1939, married a German, and stayed here. I took a picture of her and
will send it to her family so that they will know she survived the war.*

*Several emissaries from Field Marshal Kesselring's headquarters
crossed the lines today and are authorized to surrender the Nineteenth
Army. I would have been given the job as liaison, but I was away at*

the camp and it fell to Pundt. Pundt crossed the lines with them to go back to Nineteenth Army headquarters and bring General Brandenberg, its commanding general, to Innsbruck, where we move to tomorrow, for the official surrender of virtually all remaining troops opposing Sixth Corps.

The surrender of the German Nineteenth Army was a great day for the Sixth Corps, but there was even to be icing on the cake. Our troops had captured Berchtesgaden, a summer resort noted for its location and beautiful surroundings, but in recent years more renowned as the site of the Führer's luxurious two-story stone chalet on a mountain overlooking the village.

One of the chalet's remarkable features was a room (in which I had myself photographed) with a twenty-five by ten foot window presenting a breathtaking view of the village below and the snow-capped peaks of the Bavarian and Austrian Alps. Above the chalet, reached by a road

Two captured German jet aircraft near Innsbruck. This was among the earliest American images of a "secret weapon" that appeared far too late in the war to save the Fatherland. *Photo by author*

and copper-lined tunnel, was an elevator which rose 300 feet to Hitler's octagonally shaped "Eagle's Nest" at the summit of the mountain.

It was to this chalet that Chamberlain had come with an appeasement appeal and returned to England to promise "peace in our time." It was from here that the Führer and his coterie of sycophants had often directed diplomatic and military operations.

The GIs had stormed it on May 4, and on May 5, with the structure still smoldering, had raised the American flag on Hitler's private flagpole.

If May 4 was an exciting day, May 5 was a frenzied one. The corps headquarters was moved to a suburb of Innsbruck, the capital of the province of Tyrol. It was Emperor Maximilian's favorite city and was the city of Empress Maria Theresa's imperial palace. Only nineteen miles from the Brenner Pass, it connected Austria and Italy and lay cradled by the Alps in the Inn Valley. Damage was minimal except for the area around the railroad marshaling yards, which were completely destroyed. Since marshaling yards were a prime air force target in all cities, I was not surprised to find the area neighboring the yards, about a quarter of the city, in ruins. That the bombings were not indiscriminately targeted was evinced by the virginal state of the rest of the picturesque town, its tall houses and narrow streets unsullied by the savagery of war.

On our drive to Innsbruck we had come on an airfield with two jet-propelled planes. This had given me a chance to get a close look at this new phenomenon and take a few pictures. The airfield was the one mentioned in the April 26 debriefing report of the OSS agent who had parachuted into the vicinity.

The new headquarters location proved to be the Golf Hotel Iglerhof, a luxury resort four kilometers from Innsbruck, with tennis courts, a golf course, swimming and boating facilities, and a Viennese orchestra among its many enticing trappings. With the war about over, this paradise was indeed the place to await repatriation to the States.

Hardly had I settled into my quarters, not even unpacked, before I was called on to arrange billets for 550 of the German scientists who had developed the V-1 and V-2 rockets. The Russians in their advance had captured Peenemünde, the rocketry research center in northern Germany on the Baltic Sea, but as the Russians neared, Professor Wernher von Braun and his team decided their best interests lay in surrender to the Americans. Hence they were removed from Russian reach and were now en route to southern Bavaria where they were to be interrogated by thirty British and American scientists. The most knowledgeable of the Germans were then to be sifted out for transfer to the United States.

There was a fierce competition between the Americans and Russians to locate and take into custody all leading scientists in the fields of rocketry and jet propulsion before the other side could get to them. Both sides had much to learn from the Germans in these fields. Von Braun was in the first group of seven shipped to the States.

Returning from the daunting billeting problem, I questioned a civilian who was supposed to know the whereabouts of fifteen imprisoned generals, American, French, British, and Greek, plus Kurt von Schuschnigg, the chancellor of Austria before annexation. Regrettably, the man's information was not specific enough to warrant our taking any action. And as it happened, it didn't matter. The following day our troops freed them. Among the liberated was Martin Niemöller, a prominent German clergyman who was a symbol of Christian resistance and who had openly opposed the Nazi Party's attempt to render Christianity impotent. He had been arrested and imprisoned for eight years. Also freed was Leon Blum, the French premier before World War II. The Vichy government had turned him over to the Germans.

Of the two French generals set at liberty, one was Maurice Gamelin, the supreme commander from 1939 to 1940. The other was Maxime Weygand, who had taken over command from Gamelin in 1940 and then surrendered to the Germans. To humiliate the French, the surrender was arranged by the Führer to be accepted in a railroad car in the forest of Compiègne, the same railroad car in which Gamelin had accepted the German capitulation at the end of the First World War.

To polish off my first day in our Elysian command post, some headquarters personnel came on a gory scene. A Nazi Party official had shot his wife, his daughter, and himself. I was asked if I cared to search the bloody house for documents. I declined.

May 6   *Finished editing Rommel's letters.*

The product of the excerpts of Field Marshal Rommel's letters was a booklet of fifty-two legal-sized pages. The letters, which the marshal had never expected to see print, were uniquely revealing, objective, vivid, graphic, and timely. They bared his soul as his battles raged. Distributed to division, corps, army, army group, and SHAEF (Supreme Headquarters Allied Expeditionary Forces), it quickly became popular reading and requests for additional copies poured in.

Interrogated a prominent SS general, third in command to Himmler. A slimy rat. One look at the man and you knew he was not fit to live among humans.

While my diary describes the man as a "slimy rat," to this day I remember his face as resembling the snout of a pig. It was the only time in my life that I have ever taken an intense dislike to someone at first glance. He was being held under guard in the basement of a small hotel in Innsbruck that we had begun using as a detention and interrogation center. After I was through with him, he was returned to the basement and tried to escape, getting a block or two away before being recaptured. I told the guards to beat him up, the first and only time I ever ordered physical punishment for a prisoner.

With the capitulation of the German army and the complete occupation of the Fatherland, it was possible to take inventory of the camp situation. Allied forces had discovered 20 extermination camps and 165 subsidiary labor camps. In the latter, which did not practice extermination, deaths nevertheless occurred by the thousands through starvation and the epidemic spread of disease.

As early as April 5 the troops of the Sixth Corps had captured the Nordhausen slave labor camp. A photographer friend in the Signal Corps told me of the horrors within and gave me copies of photos he had taken there, some so gruesome that the backs were stamped "For Official Use Only. Not For Publication." The pictures pretty much told what would be found in other camps.

As we pushed our way deeper into the Fatherland, freeing more camps, appalling reports came to my attention. A typical one, dated April 25, and sent by Lieutenant Brook of our 103rd Division reads: "Concentration camp containing estimated 5,000 DPs [displaced persons], including estimated 600 Jews, in Landsberg. Situation regarding food, medical treatment and sanitation urgently critical. Jews dying of starvation and many insane. Much evidence of atrocious treatment."

A letter I was later to receive from Ralph LoBuono, a cousin by mar-

riage and an eyewitness, whose Seventh Armored Division reconnaissance unit freed other camps in their race toward Berlin, reads in part:

> On our way north we ran into a Jewish concentration camp. We had no
> idea if the Germans were still there, were hiding or what. Apparently
> they just left the prisoners to die. We had to break the locks to release
> them. They were a pathetic sight in their striped prison garb. Because
> they were suffering so badly from malnutrition, there was no muscle or
> flesh on them. Their wrists, elbows, ribs and knees stuck out. They were
> like skeletons covered with skin. No one should ever have to suffer like
> that.
>
> We had spare K rations on our tanks, and we gave all we had to them.
> They ate the K rations as if they were gourmet meals, putting their free
> hand under their chin so as not to lose even one crumb. One man went
> down on his hands and knees and kissed my hand. I immediately picked
> him up and told him that was not necessary. Their suffering had been
> awful. We were very happy to free them.

Typical of camp reports that came to my attention was one describing conditions at Struthof in Alsace. Its records showed that since April
1941, sixty thousand men and women had been herded within its electrified fences. Of those, fifteen thousand had been killed, most of whom
ended in the crematorium.

At the time of its capture, Struthof held 18,514 inmates, of whom
11,867 were "Aryans in protective custody," 3,720 Jews, 1,988 non-Ger-
man civilian workers from occupied countries, 342 professional criminals, 211 "dissenters," 207 prisoners of war, 74 vagrants, 28 former
Gestapo personnel, 18 German army personnel held for military offenses, 13 homosexuals, 7 clergymen, 6 Spanish Republicans, and 5
Bible students.

Its records showed that one to twelve persons were killed every night
for "attempting to escape." A gas-producing mechanism and a dissect-
ing table were housed in a unit marked "Fumigation."

Therefore, when in the last days of the war our Forty-fifth Division
forces captured the infamous Dachau camp and reporters were permitted entry, their stories of the horrors they found did not surprise
me. As early as Anzio we had heard reports of the camps, and shortly
after, in Rome, Mr. Yaselli, just returned from Germany and with good

sources, had told me the Jews in the camps were being exterminated by gas.

Several weeks after its capture, I found the time for a personal inspection of Dachau. Located outside Munich, it was the precedent for the concentration camp system established by the Nazis. Opened in 1933, at war's end it was rated among the worst extermination camps, equaled or surpassed only by Auschwitz, Lublin, and Buchenwald.

At the time of its fall, it had 65,000 prisoners on its rolls, 32,000 in the main compound and the rest in satellite work camps. Over 160,000 had been put to death in it during the Nazi regime, belying the motto worked into its iron entry gate: *Arbeit macht frei*, Work liberates. Every form of murder had been practiced here: hanging, shooting, poisoning, gassing, killing by dogs, and starvation.

Shown around the place by a former prisoner with a cadaverous head on a skeletal frame, I shook my head in disbelief as I surveyed the housing conditions.

"As bad as this place was," he assured me, "it was like a sanitarium compared to others many of the prisoners had come from."

In the Lublin and Auschwitz camps, declared my guide, millions had been killed. One method of murdering Polish girls had been to insert a rifle bore into the vagina and then fire the weapon.

Among the groups confined here, in addition to the vast numbers of slave laborers, were the better educated and influential: clergymen, labor union leaders, recalcitrant journalists, political dissidents, and myriads of others who had refused to knuckle under to the Nazi system. By the time of my visit, all the starving inmates had been evacuated, for which I was thankful. I had no need to see the actual victims.

It was horrifying enough at Dachau just to inspect the original crematorium, and then the newer, much larger one, a long low brick structure with a huge smokestack. Inside were its gas chamber and ovens.

As I pointed my camera at the attack-dog kennels, the guide commented, "Their living conditions were better than ours." The rope with which SS men were hanged for desertion or other infractions was still hanging from the limb of a tree. The spot where selected prisoners, often Russian officers, were shot through the head with a pistol was black with their blood. The great pit into which bodies were thrown gave mute testimony to the scale of death.

As I moved about photographing the immense compound with its electrified fence and the moat outside it, I asked if any prisoners had ever escaped.

"Yes," said the guide, "many, many. But not through the fence."

"Then how," I asked, thinking they had perhaps burrowed out.

"That way," whispered the guide in a reverential tone, pointing to the crematorium. "Through the chimney."

During my tour, working details of SS men under U.S. Army guard were periodically marched by.

The overwhelming evidence of what transpired here at Dachau, plus the messages that crossed my desk about the camps our troops had overrun—Schirmeck, Nordhausen, Landsberg, Struthof, among others—not to mention the photographic evidence that had come to me in the course of my work, had inoculated me forever against charges made in later years by Nazi apologists that such death camps had never existed, that no Holocaust had ever occurred.

24

The War Ends

May 7, 1945 *The European war is over. At the General Staff conference, at which I gave the world battlefront situation, the chief of staff reported the receipt of a telegram from Supreme Headquarters announcing the cessation of hostilities in Europe as of tomorrow.*

Together with Joe Haines, I inspected and rendered reports on a textile mill and a plant specializing in molybdenum, a metallic element used to toughen alloy steels. Captain Hersey, one of General Brooks's two aides, came into the war room at 4:00 A.M., while I was on night duty, and insisted I drink a bottle of champagne with him—which I did—to celebrate the armistice. The general's party broke up too early for him.

After Hitler's defeat of France in 1940, he had ordered that the bells be rung throughout the Reich for seven days of celebration. Now, with his defeat, there should have been an equivalent Allied celebration. And why not? Just days before, on April 30, hunkering down in a Berlin bunker, the mighty warlord, who had once thought himself the successor of Frederick the Great and Attila the Hun, had blown his brains out, closing out a chapter on one of the low points in the history of mankind.

But for us at Sixth Corps, the announcement of Victory-in-Europe Day produced no bell ringing and no other celebrations. If there were any at all, they were subdued. No one got drunk. Nobody danced on tables. It was just another day, but marked by a welcome relaxation. A snooze in the lounge chairs on the sun-drenched hotel porch was the extent of the jubilation. The surrender, so long in coming, and so long foreshadowed, was anticlimactic.

Before dinner I had cocktails with Count Castell, the French liaison officer, and after I had a few leisurely drinks with Major Costello and his CIC group. They were holding the mistress of Robert Ley, the head of the Nazi Labor Front (who later hanged himself in his cell while awaiting trial as a war criminal at Nuremberg). Also, they had picked up another SS general and wanted to know if I was interested in interrogating him. I wasn't. Ordinarily I had a keen interest in high-ranking officers, but with the war over I felt this particular general would be better interrogated about his crimes at higher headquarters. There dossiers were kept on such people and there the interrogator would have the advantage of the dossier in front of him as he grilled the man.

Captain John Rieger was now sent to the German Nineteenth Army headquarters as liaison and proposed that I take over the screening of all suspects—his job, and one I would have liked for a while for the varied experience—but Colonel Dixon refused to let me go.

Suspects fell into various categories: SS men masquerading as forced laborers, concentration camp guards seeking to hide their past activities, Russian traitors, German army deserters in civilian clothes, Nazi political operatives seeking to disappear in the hordes of displaced, plus a host of others.

In Innsbruck and the surrounding area, anti-Nazi informants came out of the woodwork in droves. A list of the city's prominent Nazis was assembled, and for a few days I worked with the CIC searching their homes for weapons. That job done, I spent the next days inspecting and reporting on factories, their type and production capacity, number of employees, condition of plant, amount of finished and raw material on hand, and how quickly they could be put back into operation should the U.S. Army need their production. While the war in Europe was over, the war with Japan was not, and it was thought that some of this production might be of use to us.

May 13 *My first day off in a long time. Drove jeep halfway up the mountain. Countless people in this part of the country seem to go in for mountaineering.*

On this day the 10 millionth copy of the *Beachhead News* rolled from the presses, and the paper issued a Sunday supplement. The editor had been told many times by visiting VIPs, officers, and professional journalists that the *Beachhead News* ought to tell its own unique story. It took the occasion of its first anniversary to do this.

May 16 *Down toward Brenner Pass, inspecting factories. Found a warehouse full of German signal equipment we might be able to use.*

May 17 *Drove to Füssen in Germany, over the mountains, gorgeous scenery. Inspected the roadblocks of the Thirty-fifth AA Brigade as ordered.*

People in Germany not as friendly as the Austrians. In driving across Austria and into Germany I saw a strange thing, a camel on a farm. Still can't figure out what a camel is doing in Germany.

In the evening to the Victory Ball at our hotel. Music and floor show excellent, especially a Chinese dancer, but my blind date, a nurse, was dull.

The disappointment in my blind date may have been influenced by the cherished memory of another blind date. On that occasion, a formal dance at the officers' club at Camp Chaffee, my date was a comely, willowy brunette, and rather a knockout. Enhancing her appeal was her gown, a bit of a sensation for those days in Arkansas. It was cut in such a way that two inches below the bottom of the décolletage, which was alluringly deep, there was a large diamond-shaped area exposing the navel. Somewhat apprehensive about the daring cut of the dress, I wondered how she would be received.

It was a needless concern. All my buddies, plus officers I hardly knew, kept cutting in all evening. In my remaining weeks at Chaffee, I was unable to get another date with her. That evening my stunning dance partner had dispensed her phone number like confetti.

May 18 *With Joe Haines to Innsbruck to pick up Toni Zeleminis, Joe's blind date of the night before. She's a slightly chunky girl, twenty-two, beautiful eyes, teeth, and complexion, daughter of a Latvian diplomat, speaks flawless German and British English, plays the piano, sculpts, draws, and has just about completed her medical studies. A remarkable girl.*

At the dance the previous night, I had cut in on Joe and started to speak to Toni in German. Joe grinned. "She speaks better English than you," he said as he turned her over to me.

Intrigued by the many castles I had seen, but only at a distance, during the corps's advance through Germany and Austria, I now had a chance to inspect a small one closely. It was extremely picturesque and from its strategic height dominated the surrounding area and offered breathtaking views of the pastoral countryside. It belonged to a baron, and before the war had been rented to an American banker, we were told by the dozen occupants, residents of bombed Innsbruck homes who had found succor here. Old issues of *Time* and *Life* in one of the rooms seemed to substantiate their story.

A romantic at heart, I was sorely tempted to requisition it for living quarters for myself and some of my friends, since it was so close to Innsbruck, but the pragmatist in me warned that I might be overstepping my bounds. Inasmuch as we already had luxurious quarters at the hotel, I opted to leave well enough alone.

We then went to a binocular factory and looked it over. Thinking the army might have use for its product and would like to see a few samples, I told the manager to have several pairs ready for the following day.

May 19   *Picked up the binoculars with Toni and asked her to get four girls for tomorrow's party at Colonel Dixon's. We drove up the mountain to a little church and ate a picnic supper of K rations while we discussed Germany and politics, and she told me about herself.*

Her father had been the Latvian ambassador to London before Russia forcibly annexed Latvia in 1940. Her brother, who had also been studying in Austria, had been drafted into the German army. She had no knowledge of his fate or whereabouts, another one of so many plaintive stories I had heard.

25

Disbanding the German Army

Aside from those for PWs, several types of camps had come into being as the war neared its close. The first and earliest of these were the DP camps, some of which were put into operation in the heat of battle. The displaced persons they harbored included slave laborers numbering close to 8 million from lands the Germans had conquered. As the Wehrmacht drafted educated, efficient German workers to fill the military ranks, conscripted laborers from nineteen countries, often illiterate and inefficient, were merged into the German labor force.

Swelling the ranks of the slave laborers freed by the armies of the Western powers were millions of other refugees who fled ahead of the Soviet winter offensive and flooded the Allied occupation area. Half of them were Russians and became an unanticipated long-term headache for the occupation troops. They needed much care and supervision. Ignorant of both German and English and seemingly basic sanitation, they had no jobs or homes, not even a change of clothing or blankets. Filthy and infested with lice, they continuously scratched themselves. Because many of them emanated from regions where typhus was endemic, they were also a health hazard. Spread by the louse, the disease can quickly reach epidemic proportions and threaten whole populations. Napoleon's army in Russia suffered more deaths from typhus than from combat. It therefore behooved our medical personnel to keep a sharp eye out for any outbreak. Fortunately, dusting with DDT proved highly effective.

On one of my visits to a camp, I found the DPs elated at being set free. Polkas were being danced to accordion music. Yet many dreaded the future. Some were restless, others apathetic. In many camps there were discipline problems. Telephone wires and light wires were torn out, windows broken as fast as they could be replaced. Groups ran amok, set fires, and at times raped, robbed, and murdered. If allowed to leave camp, towns were pillaged, armed gangs were formed, and banditry practiced. They endeared themselves neither to victor nor vanquished.

Force often had to be used to return Soviets to their homeland in compliance with the Yalta agreements. Many refused to go home. Our humanitarian benevolence was preferable to the reception they could expect on repatriation. So fierce was their resistance at times that in the British sector, I heard, the Tommies had resorted to killing some of these people to induce the others to submit to returning to their home countries.

Numbers of these Soviets had fled communism and sought political asylum. When returned, the Russians executed many of them on the spot. Knowing the fate awaiting them, some hanged themselves and others committed suicide in other ways.

In contrast, the displaced French, Belgian, and Dutch forced laborers were repatriated without problem just as fast as transportation could be found.

Although Germany had formally surrendered on May 8, and the herding of its troops into PW camps was in full swing, nevertheless as late as May 21 it was believed in the highest Allied circles that some Nazi forces might still be trying to get to the rumored redoubt area for a final suicidal stand. To prevent that, roadblocks had been set up.

May 21, 1945   *Had my first plane ride. Flew in a captured German plane to Kaufbeuren where I inspected the roadblocks of the Thirty-sixth Infantry Division.*

No one ever forgets his first plane ride, and certainly not if it was anything like mine. When I looked at the map and saw Kaufbeuren was on the other side of the Alps, in Germany, and here we were in Innsbruck, Austria, and it was late in the day, I said, "Colonel, with a jeep going over these winding mountain roads, even if I drive like hell, I won't get there till dark."

"Call the artillery people," was his response, "and have them fly you over."

When I arrived at the airfield, a captured German artillery observation plane, its marking painted over with the American insignia, was warming up with a pilot, a lieutenant, impatiently waiting for me. "Captain," he said, "the weather guys tell me there's a storm coming up. If we fly into it, I've got as much chance of finding that field as I have finding a pimple on a gnat's ass."

He helped me into a parachute and we climbed into a noisy plexiglass bubble on wings. Trying to hide my nervousness, but feeling first things come first, I asked, "If we have to bail out, what's the S.O.P.?"

"See that lever on the door?" asked the pilot.

"This?" I asked, motioning to the lever.

"Just put your foot against it and shove it hard."

"And then?"

"The whole door falls out."

"And then?"

"You jump, shit green, count ten, and pull that ring," indicating the chute's ripcord. "Nothing to it."

With that assurance (to him, at least), we taxied up the field a short distance and were quickly airborne. Wafted up and down by sudden mountain drafts, the little plane sometimes seemed to want to fall into the trees. Every few minutes, it seemed to me, if the plane had had an open window, I could have reached out and caught a handful of pine needles.

As we were landing, lightning was forking through the dark clouds racing toward us, and the first drops of the storm, which was to last a couple days, pelted the plane.

Never having flown before, and not knowing how my stomach would react, I had taken the precaution of putting in my pocket a small rubberized folding travel bag. But in the air apprehension had been supplanted by exhilaration. So absorbed was I in the flight that I forgot about my stomach. And when I pictured our antiaircraft guns popping away at this cub plane as the pilot and his observer sought to guide the German artillery fire, I mentally took my hat off to the crew. They had earned their nightly *Bier und Bratwurst*.

After I finished my inspection, I spent the night at division headquarters, planning to fly back to Innsbruck in the morning. In the morning, however, it was storming badly. I borrowed a jeep and drove for hours through the rain to return to corps headquarters. There, after the bitterly cold and nasty trip, I found a message telling me to report the next day to Seventh Army headquarters with my team.

No longer was I member of the Sixth Corps headquarters, and my residence in its heavenly haven had come to its end.

I made the rounds, bidding farewell to friends. As I came to CIC, I found them carrying out a young woman employee. She had just drunk iodine. It was said the earlier bombing of Innsbruck had driven her to the brink of insanity and now she had suddenly snapped.

That evening a staff farewell dinner was thrown for General Brooks, who was returning to the States. Brooks thanked us for the support we had given him, particularly singling out Colonel Langevin and his crystal ball. The occasion offered me a last chance to talk to him. After congratulating him on his speech, I apologized again for the gaffe that haunted me: Introducing Field Marshal List to him as Field Marshal Rommel. With a pat on the back and a mile-wide smile of absolution, he said, "Son, it didn't lose us the war now, did it?"

Although rest for the weary was overdue, it was not in the cards for me. While most of the army could settle in and wait to be returned to the States, for those of us in intelligence there was much work still to be done. The Third Reich's capitulation raised sharply the demand for German-speaking intelligence personnel. The defeated army, now gathered into numerous prisoner of war camps throughout the land, remained to be demobilized, a process that would take months. All levels of government had to be cleansed of Nazi officeholders and refilled with anti-Nazis or at least non-Nazis, a formidable challenge for the American Military Government staffs.

In the search for those who had committed criminal offenses, every war prisoner had to be screened before being handed his discharge papers. To assist us, Washington provided a thick ledger with the names (alphabetically listed), descriptions, and other pertinent information of war crimes suspects. This had been compiled by a special agency from data earlier forwarded by all intelligence sources. Those to be detained ranged from the top Nazi leadership and Gestapo agents to local leaders of the Hitler Youth, the Peasants' League, and the Labor Front. General Staff officers, concentration camp guards, female members of the

SS, and senior noncoms were among others to be automatically arrested. Depending on the category, the arrested went to war crimes camps or to internment camps.

With my release from Sixth Corps headquarters and my fighting days over, I started out, together with Sergeants Rothschild and Lowensberg, for the headquarters of the Seventh Army in Augsburg, Germany. Getting there entailed a beautiful drive. En route we saw in the distance the mountaintop castle of Mad Ludwig II, a fantastic baroque edifice. I was tempted to inspect it but could not spare the time.

Arriving at army headquarters, I found our orders had already been cut. We were to report to Salzburg, Austria, a hundred miles east, and screen sixteen thousand PWs preparatory to their being discharged. Another officer and several noncom interrogators would join me there and be part of my staff.

By lunchtime we reached the outskirts of Salzburg and found the headquarters of one of Sixth Corps's seasoned divisions, the stalwart Third Infantry, the army's most decorated division, settled in princely comfort in the summer palace of the Habsburgs. (As noted earlier, battle-hardened units did not live in tents if they didn't have to.) No one could begrudge this division—which had bled in North Africa, Italy, France, Germany, and Austria—its costly-wrested comforts.

After a meal and a brief meeting with friends, we drove on to Salzburg proper. The birthplace of Mozart and the musical capital of Europe, it was idyllically situated on both banks of the Salzach River and lay in a valley dominated by the snow-capped Alps. Spotted throughout the city were many churches, and picturesquely overlooking them was the Hohen-Salzburg fortress, which for a thousand years had been the home of the powerful prince bishops of Salzburg. Like lovely and romantic Heidelberg and Innsbruck, my men and I agreed, this would be a pretty place to laze away the days until repatriation.

On our arrival at the PW camp, I was agreeably surprised to find the ranking German officer had appointed himself temporary commandant and had the prisoners well organized. With the help of PWs pressed into service as clerks and runners, we screened 1,800 men by nightfall, and the following day we screened another 2,500 men, culling out a good number of the morally anesthetized Dachau concentration camp guards. They had been captured when units of our Forty-fifth Infantry Division liberated the infamous camp. Unmoved by their sudden obsequiousness and buttery profession of admiration for their captors, *I signed their arrest reports with pleasure,* to quote a snippet from my diary note for the day.

Months later, on March 12, 1946, at another camp, my diary entry for the day reads: *Right now we're interrogating 11,000 SS men. These are Hitler's Supermen, many of whom guarded the concentration camps. They are the subnormal who killed, tortured, shot, starved, poisoned, hanged, knifed, and beat up millions of Jews, German anti-Nazis, and intellectuals who would not knuckle under. They are the ones who were Naziism's greatest prop, the perpetrators of history's colossal Schweinerei* [a German colloquialism for filthy mess].

Now, as we interrogate them, admittedly harshly, and faced with the probability of being charged with war crimes and possibly being executed, they shake, cringe, wheedle, and snivel. The Supermen don't feel so super any more.

The next day we booked another 160 automatic arrestables in various categories, among them two generals from Vlasov's army and an SS colonel who tried to prove to me that he was not SS and was given short shrift.

In the weeks and months ahead there were days when my hand ached from the pile of arrest reports that required my signature, together with rank, branch, and serial number. Once, to solve the problem of the aching hand, I had a rubber stamp made, smugly assuming I had outsmarted the system, only to have army headquarters fire the reports back to me "as not in conformity with policy."

The interrogating procedure was simple and fast. Each prisoner was given a deceptively innocuous-looking questionnaire, called a *Fragebogen* in German, to fill out. It required of the respondent a wide variety of information, including a list of all his memberships in National Socialist and military organizations, his associations, and employment and salary history back to the pre-Hitler period.

On entering our offices, the man was ordered to remove his shirt and raise his arms. If the telltale SS blood-type tattoo was found on his inner upper arm, he was automatically detained, and if high enough in rank, arrested.

If he passed that inspection, he gave his *Soldbuch* and *Fragebogen* to an interrogator. Together they provided a résumé of the man's life.

Few were aware of the investigative power of the *Fragebogen* tool and the incriminating nature of the questions. The responses quickly uncovered overt Nazis, sympathizers, and individuals who had benefited materially from the Nazi regime.

The time spent on interrogation, and the degree of probing, were generally commensurate with a man's rank. Among the lower ranks, a cursory glance at the man, the *Soldbuch*, and the *Fragebogen* was usually sufficient to win him his discharge papers. If his home was in our army area, he was given half a loaf of bread and a pound of lard for the trip, and a truck ride to his destination. If he lived outside our area, he went to one of several small temporary camps to await transportation.

When the screening team had a borderline case, and this was frequent, the man was passed on to me. Playing God was never my idea of a good job, but the buck stopped with me and caused me much anguish. Rarely did a day pass that I did not pray for Solomonic wisdom.

The nature of the work was such that one could not for long sustain a spirit of vindictiveness. One could not fail to have compassion for the high number of sick, starved, wounded, and crippled. I had no rancor in my heart for these soldiers, although I had come to hate the system they had been fated to defend. To one who had been raised to believe all men are creatures of God, these lines were an intensely poignant sight. Observing them, a spectacle to be indelibly etched in the mind, one had to ponder human resilience in the face of crippling injury, illness, starvation, and the absence of almost all creature comforts. Yet these men were anxious to get home to start life anew. Marveling at the tenacity of the human spirit, I ordered that the badly wounded, the amputees, and the seriously ill be culled out for quick release.

As Germany slowly began its return to normalcy, and the populace became aware of the *Fragebogen*'s inquisitorial purpose, it became a source of humor in skits in German shows. At one such show I attended—the only American officer present—an actor directed his humor at the *Fragebogen*, and suddenly and fearfully, all eyes in the small auditorium were turned to me, expecting, no doubt, that I would jump up, halt the proceedings, and put the actors under arrest. When I made no such move, the audience became aware that it had just had a taste of free speech, something that had gone out when the Nazis came in.

For the big job ahead, army headquarters reinforced my team with several noncom interrogators and a Lieutenant Phillip Rothman.

The evening that Rothman reported for duty with me there were no enlisted men around to help him with his baggage, so I offered to lend him a hand. To my dismay, among the officer's bedding roll, musette bag, and normal baggage, there was a footlocker filled with books, so heavy that a pair of elephants would have been more fitting bearers. Entry to the house requisitioned for quarters was up a long flight of stairs. By the time we got the footlocker to his room, I was afraid we had developed hernias.

About thirty, classically handsome, with dark wavy hair, Rothman was a professional educator, with a gentle soft-spoken manner. He was fluent in both French and German and had been following a long-time schedule of reading, he told me. A certain amount of time, in months or years, was allotted to different literatures: so much for the Elizabethan, so much for early American authors, so much for the French dramatists, so much for the German writers, the Russian writers, and

Five thousand prisoners line up for cursory physical examination before interrogation leading to discharge or transfer to internment or war crimes camps. *Photo by author*

Hitler's waning fortunes were exemplified by some of the prisoners we were taking in the spring of 1945. The soldier at left is fifteen, the one on the right fifty-five. *Photo by author*

so on. The war, he remarked, proved an annoying interruption to his schedule. I expressed sympathy but inwardly said, in the forthrightness characteristic of army patois, "Tough shit! Whose life hasn't been disrupted?"

He was delighted to learn that the one book I had lugged throughout the war was a leather-bound copy of Shakespeare's complete works, which I had opened only once or twice, and which he promptly borrowed.

The fear that I had been sent a prima donna quickly evaporated. As we got to know each other, I discovered that Rothman, brilliant, yet self-effacing, had been a child prodigy. At the age of fourteen he had written a play that attracted the notice of the New York Theater Guild, but when a boy in knickers appeared at their office to discuss its production, the producers refused to believe he was the author. At the age of eighteen he had graduated from Harvard, and he later studied at Columbia.

Every move from one camp to another required a search for new living quarters. Entering the house, Rothman and I would conduct an inspection. While I checked out the number and size of the rooms and decided how they would be used, Phillip would first search for a piano, an instrument he played and loved. On finding it, he would tickle the keys a bit to check the tone and then inspect the sheet music available.

Knowledgeable in art, Phillip would inspect the paintings and prints on the walls of our new quarters. Then he would join me at the bookshelves, or in the library if it were a more sumptuous home, for an examination of the reading matter. The books pretty much clued us in as to the type of occupants.

May 29   *All kinds of people, from privates to generals, from paupers to the rich, present me with their problems. . . . Each thinks he has a special problem and warrants special treatment.*

In addition to German soldiers, the cage held numerous civilians who had been indiscriminately scooped up. One such innocent was the tutor of Austrian chancellor Schuschnigg's sons. Some owed their incarceration to the German fondness for titles and uniforms. A doorman at a hotel, apartment house, or theater often had a jaw-breaking title and a uniform worthy of a spoof in a musical comedy. When they protested their arrest, because of the language problem, the captor's attitude was, "Tell it to the judge."

On a visit to corps headquarters to pick up the team's mail and attend a dance, I was told by Colonel Dixon that the CIC brass from army headquarters, who were inspecting the various camps, found mine the most efficiently run and productive. He wanted to know if I wanted to be reattached to corps. I thanked him for the offer, but I liked running my own operation and the degree of independence it afforded me. Soon after, Signal Corps photographers took stills and movies of my staff screening the prisoners, probably as part of a training film. One shot was of me giving the German camp commander his orders.

June 2   *Interesting talk for hours last evening with Rothman, my lieu-*

tenant, about professors we both had at Columbia and reminiscences of Columbia life.

Finished the prisoners in this camp. Leaving today for Heidenheim, Germany, on a new assignment, via Innsbruck and Augsburg.

According to information I received at this time, I was to screen 335,000 PWs at a camp in Heidenheim, Rommel's birthplace, and my staff would be enlarged by additional interrogating officers and noncoms.

Among the memories I took from the Salzburg camp was a particularly unpleasant one. A PW searching through a trash box outside my office window picked up a hand grenade. It went off and blew out the man's guts, killing him. There was suspicion among some of the staff that a die-hard Nazi had placed it there with me in mind when the opportunity afforded. Prisoners, I was to find out in the next camp, were often inadequately searched by the guarding troops.

On arrival at Heidenheim I checked in at the headquarters of the brigade that was to supply the guard troops for the camp. The brigadier general in charge, a friendly bear of a man named Ennis, seeing me talking with his executive officer, came over, had me explain our work and requirements, and invited me to eat at his mess.

Through with the formalities, Rothman and I moseyed about. Opulent, with rich baroque furnishings, it appeared to have been a private club. We were told it was the only building in the shot-up town with hot water. On the second floor we found living quarters, and Rothman was about to take a bath when the general came in from another room. Without knowing it, we had been in his apartment.

In the next days one of us would suddenly say to the other, "Hey, how about a hot bath?" And we would go into spasms of laughter. In reality, an invitation to the general's tub would have been even more appreciated than the invitation to eat at his mess.

We requisitioned two houses in the vicinity of the camp. In the one, whose owners had young children, we ran across a shelf of school books. One of the volumes, an elementary mathematics text, had examples such as this: An Aryan housewife goes to the Jewish butcher to buy a kilo of meat. The Jewish butcher has a dishonest scale and the kilo of meat she trustingly sought weighs really only seven-eighths of a kilo. By what percentage did the dastardly Jewish butcher cheat the trusting Aryan housewife? Much of the book contained pages of similar anti-Jewish propaganda designed to instill prejudice in the young while simultaneously teaching mathematics.

The second house, meant as billeting for the officers, was an upscale one. As in many of the more luxurious homes, there was a wall of antlers and a large skin, a favorite type of decoration in such residences: proud, conspicuous, and irrefutable proof of the owner's hunting skills.

This house was owned by a Frau Trost, a stately, cultured woman in her mid thirties, who had studied painting in Paris and spoke excellent French, a language with which Phillip, whose mother was French, was especially comfortable. Frau Trost was artistically talented, and part of the decor of the house consisted of her paintings and etchings.

One evening, having just drawn my PX rations, I offered her a cigarette and invited her to share my bottle of American 3.2-percent-alcohol beer. As we smoked, she sipped the beer critically, commenting that it did not match the prewar German beers but was better than the ersatz brew currently produced.

Asked about her husband, she told me he was a major in the army, had survived the war, and was now a prisoner. After a few searching questions to determine if there were any impediments to his early release, she revealed that he had a middling rank in the Nazi Party. "Why?" I asked. "You appear much too intelligent a woman, and I assume the same of your husband, to have swallowed the claptrap spouted by Hitler and Goebbels."

She sighed. "You would have had to live here to understand. My husband and my father-in-law could not have kept their business unless they kept quiet and joined the party."

Her response would have been understood by Betty Trippe, the wife of Juan Trippe, founder of Pan American Air Lines, who noted in her diary in 1936 when Pan Am was negotiating in Berlin for landing rights: "Our German friends were tight-lipped concerning any reference to Hitler and the political situation. They did say there was no opposition party because anyone who dared to speak against the government was reported and severely dealt with, which often meant death or a mysterious disappearance."

The Trosts owned the local brick and roof-tile kilns, whose products were in great demand then and would be for years to come as the Germans repaired their war-damaged homes, factories, and public buildings.

These were typical of the large houses we requisitioned as living quarters. Because the cities were largely demolished, we usually found such houses in the less damaged outskirts. *Photo by author*

The story was not dissimilar to that of my host Herr Hut in Alsace. Nor was it unlike the story of a Herr Ohl I was to meet. A highly placed executive with the Würtemmberg Metallwaren Fabrik, with a rank in the Nazi Party, he had, at the risk of his life, helped Sergeant Joe Lowensberg and his family escape from Germany.

Leica cameras were among the most sought-after trophies in World War II. It seemed every soldier, from private to general, badly wanted one of these much-vaunted instruments, which were renowned at the time as the best 35-millimeter cameras in the world. When the Germans learned of the GI hunger, the cameras were often hidden in fear of expropriation. I, too, would have liked one, so I asked Frau Trost if she had any idea where I might get one. To my surprise she replied that she had one, a late model, and I could have it. "It is hidden in the coal pile," she said, "I will get it for you in the morning."

"No," I said, "I can't accept yours. But thank you."

"But I want to give it to you," she insisted. "You have been very kind to let us stay here."

Besides herself there were two young children and her mother. In view of much callous and sometimes brutal GI behavior in those first weeks after the end of hostilities, I could understand her gratitude. I still refused the camera, even though Military Government had earlier ordered that all cameras be surrendered. Not until I was about to leave Germany did I finally get a Leica.

Although it violated security rules, I could never bring myself to throw families out of their homes. The houses we took over were generally large ones. My practice was to take the space we needed and confine the family to the other rooms.

A call from army headquarters informed me that the first batch of prisoners would not arrive for another seven or eight days. This gave us in effect a week's vacation. During this time I went to corps headquarters for supper and a party for Colonel Langevin, my boss for seventeen months, who was going back to the States. As I bid him farewell, he praised me lavishly, which I appreciated since effusiveness was not normally a part of his personality. Inwardly, though, I was nettled that he had not recommended me for the Bronze Star. My attitude toward medals had not changed, but since Bronze Stars were being awarded to some of the officers with whom I had worked, I was disappointed that I had not been awarded the recognition that I felt was my due. What I did not know at the time was that the colonel had indeed recommended me, but because I was no longer attached to corps and moved about so often, no medal had reached me. Eventually two Bronze Stars caught up with me, one a few weeks later at corps headquarters and the other months later in the repatriation process—each with the same citation.

A few days into the work at the Heidenheim camp, a German officer asked his interrogator if he was obliged to surrender his pistol. Told of this, I was angered by the sloppy searching of the PWs, and recalling the hand grenade incident at the Salzburg camp, I selected a strapping German sergeant and stationed him at the entrance to the interrogation offices with strict orders to collect all weapons. In short order he had half a dozen pistols and a mess of knives, daggers, and cameras.

July 1 *Rothman had an accident, overturned jeep, nobody seriously hurt. Investigated scene. Found driver, Lowensberg, had hit a big rock on the shoulder of the road.*

July 3 *To Augsburg with Rothman. On the way back, while driving the BMW at 60 mph on the wet road, a farmer's horse ahead started to bolt and buck as he heard us coming. I swerved to avoid hitting him and the car skidded crazily. For a moment it seemed our number was up. We wound up in a ditch, almost overturned. Neither Rothman nor I was hurt, and I managed to get the car out without damage.*

Somewhere in the Pentagon archives there must be a breakdown of the number of casualties that were battle related and those that were simply traffic related. In the course of the thousands of miles I drove in the pursuit of my work, plus those not work related, and for which I often used a BMW confiscated from a captured German major, I was involved in several accidents. One of the most serious occurred when I was driving with a Lieutenant Hecht and Sergeant Rothschild and headed for Bad Schwalbach. It had drizzled earlier and the road was wet with a mixture of rain and gasoline dripped by tanker trucks supplying fuel to the airfield at Frankfurt. I saw the glistening slippery mixture on the road ahead and quickly slowed from fifty to twenty miles per hour, but still not slow enough. The jeep fishtailed as I braked and then spun into a series of 360-degree turns, slid off the road, and overturned. Luckily the roof was up and, notes my diary, *miraculously, we crawled out disheveled but unhurt. As we were working on the jeep, which was pretty well wrecked, a major's jeep skidded off the road and overturned. He suffered a broken leg.*

The jeep had many admirable qualities. Its short wheelbase, however, made it extremely susceptible to skidding under slippery conditions.

With the war over, there was much racing around by the occupation troops and the accident rate soared alarmingly. So serious did it become that the ordnance people developed schemes and gimmicks to encourage safer driving and lower the number of damaged vehicles that had to be repaired or replaced.

One type I recall: Located at a central point in town, usually the square, there was a mound of earth topped by a cross with a wreath. A few feet from it was a demolished jeep. Nailed to a post or a nearby tree was a sign with a Burma Shave–type jingle:

> Here lies the body of GI Joe
> He broke his neck while on the go.
> His nickname was Speedy
> His last name was Burney
> He's had it, brothers
> His sentimental journey.

Although these exhibits were intended only as warnings to army drivers, the local people often accepted them at face value and in sympathy placed flowers on the "grave" of GI Joe.

Another effort to cut down driving speeds was a multiplicity of signs posted by the MPs:

> SPEED LIMITS
> TRUCKS 30
> JEEPS 40
> JAIL 45

The task of organizing a PW camp usually fell to the American commander of a battalion stationed in the area. He was responsible for searching, guarding, and feeding the PWs. Invariably he spoke no German, had no experience in this kind of thing, and was thankful for my help.

The simplest and most efficient way to organize the camp, I would tell him, was to have the highest-ranking German officer do it. The officer, appointed commandant, would establish a cadre of junior officers. These would seek out the cooks and establish a mess, ferret out the doctors and set up a dispensary, set up rosters for camp chores, find mechanics to service our vehicles, and otherwise organize matters for efficient operations.

I would send an order to the *Bürgermeister* of the local town to furnish us with several hundred books from the town library to be used as the camp library. He would be told to supply us with whatever number of typewriters were needed, as well as paper, carbon paper, cooking utensils, tools, and so forth.

Each morning, for a half hour or so, the American commander of the guarding battalion, the German camp commander, and I would meet. The German would receive his new orders and be asked about his problems. These would usually be requests for supplies of one kind or another. The dispensary, for example, might need certain drugs. I would requisition them from the local hospital. Sometimes, when we were stymied, the German might suggest a solution, or the problem might be passed on to the *Bürgermeister*.

The *Bürgermeister* came in handy in other ways. In the town near-

Motor pool at Internment Camp 97. The car is my captured BMW, its original German camouflage painted over with American insignia. The man in the center is a German ordnance general who volunteered to service the car personally. The staff's jeeps were named Ban Day, Ban Day II, and Ban Day III. At the intelligence school in Maryland, every eighth day was a free one and called Ban Day in honor of General Banfield, the school's commandant. *Photo by author*

Lieutenant Phillip Rothman, my second-in-command, with Dina. *Photo by author*

est the camp, he was ordered to supply us with whatever we needed in the way of household help.

Since we American interrogators all spoke German, the help found it pleasant and rewarding to work for the "Amis." The benefits included free meals, a matter of some consequence in a near-starving country, plus gifts of cigarettes, candy, and assorted hard-to-get sundries. The German staff, in turn, bent over backward to furnish us with useful local information. Where, for instance, come winter, could one get skis and ski boots made? Where could I get a new briefcase? What was manufactured locally that could be bought and sent home, such as glassware, toy electric trains, cuckoo clocks, and other items?

In the course of my work since being detached from the Sixth Corps, I had acquired two appendages, both lovable and intelligent. One, Hans, was a handyman, one of our former PWs. The other was a dog, a young Irish setter, Dina by name, that I eventually brought back to the States with me. Hans took especial pleasure in grooming and playing with her, teaching her a wide repertoire of tricks. The one that always evoked a roar of laughter when I entertained friends was to ask her, "What do the girls do in Germany?" At this she would roll onto her back and spread her legs. The more bottles of wine that were consumed, the more was Dina called on to respond to this question.

I first employed Hans in Salzburg after discharging him from the army. He was a cheerfully hard worker, talented and efficient, the first one up in the morning and the last one to bed at night. He made himself indispensable and wormed his way into all our hearts. He became my majordomo and took charge of the household staff.

Hans came from East Prussia, now Russian-occupied, and had lost contact with his family there. He had the Führer's size and build, sported the same absurd mini-mustace, and when his hair wasn't slicked down, had a forelock just like Hitler's. He could have been used by German security as the dictator's double.

A few times I had the fleeting thought that I might be harboring the Führer, since there was some doubt at the time that he was really dead. What an ignominious end to my army career, I thought, if this should turn out to be the case. Several times I discreetly, and not so discreetly, probed into Hans's background.

Competent and resourceful, Hans efficiently tackled every job I gave him. He was a baker by trade, and everything he baked for us was mouth-watering. It was his baking, I think, more than anything else, that assured me he was not the Führer. Rothman had jokingly suggested we check his wallpapering ability, since Allied propaganda had often referred to Hitler as a former wallpaper hanger.

"If this fellow turns out to be Hitler," I said consolingly, "we'll both go down in history."

"Yes," said Rothman, with a grimace, "for being personally executed by Eisenhower."

My favorite recollection of Hans concerns an incident that occurred that winter. It was a bitterly cold one, and the shortage of coal so severe that we heated the house—as usual, a large one—mostly with wood. To that end I had the *Bürgermeister* send us three men for a few days to chop wood.

Coming home one evening, I found the household staff in a state of excitement. While the woodcutters had been at the house, a cook had her watch stolen. The next day the maid noticed that her diamond pin was missing.

I discussed the matter with Hans. He said he thought he knew the thief and asked me to let him handle the matter.

The next evening I came home to find the staff jubilant. The missing articles had been returned. "Who took them?" I asked Hans. "The fellow you thought?"

"I'm not sure," said Hans.

"Then how did you get them back?"

"In the morning," replied Hans, "I accused them of stealing. They denied it. I said, 'Listen carefully! The captain has a terrible temper. You have never seen him, because he has gone to work before you get here, and you are gone before he gets back. But one look at the man, just one look, and you can see that he would rather kill than eat. At his last station he shot two men who worked for him and stole a can of gas from his jeep. He didn't know which man was guilty, so he shot them both. He does not tolerate stealing! I advise you to return the jewelry. After lunch go to your homes and bring it back. Put it on the kitchen table. I don't care who took it. Nobody will be in the kitchen to see which of you took it. Just remember, if that jewelry is not returned, the captain will shoot you like that!'" and Hans snapped his fingers.

I doubled up with laughter. "Hans," I said, "I'm not sure if I should reward you with a bottle of champagne or shoot you for your cock-and-bull story to these men."

"Gnädiger Hauptmann [merciful captain]," said Hans with twinkling eyes, "I vote for the champagne."

The staff all joined in the laughter and I broke out several bottles of our best.

Some months after I returned home, I received a letter from Hans telling me he had been reunited with his family.

My handyman and majordomo Hans, a discharged PW. You can see why I at first wondered if I might be giving succor to Hitler.

July 31 *While at army headquarters Captain Snedal told me that I had been recommended as the C.O. [commanding officer] of a seven-officer, twenty-man MIS detachment at army headquarters. I told him I didn't want the job, preferred the liberty my present work gave me.*

CIC at army wants me to take over a camp of internees, 3,500 strong, at Neustadt, a little town near Marburg. Will do.

August 5 *Visited the camp, found conditions poor but not hopeless. The guarding battalion staff looks about the same.*

Among those held at Neustadt, near Ludwigshafen, were 218 generals. Often the camps we took over were former German army installations that were in reasonably good shape. This, though, was not always so. This internment camp was a case in point. Construction was not in my bailiwick, but impatient with the rate repairs were going, I stepped in.

August 10   *The second barbed wire fence is being erected at the camp. Floodlights and an electrically charged fence are being installed.*

August 14   *We've got civilian carpenters starting work on the barracks. The camp is a series of dilapidated barracks and one building simply must be renovated for offices. I'm getting some supplies, mostly by hook or crook. The Military Government in Marburg wouldn't let me take any of the stock I found at a construction firm. Says it's all frozen for civilian use.*

August 15   *Swiped paint, glass, chairs, insulating board, turpentine, electrical fixtures, wood, nails, hinges, door knobs, filing cases, desks, bulbs, wire, etc. from the captured ammunition factory nearby.*
   Have arranged to pay the carpenters, electricians, and painters by letting them take some supplies for themselves. They can't buy the stuff at any price.

Suddenly, now, we were awash with news. First we heard over the radio that Japan had surrendered unconditionally. Second, my right-hand man, Lieutenant Rothman, received orders to report to the army's Biarritz University.

Early in our association, I had found him an intelligent, conscientious, and hard-working officer and had him promoted to first lieutenant. My own long delay in attaining that grade still rankled. I did not want this to happen to him. Although we had developed a strong bond, had become good friends, Rothman had his heart set on teaching at Biarritz. He hated the work we were doing, although he was good at it, and I fully understood and sympathized with his position. We had numerous discussions about the dilemma of having to place people into categories based on fixed rules, which at times so egregiously offended my sense of justice that I often felt it necessary to bend them. A case in point: One morning I had a small, handsome Russian boy of fifteen standing before me. His story in a nutshell was that his father had been killed in the Russian army when he, the son, was twelve, and his mother had died about the same time. Out of food and hungry, he had gone to some German soldiers occupying the area. They took him on as a stable boy, gave him a uniform, and fed him. He stayed with them and was ultimately captured with them. Now, if he was released, he told me, he would go to the farm of the major under whom he had worked, the major having promised to employ him after the war.

According to the rules, he should have been returned to Russia. There he would have been executed for treason. So I changed his papers to read, where it asked nationality, "German"—effectively making him a German citizen—and discharged him.

A scholar and humanist, Rothman found the work with its arbitrary decisions painful and distasteful, despite my granting him wide latitude in applying the rules. "There, but for the grace of God, go I," he would often remind me and asked, in view of my understanding of his feelings, to recommend his transfer to Biarritz. In time I was able to effect his transfer.

Third, hardly had I bid Phillip good-bye when, without any previous warning, I received the news that I was to report to Military Intelligence Service headquarters preparatory to repatriation. With the end of hostilities in Europe, Washington began its demobilization program to equitably select overseas troops for return to the States and discharge. It was based on a scoring system that determined a man's total points, taking into account numerous factors. One point was awarded for every month's service, one point for every month overseas, and five points for every battle star. A battle star was earned for each campaign in which a serviceman had fought. A decoration added additional points, and so on. Since I had been in five or six campaigns and had also been awarded the Bronze Star, I came up for fairly early discharge.

In Paris, at Military Intelligence Service headquarters, I first checked my mail slot. There I found a note from Rothman. The contents were too sentimental and flattering for him to tell me to my face. And he again thanked me for arranging his transfer.

That evening, going to the hotel in which I was billeted, I found I had been assigned a room with two beds. On one was another officer's luggage, but no sign of the man, even that night when I retired late. But who should walk in the following morning? Alex Shayne!

He had gotten married, he told me, and had been here for several days but was spending the nights with his bride elsewhere. His wife,

Alex said, had been a Russian parachutist and was captured by the Germans. He met her in a camp in the course of his work. A British officer working in the same camp was also smitten by the girl. Noticing that they were in competition, the Englishman asked Alex his intentions. Alex said he wanted to marry her. "In that case, old man," said the Britisher sportingly, "she's yours. My intentions were not that honorable."

To get his bride across the German-French border, the first step toward America, had been relatively easy. Alex had hidden her in the back of his jeep, piled blankets and baggage on top of her, and being an American officer, was only perfunctorily checked at the border.

The difficulty now was getting a passport for her. The Russians, in the days of Stalin and long after, did not readily permit emigration, to put it mildly. And for a Russian soldier to marry an American and go to the United States was in no way acceptable.

How to get her from France to the United States? Despite all of Alex's pleadings, the American embassy said it could be of no help, the thing was impossible. The Swedes had also been of no help. In desperation Alex was now trying to make the acquaintance of pilots flying to the States, hoping to find one who would smuggle her aboard a plane. If he could manage that, his sister, a pediatrician in Brooklyn, would meet her and take care of her until he arrived.

Later in the day I met Alex's wife, Valeria, a tall, slender, extraordinarily beautiful young woman, pleasure-hungry and simply drunk with Paris.

When Alex suggested doing the town that evening, I had to plead poverty, having sent my money home ahead of me, keeping only enough for the minor expenses I expected on the trip.

"If money is the problem," cried Alex, bursting into laughter, "there is no problem!" He reached under the bed, pulled out a bulging shoe box held together by thick rubber bands, and tossed it to me. "Help yourself!"

The box was crammed with bundles of German-mark invasion currency that the American forces circulated in Germany and which, by American decree, the Germans were forced to accept as legal tender. Alex's bills, however, were not those issued by the American army, but were those printed by the Russian government with American plates.

They looked the same, and that the source of issue was Russian could be told only by a dash printed ahead of the serial number.

In congressional testimony years later, it developed that an assistant secretary of the treasury, Harry Dexter White, a Communist sympathizer, had ordered the printing plates shipped to Russia and, after the war, the Russian troops in Germany, who had not been paid for years, were paid all their back wages at once. Since the Soviet paymasters would not convert the military currency to rubles, the Red soldier was forced to get rid of his invasion marks in Germany before he was repatriated and they became worthless. Like a kid in a toy store, he bought everything in sight. Ball-point pens, a recent American invention, were sold to him for $500. A GI's old watch, even a three-dollar Mickey Mouse watch, was good for $500 or $600 or sometimes $1,000. (Many of the Russians were illiterate peasants who could not tell time but were fascinated by the ticking of a watch when held to the ear.) Equally outrageous prices were paid for cigarettes, candy, soap, and almost anything else a U.S. soldier was willing to sell. During this period of liaison with the Red Army, Russian-speaking Alex, while the sun shone, made hay.

That night we did Paris in style. Valeria, stunningly outfitted in Parisian finery, paid for with francs converted from her countrymen's invasion marks, had a ball.

The following day, reporting to my superiors, I was handed my orders to return to the States and simultaneously implored to volunteer for another six or eight months' service, since there was an appalling lack of German-speaking intelligence officers for the work still to be done.

I went to lunch and weighed the pros and cons of returning to the States versus staying in Germany for another few months. The appeal to my patriotism, to help out the army during its shortage of German-speaking officers, was one of the factors in my decision. The decisive one, though, was my desire to research the Field Marshal Rommel story. I sensed a tragic drama of Shakespearean dimensions in the murder of this general, who had a deep moral belief in the warrior's code of honor and was famous for his chivalry, his fingertip sensitivity, and savviness on the battlefield. Designed to deceive the German people, the German army, and the world, the murder and camouflaging state funeral were carefully scripted by the Führer and his cohorts down to the minutest detail. Despite the meticulous orchestration, the drama developed a few glitches, I was to learn, among them the arrival of Hitler's wreath at the railroad station in Ulm while Rommel was still alive.

My desire to get to the bottom of the story had never abated. I found myself in constant ruminative preoccupation with the man, the event, and the reasons for it. But at war's end I was far from Herrlingen, and the pressure of my duties left little time for searching out the sources that could supply the information.

Now, however, I was no longer working in camps in Austria, but in camps in the province of Württemberg, Rommel's home grounds, and within a reasonable driving distance of his home. My rejection of the seven-officer, twenty-man command at army headquarters was partly due to my belief that it would tie me down and hinder my search for the Rommel sources once I began the hunt.

For the remainder of 1945 and until April of 1946, I supervised interrogation in prisoner of war, internment, and war crimes camps. Then the scope of my work was broadened.

April 24, 1946 *The G-2 of the Ninth Infantry Division, to which the Intelligence Detachment is now attached, insists that I take over operational control of the interrogation in the internment camps and hospitals, not only in the Ludwigsburg area, but also of those in the Bad Mergentheim and Karlsruhe areas.*

Spent the day visiting several of the camps and getting oriented.

Despite the change in my duties, I was able to continue my research. On weekends, and occasional weekdays when work permitted, I chased down the sources for a book on Rommel, wanting to obtain the facts while memories were still fresh. Several times I conferred at great length with Mrs. Rommel, on one occasion arriving at 10:00 A.M. and not leaving until 1:00 A.M. the following morning.

From Mrs. Rommel I learned the address of General Hans Speidel, the marshal's chief of staff during the Normandy fighting, and a man with impeccable credentials for a professional assessment of Rommel. Despite the difference in our nationalities, ages, and ranks, we quickly developed a warm friendship and spent many weekends together.

Left to right: General Speidel, Mrs. Rommel, the author, Mrs. Speidel, the Speidel's daughter Christa, and Mr. and Mrs. Firnhaver (friends of the author), May 26, 1946. *Photo by Manfred Rommel*

Another primary source was *Hauptmann* Hermann Aldinger. A friend of the marshal from World War I days, he had been Rommel's *Ordonnanzoffizier*, a combination aide, private secretary, personal assistant, and in Rommel's case, confidant.

Professor Dr. Kurt Hesse, an internationally known military historian and longtime friend of Rommel, and the man the marshal had agreed would be his official biographer if he did not survive the war, discussed the general with me at great length in several meetings.

When he learned that I was digging into Rommel's curious death, Professor Dr. Albrecht of Tübingen University, Rommel's personal physician, was eager to see me and refute the official Nazi-originated story that the marshal had died of a heart attack.

Oskar Farny, one of Rommel's closest friends and the man to whom he confessed the day before his murder that he felt his death, instigated by Hitler, was imminent, was my host for a weekend visit.

While these were the main sources, there were many others, but by June I felt I had gotten the complete picture and returned to the States.

The book I wrote could find no publisher. While all agreed it was a fascinating story, a common thread ran through all the rejections: "We feel there is no market at this time, so soon after the war, for a book that deals so favorably with a German militarist."

Forty-seven years later, in 1993, I dug out the manuscript, and in October 1994 the story, *Discovering the Rommel Murder*, was finally published.

Reflection

Well do I still recall on the homeward voyage standing at the rail with my shipmates as we eagerly waited for the Statue of Liberty to come into view. With the ship nearing its destination, I reflected on my four and a half years of army service. I made a mental list of the relatives and friends in civilian life who had died in the service, then added my army comrades who had been killed or wounded. It was a long list. As I removed my glasses to wipe the tears welling in my eyes, I was reminded again of the words of Wellington: "Nothing except a battle lost can be half so melancholy as a battle won."

And then I considered the flip side: How many men had *I* killed or maimed? I could say none, but would that be the truth? Yes, I fired no bullets, not even one, but what about the questions I fired? The information suctioned from prisoners resulted in the death of many of their brethren. I can yet remember, clearly, saying to a PW, a swaggerer, "You are lucky. As a prisoner, you will now get hot meals. I guess you don't remember your last hot meal."

"Oh yes," he said arrogantly, falling into the trap. "We got hot meals every night."

"Every night!" I ejaculated, feigning surprise.

"At six o'clock, right here, behind the cemetery," said the German, pointing to the spot on the map.

I phoned the artillery with the map coordinates, and that evening at six they put a TOT (time on target) on the location, all shells landing simultaneously, giving the enemy no time to dive for cover.

How many were killed or wounded? I don't know.

The information we siphoned from captured documents certainly led to the death of many. The citation with my Bronze Star singles out only a few of my contributions to the war effort. One sentence says of me, "While on Anzio Beachhead he was the first to evaluate captured map overlays showing the disposition of component units of the enemy, making it possible to neutralize their fire."

Reduced to plain English, this says I made it possible for us to kill them before they killed us.

So how many had I killed? Was it tens? Hundreds? Thousands? I have no idea, and if I could find the answer just by pushing a button, I would not push that button. The information I passed on to the men who did the actual bombing, shelling, and rifle firing certainly resulted in great numbers of casualties and much suffering for the families of these wounded and dead German soldiers.

It is sad that armies, as a result of the failure of their political leaders to come to terms, are made up mostly of good, decent men forced by the nature of war to commit terrible acts against one another. This folly was brought home to me many times during the war, and poignantly at a social gathering some years after the war by a young attorney who had been an infantry lieutenant. He told me of a nighttime reconnaissance patrol he had been leading when he ran into a German patrol. Both he and the enemy point man fired simultaneously. The German, however, stumbled as he fired and missed, while the lieutenant's shot found its mark.

"I went through the guy's pockets," said the lieutenant, "and took his wallet and papers. In the morning I examined the stuff with one of my men who spoke German. There were pictures of his wife and kids, and a letter from his wife. He deplored the war, couldn't wait for it to end. In my pockets I also had pictures of my wife and kids, and a letter from my wife. With a change of names, the letters could have been substituted for each other."

"I kept the stuff," continued the lieutenant, "and after the war I wrote his wife. It was the toughest letter I have ever written. I tried to tell her how sorry I was, and I enclosed the pictures and her letter. She wrote back, thanked me. She assured me she understood the bestiality of war, that it was him or me, and forgave me for killing her husband. I can't tell you," said the lieutenant, tears inching down his cheeks, "what a weight it took off my shoulders.

"You know," he continued, after a pause to gather himself, "war is so, so . . . [he struggled to find the word, and finally] *so fucking stupid! So fucking, fucking stupid!*" It was the most vituperative expression he could come up with, and I sensed it still fell far short of the vitriol buried in his heart. Five decades have gone by since the end of the Second World War. Now that the passions have subsided, it is not uncommon for the former adversaries to meet in the military cemeteries at the anniversary of battles to jointly commemorate the fallen. They mingle as they walk among the gravestones recalling their dead. Often victor and vanquished join in embrace and tears and agree with the tottering, withered British veteran who, in October 1992 at the fiftieth anniversary of the Battle of El Alamein, surveyed the ocean of grave markers and put it all in three words. "What a waste!" he said, with dimming eyes. "What a waste!"

Many decades before, after the armies of Emperor Napoleon III of France and Emperor Franz Josef of Austria had engaged in battle in northern Italy, it was left to the nurses in Castiglione to succor the wounded of both sides. To a Swiss who had watched the fighting from afar and was now helping attend the wounded, the nurses said sadly of their dying patients, *"Tutti fratelli"* (They are all brothers). The comment inspired this observer, the Genevan Jean-Henri Dunant, to found the International Red Cross.

With the passage of time, I have heard many old soldiers reminisce about aspects of army life they enjoyed and miss: the camaraderie, the practical jokes, the general hijinks. I have never heard one who missed the killing. All would agree with Erasmus, who said centuries ago, "War is delightful only to those with no experience of it."

Every night in my prayers, during my combat days, as I drifted off to sleep, I thanked God that I was not called on to *visibly* kill another human face to face. Not once did I have to point my gun at another man. Yet, come the morning, my brain would snap to attention and tell me it was time to get up and get on with the job of *invisibly* killing him, the German, my enemy. My situation was analogous to the judge who sentences a man to death but does not have to watch the execution. He feels his act is just, yet is repelled by the consequence.

In a philosophical discussion with General Hans Speidel that ran late

into the night, we pondered man's eternal fascination with war, a fascination dating from the time of primitive man using sticks and stones
to modern man employing overpowering gunpowder-based weaponry
augmented by the latest scientifically based technologies. From time
immemorial, we decided, men have had an enormous talent for savagery, something that has never had a chance to atrophy for lack of use,
leaving only the art of politics at the highest levels to keep it in check.
Consequently, through the ages war has been accepted as a last-resort
anthropological ritual, the only means by which human disputes can
be settled.

Discussing the individual soldier, we wondered under what circumstances adrenalin would flow faster: when a man is engaged in one-to-
one combat, is facing death by a dropping bomb or the random shard of
a shell, or little short of suicide, is crossing a minefield defended by
barbed wire and entrenched machine guns?

We wondered why battle brings out the best and worst in man. And
how does one explain the capricious fates that decide which men will
die and which will live? And how explain why most men who survived
the killing fields are riddled with ambivalence: not wanting to have
missed the experience, yet not wanting to repeat it?

Why does the German veteran want to be buried with the haunting
strains of "I Had a Comrade" and the American veteran to the bugler's
heart-wrenching "Taps"?

And yet, while war is hatred and fear, weariness and filth, cowardice
and heroism, why is professional soldiery an honorable calling? We reflected on these questions and others. On one point we differed. I felt
the American development of the atomic bomb made us such a domi-
nant power that we could force nonmilitary solutions in our areas of
interest. Speidel disagreed. He predicted that in time the bomb would
be developed by other countries and a proliferation would follow. "You
will see," he said, presciently, "it will become a dangerous world. You
will regret ever having invented that weapon."

All this having been said, I would like to end with a personal note
for my children and grandchildren, and that is the hope that when I
pass on I will be able to leave you a few dollars. But if I could leave you
a world destined to be perpetually at peace, then, then, would I be leaving you the best of legacies!

2/99

B
Marshall

Marshall, Charles F.

A ramble through my
war.

$29.95

DATE			